The Kids' Book of the
50 Great States

A State-by-State Scrapbook Filled with Facts, Maps, Puzzles, Poems, Photos, and More!

NEW JERSEY

WASHINGTON

HAWAII

MISSISSIPPI

NEW MEXICO

SCHOLASTIC
PROFESSIONAL BOOKS

New York ★ Toronto ★ London ★ Auckland ★ Sydney

Acknowledgments

The editors are mightily grateful for the selfless and invaluable contributions of Louise Spigarelli, social studies teacher at St. Mel's Elementary School in Dearborn Heights, Michigan.

We would also like to extend a special thank-you to Lois Lenski Elementary School in Littleton, Colorado; Dr. Barbara E. DeSpain, principal; Marcia Parrish, librarian; and Marion Honemann, teacher. These individuals were instrumental in helping us pilot this project with fifth graders. The teachers, librarians, and their students helped us decide what kids wanted to know in this book. Working with their students, they prepared some examples for the 50 states.

In addition, we want to thank all the schools across the nation that accepted our challenge to be involved with this book. Teachers and students developed the plan for our course of action through trial and error. They were superwilling to do the rewrites that created an innovative project. Working together, we all learned a great deal and helped one another.

Judith H. Cozzens, *Project Coordinator*

Mae E. Davies, Helen C. Healy, and
Shirley P. Merdes, *Consultants*

Project direction and content editing by Elaine Israel.

Cover design by Katherine Massaro.

PHOTO CREDITS Front cover: Coyote: © Tim Davis/ Photo Researchers, Inc.; flower: © Rhoda Sidney/Stock Boston; cowboy: © 1997/Comstock; kids with snowman: © 1996 John Terence Turner/FPG International; Statue of Liberty © 1995/Comstock. Back cover: Native American: © 1992 Travelpix/FPG International; surfer: © 1997 Telegraph Colour Library/FPG International.

Interior design by Ellen Matlach Hassell for Boultinghouse & Boultinghouse, Inc.

Interior photos and illustration courtesy of the participating classrooms.

ISBN 0-590-99621-5

# Contents

Quick—what's the seventh largest state? The fifth smallest? Which one's known as the Goober State? Do you know the state drink of Oregon? How about the state fish of Hawai'i? If you answered Nevada, New Jersey, Georgia, milk, and the humuhumunukunukuapuaa, congratulations. You're among the geographically gifted. But if some of those had you stumped, you may want to check out this book. It's packed full of fascinating facts about the United States—all 50 of them.

SOUTH DAKOTA

For instance, ever wonder where the first McDonald's opened? Just turn to page 26. Where earmuffs were invented? (page 81) Which state's the proud owner of the world's largest baseball bat? (page 75) Or which state grows the most popcorn? (page 63) You'll find all the answers right here.

But there's more to this book than tantalizing trivia. As you flip through the pages, you'll learn about the history of each state, meet some famous folks who call it home, witness its weather, and catch a glimpse of its wildlife. There are also maps and snapshots of the dazzling sights that draw tourists from near and far as well as related addresses and Web site listings to find out more. Not to mention songs, puzzles, book reviews, and jokes to keep you singing, guessing, reading, and laughing about each state.

Reading *The Kids' Book of the 50 Great States* is like taking a cross-country trip without having to get in a car. Take in the awesome views as you cruise down California's coast, visit one of New Mexico's 25 Indian reservations and pick up a few words in Navajo, take a dip in one of Michigan's 10,000 lakes, gaze at the gators lurking in Florida's swamps, learn to dance the fais-dodo in Louisiana's Cajun country, grab a

NORTH CAROLINA

4

ALASKA

WISCONSIN

slab of sweet potato pie as you swing through Alabama, or head up north and learn to talk like a Mainer. (Ayuh, the bugs here are wicked good.) You get the idea.

Your tour guides are kids just like you. We held a national contest and asked students around the country to tell us about their state. Then we chose the best entry from each one (a difficult job!). More than 1,000 third-through seventh-graders from coast to coast rose to the challenge. They called their state officials, interviewed prominent people, pored over documents and books at the local library, and took field trips to investigate tourist attractions. Kids looked for information that was both serious and silly, interesting and outlandish. They drew pictures and maps and gathered photographs. Then they compiled all the information into an eye-catching, fun-to-read format, and put them all together to make this book.

You probably already know why your state's great. But there are 49 others to explore. Before you've reached the last page of this book, you'll know that Alaska is twice the size of Texas, that Georgia's the biggest state east of the Mississippi, and that 37 Rhode Islands would fit inside the state of Montana. With *The Kids' Book of the 50 Great States* as a resource, you'll soon be acing geography tests, impressing your parents, outsmarting your teachers, and—perhaps best of all—discovering what makes our country a pretty amazing place to live.

So get ready to hit the road and boost your brain power. We promise you an adventure you won't forget.

Enjoy the trip!

The Editors

LOUISIANA

The Kids' Book of the 50 Great States

Alabama

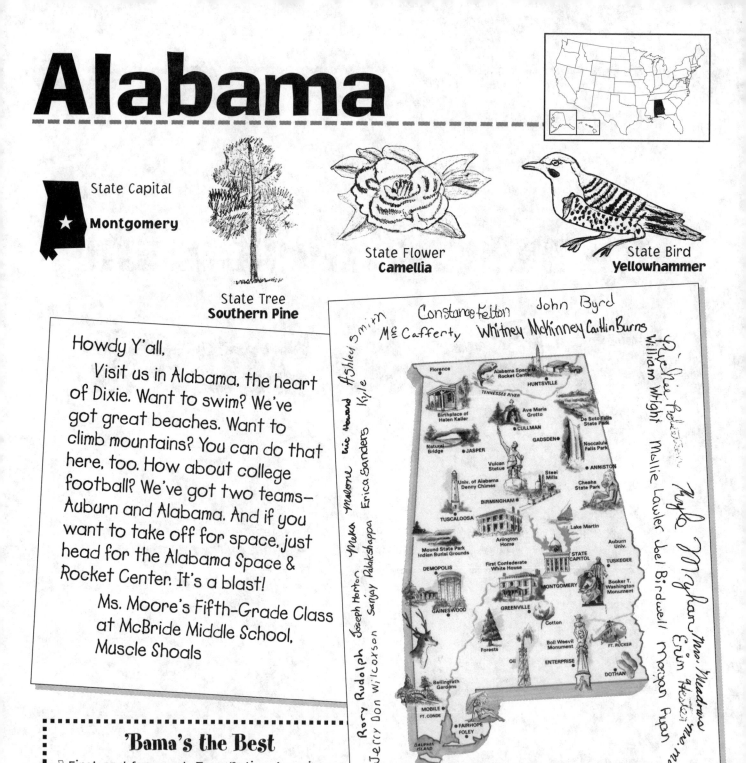

State Capital
★ **Montgomery**

State Tree
Southern Pine

State Flower
Camellia

State Bird
Yellowhammer

Howdy Y'all,

Visit us in Alabama, the heart of Dixie. Want to swim? We've got great beaches. Want to climb mountains? You can do that here, too. How about college football? We've got two teams—Auburn and Alabama. And if you want to take off for space, just head for the Alabama Space & Rocket Center. It's a blast!

Ms. Moore's Fifth-Grade Class at McBride Middle School, Muscle Shoals

'Bama's the Best

⌂ First and foremost. **Four** Native American tribes—the Cherokee, Chickasaw, Choctaw, and Creek—have lived in Alabama.

⌂ Alabamians go way back. Humans **lived** in northeast Alabama from about 6000 B.C.

⌂ Voilà! The **earliest** permanent settlement was made by the French, who landed on Dolphin Island in 1701.

⌂ Don't get bugged off! Alabama was the **first** state to have a monument to an insect, the boll weevil.

⌂ Say "yum" if you love peanut butter. This is where George Washington Carver discovered **more** than 300 uses for peanuts and **more** than 50 for sweet potatoes.

⌂ It's out of this world. Huntsville has the **largest** space museum in the world.

⌂ Duck! The nation's **largest** stalagmite is in a cave at Cathedral Caverns.

BORN IN ALABAMA

Julia S. Tutwiler (1841–1916) improved the lives of many Alabamians. She helped educate women and taught them how to be teachers at a time when that was unusual. She also worked to better the horrible conditions in state prisons.

W. C. Handy (1873–1958) played the cornet and composed music that still makes us hum. One piece he wrote was "St. Loius Blues." He went to public schools, but most of his education came from his father and grandfather, who were both clergymen.

Helen Adams Keller (1880–1968) became deaf and blind when she was a baby. But she grew up to be a writer and speaker known around the world. The person who taught her and helped guide her through life was Anne Sullivan.

Jesse Owens (1913–1980) outran terrible poverty and prejudice against black people to become an Olympic Games champion. The records he set remained unbeaten for many years.

Rosa Louise Parks

W. C. Handy

Helen Adams Keller

George C. Wallace

Rosa Louise Parks (1913–) was on her way home from work as a housekeeper when she sat in an empty seat on a bus. She was arrested! That was in 1955. The seat was meant for white people only. Black people, like Mrs. Parks, had to go to the back of the bus—even if there were no seats there. Rosa Parks's courage in defying segregation made her a heroine of the civil rights movement.

George Corley Wallace (1919–) was the governor of Alabama from 1963 to 1967. At the time, he strongly supported keeping black people and white people separate. This was called segregation. It was against the law and treated black people as second-class citizens. We are thankful those days have changed forever!

Ralph Abernathy (1926–1990) was a man of peace. A Baptist minister, he became the head of an important civil rights group.

Hank Aaron (1934–) was a baseball player nicknamed "the Hammer" for the way he whacked out hits. His 715 home runs beat the record of Babe Ruth, a legendary player. But he didn't stop there. When he retired, Aaron's record stood at 755 home runs.

Are you hungry? Fix yourself some
'Bama Sweet Potato Pie

YOU NEED:

Enough sweet potatoes to make 1 cup mashed
1/3 cup butter or margarine
2 eggs
1/3 cup milk or half & half
Pinch of salt
1/2 teaspoon ground nutmeg
1/2 teaspoon cinnamon
1 teaspoon pure vanilla extract
1 cup (or less) sugar
1 unbaked 9-inch pie shell

WHAT TO DO:

Cook and mash sweet potatoes.

Beat eggs.

Melt butter.

Combine sweet potatoes with all ingredients (except pie shell), blending well with electric mixer or by hand. Pour into pie shell.

Bake in preheated 400°F oven about 30 minutes or until golden and puffy.

Serve alone or topped with whipped cream.

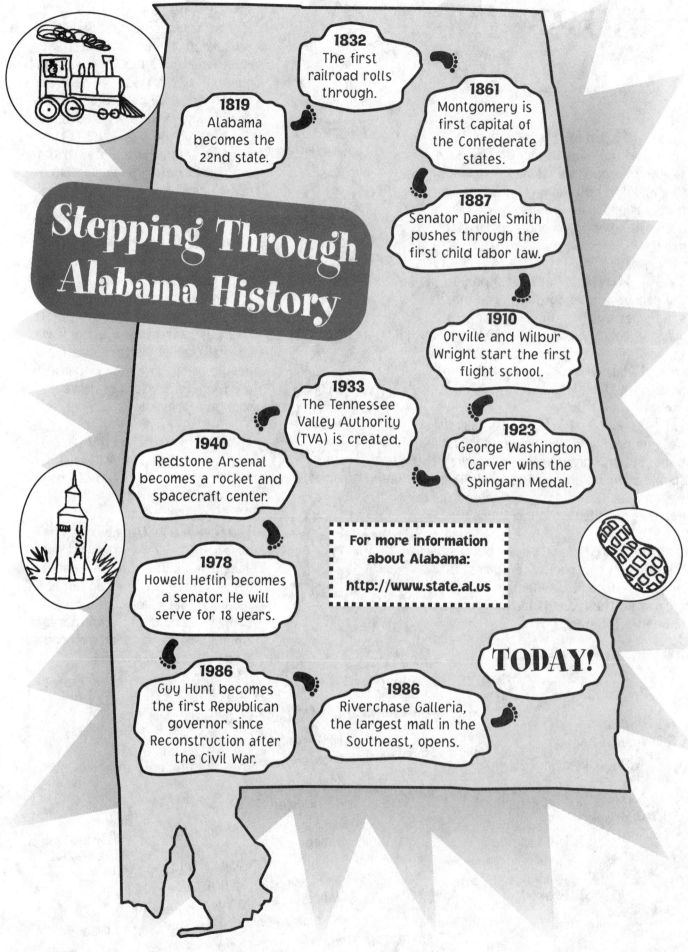

Stepping Through Alabama History

1819
Alabama becomes the 22nd state.

1832
The first railroad rolls through.

1861
Montgomery is first capital of the Confederate states.

1887
Senator Daniel Smith pushes through the first child labor law.

1910
Orville and Wilbur Wright start the first flight school.

1933
The Tennessee Valley Authority (TVA) is created.

1923
George Washington Carver wins the Spingarn Medal.

1940
Redstone Arsenal becomes a rocket and spacecraft center.

For more information about Alabama:

http://www.state.al.us

1978
Howell Heflin becomes a senator. He will serve for 18 years.

TODAY!

1986
Guy Hunt becomes the first Republican governor since Reconstruction after the Civil War.

1986
Riverchase Galleria, the largest mall in the Southeast, opens.

Places to Wander

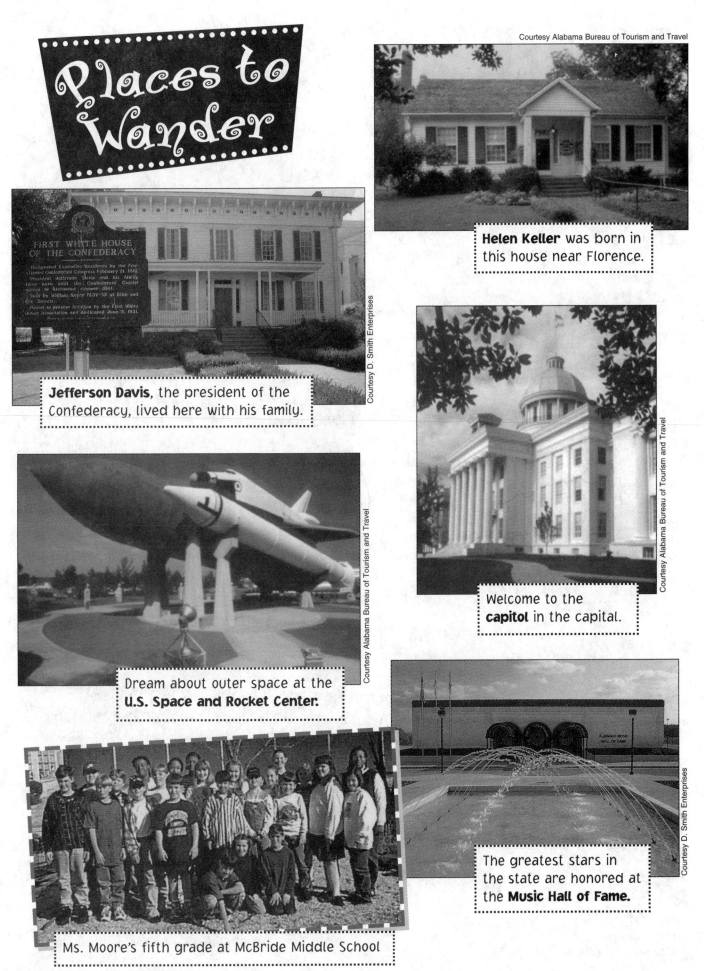

Courtesy Alabama Bureau of Tourism and Travel

Helen Keller was born in this house near Florence.

Courtesy D. Smith Enterprises

FIRST WHITE HOUSE OF THE CONFEDERACY

Jefferson Davis, the president of the Confederacy, lived here with his family.

Courtesy Alabama Bureau of Tourism and Travel

Welcome to the **capitol** in the capital.

Courtesy Alabama Bureau of Tourism and Travel

Dream about outer space at the **U.S. Space and Rocket Center.**

Courtesy D. Smith Enterprises

The greatest stars in the state are honored at the **Music Hall of Fame.**

Ms. Moore's fifth grade at McBride Middle School

Alaska

State Capital
Juneau

State Flag

State Flower
Forget-Me-Not

State Bird
Willow Ptarmigan

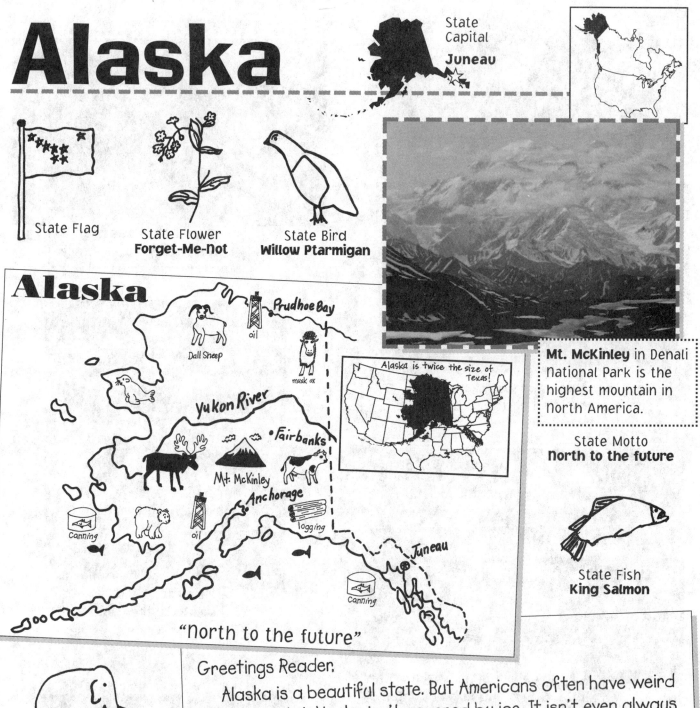

Alaska

Prudhoe Bay

oil

Dall Sheep

musk ox

yukon River

Fairbanks

Mt. McKinley

Anchorage

Canning

oil

logging

Juneau

Canning

Alaska is twice the size of Texas!

"north to the future"

Mt. McKinley in Denali National Park is the highest mountain in North America.

State Motto
North to the future

State Fish
King Salmon

State Fossil
Woolly Mammoth

State Marine Mammal
Bowhead Whale

Greetings Reader,

   Alaska is a beautiful state. But Americans often have weird ideas about it. Alaska isn't covered by ice. It isn't even always cold. Winter temperatures may dip to -45°F, but Fairbanks sometimes has 30°F winter days. Summer days can be as warm as 90°F. People hardly ever live in igloos or icehouses. And they don't share their homes with penguins and polar bears. Igloos are used only as temporary houses on long hunting trips or during blizzards by the Inupiat or Yupik native Alaskan people. We live in regular houses and apartments! If you look on most maps, Alaska seems the same size as Texas. Wrong! Alaska is really twice as big as Texas in land area.

   Mrs. Leipzig's class, Denali Elementary, Fairbanks

Alaska Talk

Bush: Remote places not served by roads

Blanket Toss: A game in which a person is tossed into the air from a blanket held by many people. It's also a way to spot animals in the distance.

Lower 48: Name for connected 48 states (not Alaska and Hawaii)

Mukluks: Warm, often knee-high, boots made from seal or caribou skins

Ptarmigan: (TAR-mi-gun) Alaskan bird with feathered feet

Qiviut: (KIH-vee-oot) Soft musk ox fur that is spun into knitting yarn

Mukluks

Awesome Alaskans

Alaska is proud of the author **ARNOLD GRIESE**. He and his family moved to Alaska in 1951. He taught school in the Athabaskan village of Tanana and at the University of Alaska Fairbanks. In appreciation of the Athabaskan people, he has written many children's books about them and their culture. *Anna's Athabaskan Summer*, *The Wind Is Not a River*, and *At the Mouth of the Luckiest River* are great books that he has written.

We're glad that **RIE MUNOZ** came to Alaska in 1950 on vacation—and stayed. Since that time she has been a newspaper reporter, a teacher, and an artist. Rie does field sketches of scenes and people in Alaska. She then returns to her studio to paint those scenes and also uses the stone lithograph and silkscreen processes. Rie Munoz also illustrates children's books.

SUSAN BUTCHER came to Alaska and took up the sport of dog mushing. Since then she has raced from Anchorage to Nome 17 times and finished first three times. She raises dogs at her kennel

about 100 miles north of Fairbanks. She says that she loves dog racing and the companionship of dogs. Susan Butcher spends lots of time supporting the Iditarod, our famous sled race.

JAY HAMMOND was governor of Alaska from 1974 to 1982. He helped protect and develop the Permanent Fund, which controls money from oil. He has been a bush pilot, trapper, commercial fisherman, and wilderness guide. He went from living in the governor's mansion to his retirement home, a log cabin on Lake Clark.

BENNY BENSON was born in Chignik, a town in southern Alaska, in 1913. When he was 13 years old he entered a contest to design Alaska's state flag. His design won! As an adult, Benny Benson was an airplane mechanic in Kodiak. He died in 1972.

Did you know...?

- The remains of seven kinds of dinosaurs have been found in Alaska.
- Juneau, the capital, can be reached only by air or water.
- Alaska has two time zones.
- Of the 20 highest peaks in the United States, 17 are in Alaska.
- Alaska has more active glaciers and ice fields than in the rest of the inhabited world.
- Alaska has the northernmost and westernmost points in the United States.
- Alaska was sold by Russia for 2 cents an acre.
- Alaska is the only state in which the citizens receive part of the state's profit from oil.

Mushing Through Alaska's History

40,000 to 50,000 years ago the ocean water level dropped about 500 feet. This allowed people and animals to cross the Bering land bridge from Asia to North America.

1741 Vitus Bering explores with Aleksei Chinkov. They land on Kayak Island, Alaska.

1799 The Russians charter the Russian-American Company to bring the fur trade under their control.

1867 William H. Seward, the secretary of state of the United States, buys Alaska from Russia for $7,200,000.

1878 The first salmon canneries are built.

1902 Gold is discovered near the Tanana River and Fairbanks grows on its shore.

1884 Laws establish public schools.

1923 The Alaska Railroad is completed linking Seward, Anchorage, and Fairbanks.

1899 Gold is discovered on the beaches of Nome.

1978–1980 The U.S. Congress and President Jimmy Carter protect natural resources on one quarter of Alaska's land.

1942 The Alaska Highway is completed.

1959 Alaska becomes the 49th state.

1964 An earthquake destroys parts of Anchorage and Valdez.

1968 Oil is discovered in Prudhoe Bay.

1977 The TransAlaska Pipeline is completed to carry oil from Prudhoe Bay to Valdez.

1989 *Exxon Valdez* accident spills about 11,000,000 gallons of crude oil.

This family's car journey began in Dawson Creek and ended in Fairbanks.

AVERAGE DAILY TEMPERATURE IN ALASKA FOR 1996

Temperature Range (°F) by Month

Month	Temp (°F)
Jan	0
Feb	9
Mar	30
Apr	48
May	61
Jun	70
Jul	74
Aug	61
Sep	49
Oct	21
Nov	5
Dec	-3

Alaska Division of Tourism • PO Box 110801 • Juneau, AK 99811-0801
http://www.state.ak.us/tourism

The sun is shining, and it is −17°F! Mrs. Leipzig's class is outside for recess.

A grizzly bear runs across the tundra, Arctic land with no trees, in Denali Park.

An Alaskan Album

The Yukon Quest is a 1,000-mile sled dog race from Fairbanks to Whitehorse, Yukon Territory, Canada.

At Alaskaland, Fairbanks, people learn about animal pelts at a cache, a log building built on tall poles that is used for storing supplies.

"Gee," yells the dog musher to his team.

Did you know that moose live in cities and chew on people's trees for food?

Alaska, Alaska

Alaska, Alaska.
The summer sun shines on and on.
Alaska, Alaska.
The sled dogs mush the winter trail.
Alaska, Alaska.
The northern lights glow in the winter's darkness.
Alaska, Alaska.
We all take pride in you.
—Jocelyne Fowler

Arizona

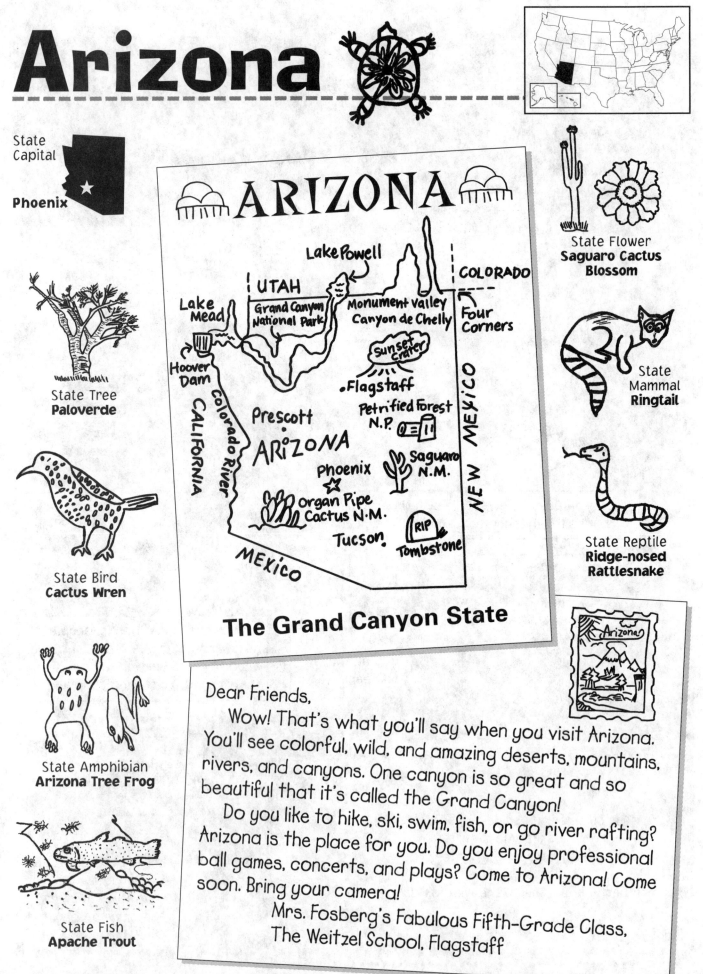

State Capital
Phoenix

State Tree
Paloverde

State Bird
Cactus Wren

State Amphibian
Arizona Tree Frog

State Fish
Apache Trout

ARIZONA

Lake Powell
UTAH
COLORADO
Lake Mead
Grand Canyon National Park
Monument Valley
Canyon de Chelly
Four Corners
Hoover Dam
CALIFORNIA
Colorado River
Sunset Crater
Flagstaff
Petrified Forest N.P.
Prescott
ARIZONA
NEW MEXICO
Phoenix
Saguaro N.M.
Organ Pipe Cactus N.M.
Tucson
RIP Tombstone
MEXICO

The Grand Canyon State

State Flower
Saguaro Cactus Blossom

State Mammal
Ringtail

State Reptile
Ridge-nosed Rattlesnake

Dear Friends,
   Wow! That's what you'll say when you visit Arizona. You'll see colorful, wild, and amazing deserts, mountains, rivers, and canyons. One canyon is so great and so beautiful that it's called the Grand Canyon!
   Do you like to hike, ski, swim, fish, or go river rafting? Arizona is the place for you. Do you enjoy professional ball games, concerts, and plays? Come to Arizona! Come soon. Bring your camera!
   Mrs. Fosberg's Fabulous Fifth-Grade Class,
   The Weitzel School, Flagstaff

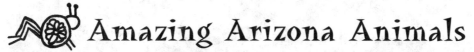

Amazing Arizona Animals

Gila monsters are the only poisonous lizards in the U.S. Only one foot long, they have poison in the glands of their jaws. Gila monster skin is shiny black and yellow.

Ringtails are mammals that live in Arizona canyons. The animals are brown or gray with a black-and-white banded tail. They are up to 30 inches long and weigh about 2.5 pounds.

Apache trout live in streams in high elevations. They are yellowish bronze with many dark spots. In the wild, adults grow to be eight inches long.

California condors have flown back from the brink of extinction. Six condors raised in captivity were released near the Grand Canyon in 1996. With wingspans of nine feet, condors are the largest birds in North America. They eat carrion (dead animals)—one way to keep their habitat clean.

Cactus wrens are birds with white and black spots on brown-and-white feathers. Adults are seven to eight inches long. As protection from predators, the wrens build their nests in cacti and eat insects, seeds, and fruits.

Javelinas are black-and-gray pig-like animals that have a snout and hooves. Javelinas weigh 25–60 pounds and grow to be about 36 inches long. They live in deserts and grasslands and eat many plants including cacti.

Arizona tree frogs are tiny amphibians that live in oak, pine, and fir forests 5,000 feet above sea level. Only two inches long, the tree frogs are colored green, bronze, and gold as camouflage from predators. They are nocturnal and eat insects.

Ridge-nosed rattlesnakes are small, only three or four ounces and about 24 inches long. They are brown with white stripes on their faces. These rattlesnakes live in cool canyons among oak and pine trees and eat lizards, centipedes, mice, and even other snakes.

Famous Arizonians

Bruce Babbitt is descended from pioneers who settled in northern Arizona. As a boy, he hiked in the Coconino National Forest around his home in Flagstaff. After two terms as Arizona's governor (1978–1985), he became the U.S. secretary of the interior under Bill Clinton. Part of Babbitt's job has been to watch over America's national parks and monuments, including those in Arizona that he came to love as a child.

George Kirk is a living legend. During World War II (1939–1945), he was a member of the U.S. Marine Corps and served as a radioman in the Pacific. As a Navajo Code Talker, he used a secret code that was based on the Navajo language. Because the Navajo Code Talkers were reliable, accurate, and fast in relaying messages, they saved many American lives. The code was never broken.

Sandra Day O'Connor grew up on the Lazy B Ranch in Greenlee County in southeastern Arizona and wanted to become a cowgirl. But she changed her mind and made history instead. In 1981, she became the first female justice on the U.S. Supreme Court.

Corporal Dinah Gillette, a member of the Butterfly Clan of the Hopi Indian tribe, is an officer of a program that helps thousands of children learn to resist drugs and violence. Her home is on First Mesa in the village of Sichomovi in northern Arizona.

Jan Romero Stevens explores her Hispanic heritage and life in the Southwest in her adventure stories. Her three books for children are *Carlos and the Squash Plant, Carlos and the Cornfield*, and *Carlos and the Skunk*. The books are written in Spanish and English. The books feed readers' stomachs as well as their minds! In each, Stevens includes a delicious Southwestern recipe that readers can try.

Raft Down the River of Time

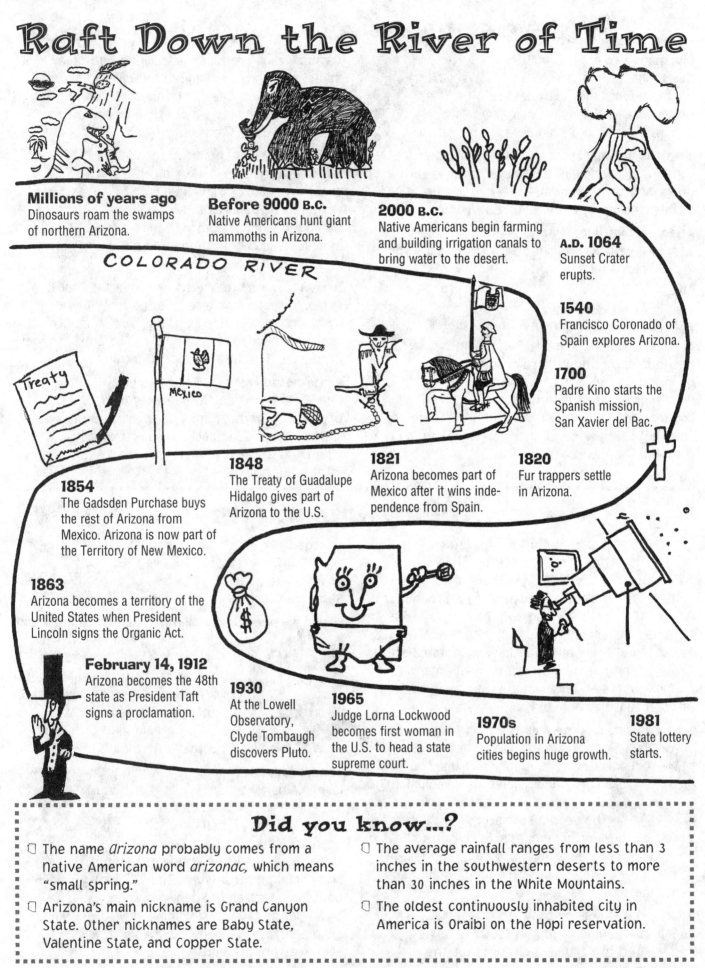

Millions of years ago
Dinosaurs roam the swamps of northern Arizona.

Before 9000 B.C.
Native Americans hunt giant mammoths in Arizona.

2000 B.C.
Native Americans begin farming and building irrigation canals to bring water to the desert.

A.D. 1064
Sunset Crater erupts.

1540
Francisco Coronado of Spain explores Arizona.

1700
Padre Kino starts the Spanish mission, San Xavier del Bac.

COLORADO RIVER

Treaty

Mexico

1848
The Treaty of Guadalupe Hidalgo gives part of Arizona to the U.S.

1821
Arizona becomes part of Mexico after it wins independence from Spain.

1820
Fur trappers settle in Arizona.

1854
The Gadsden Purchase buys the rest of Arizona from Mexico. Arizona is now part of the Territory of New Mexico.

1863
Arizona becomes a territory of the United States when President Lincoln signs the Organic Act.

February 14, 1912
Arizona becomes the 48th state as President Taft signs a proclamation.

1930
At the Lowell Observatory, Clyde Tombaugh discovers Pluto.

1965
Judge Lorna Lockwood becomes first woman in the U.S. to head a state supreme court.

1970s
Population in Arizona cities begins huge growth.

1981
State lottery starts.

Did you know...?

☐ The name *Arizona* probably comes from a Native American word *arizonac,* which means "small spring."

☐ Arizona's main nickname is Grand Canyon State. Other nicknames are Baby State, Valentine State, and Copper State.

☐ The average rainfall ranges from less than 3 inches in the southwestern deserts to more than 30 inches in the White Mountains.

☐ The oldest continuously inhabited city in America is Oraibi on the Hopi reservation.

Hi! We're Donna Fosberg's fifth-grade class at the Weitzel School in Flagstaff, Arizona. But you can call us "Fosberg's Fabulous Fifth."

Arizona Scenes

Snow in Arizona? People who live in Arizona's mountains experience all four seasons.

About 50,000 years ago, a 600-million-pound meteor fell to earth east of what is now Flagstaff. The meteor left a crater that is so much like the moon's surface that astronauts trained there.

Here you can see a mule deer walking through the Sonoran Desert. Do you see saguaros in the background and prickly pear cactus in the right foreground?

The beautiful San Francisco Peaks are in northern Arizona near Flagstaff. The peaks are remnants of an ancient volcano.

The Grand Canyon is one of the great wonders of the world. Much of it is in northwest Arizona. It took the Colorado River millions of years to carve out the canyon, a layer-by-layer record of Earth's geologic history.

Did you know...?

- The hottest recorded temperature was 127°F, on July 7, 1905, at Parker.
- The coldest recorded temperature was −40°F, on January 7, 1971, at Hawley Lake near McNary.
- The highest point is 12,633 feet above sea level on Humphrey's Peak in northern Arizona.
- The lowest point is 70 feet above sea level near Yuma along the Colorado River.

For more information about Arizona: http://www.state.az.us/

Arkansas

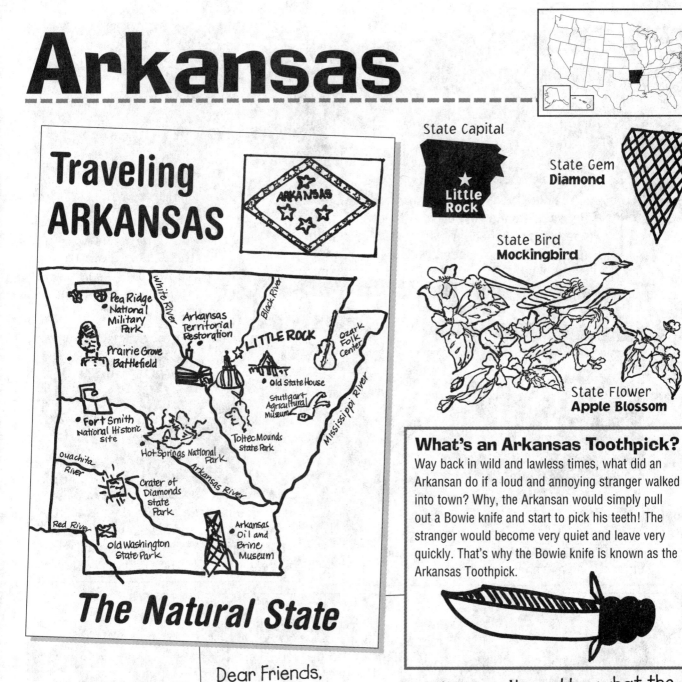

Traveling ARKANSAS

ARKANSAS

Pea Ridge National Military Park
White River
Black River
Arkansas Territorial Restoration
LITTLE ROCK
Ozark Folk Center
Prairie Grove Battlefield
Old State House
Fort Smith National Historic Site
Stuttgart Agricultural Museum
Mississippi River
Ouachita River
Hot Springs National Park
Toltec Mounds State Park
Crater of Diamonds State Park
Arkansas River
Red River
Old Washington State Park
Arkansas Oil and Brine Museum

The Natural State

State Capital
Little Rock

State Gem
Diamond

State Bird
Mockingbird

State Flower
Apple Blossom

What's an Arkansas Toothpick?

Way back in wild and lawless times, what did an Arkansan do if a loud and annoying stranger walked into town? Why, the Arkansan would simply pull out a Bowie knife and start to pick his teeth! The stranger would become very quiet and leave very quickly. That's why the Bowie knife is known as the Arkansas Toothpick.

State Tree
Pine

Dear Friends,
Wish you were here in Arkansas. No matter what the season, our state has beauty as far as the eye can see. In the summer, our blue waters sparkle. In autumn, our trees glow in shades of red, orange, and brown. Winter glistens with powdery white snow. And the pink apple blossoms of spring are soft and new. Hike in our mountains, swim in our lakes, or bathe in the hot springs. You can even dig for diamonds. No wonder we're called the Natural State! Your stay will be magical.
Mrs. Cockerham's Library Classes,
Jessieville Elementary, Jessieville

We got this letter from the President of the United States. He's from Arkansas, too.

Students of Mrs. Cockerham
Sixth Grade Library Class
Jessieville Public School
Post Office Box 4
Jessieville, Arkansas 71949

Dear Students:

Thank you for writing to me. I'm glad that you want to learn more about my home state of Arkansas.

The first people to live in Arkansas were Native Americans, and the word "Arkansas" comes from their Algonquin language. On June 15, 1836, Arkansas became the 25th state admitted to the Union, which is why the Arkansas state flag has a blue diamond formed by twenty-five stars. The diamond on the flag symbolizes Arkansas as the only diamond-producing state in America.

Arkansas' state bird is the mockingbird, its state flower is the apple blossom, and its state motto is "The Natural State." Little Rock, a beautiful city on the Arkansas River, is the capital where I lived for twelve years when I was governor.

I am proud to be a fifth generation Arkansan. I was born in Hope, Arkansas, and moved to nearby Hot Springs when I was seven years old. I enjoy all that Arkansas has to offer: scenic beauty, rolling mountains, cascading rivers, and a determined people. I encourage you to visit your local or school library to learn more about all of our fifty wonderful states.

Thanks again for taking the time to write.

Sincerely,

Bill Clinton

State Rock
Bauxite

State Insect
Bumblebee

State Musical
Instrument
Fiddle

The Arkansas Traveler

On a lonely road quite long ago
A trav'ler trod with fiddle and bow;
While rambling thru the country rich and grand,
He quickly sensed the magic and the beauty of the land.

Arkansas

DID YOU KNOW?

- Arkansas is the home of Mountain Valley Spring Water, which is bottled in Hot Springs and sold around the world.
- Arkansas is the winter home of the bald eagle, national bird of the United States.
- The state's most popular vehicle is the Chevy Pickup.
- Arkansas has the only diamond mine in North America. You can visit it in Murfreesboro.
- One nationwide business with headquarters in Arkansas is Wal-Mart. It was founded by Sam Walton in Bentonville, a town in northwest Arkansas.

- Arkansas is famous for its water springs, which many people believe help cure certain ailments. Eureka Springs has more than 65 springs.
- Arkansas fought on the Confederate side during the Civil War (1861–1865). In 1864 and 1865, the state had both a Union and a Confederate government.
- The name *Arkansas* comes from a Indian word that means "land of downstream people."
- Little Rock has been the state capital since 1821. The capitol building is modeled on the U.S. Capitol in Washington, DC.

Famous Arkansans

Isaac Parker, known as the "hanging judge," brought law and order to the wild American frontier during the 1800s. He sentenced 160 men to death; 79 were hanged. At that time, sentences could not be appealed, except by the U.S. President.

In 1932, **Hattie Caraway** of Jonesboro became the first woman elected to the United States Senate. Two of her favorite causes were helping Arkansans during the Depression in the late 1900s and early 1930s when times were very hard and protecting the rights of women.

Douglas MacArthur, born in Little Rock in 1880, was one of the leading American generals of World War II (1939–1945). He was cited for bravery seven times, decorated 13 times, and wounded three times. After the war he administered American-occupied Japan. He died in 1964.

William Jefferson Clinton, 42nd president of the U.S., is the man from Hope. He was born in that Arkansas town in 1946 and attended high school in Hot Springs, where he grew up. Though he went to university in other parts of the nation and in England, he has never forgotten his roots. It was in Arkansas that he recovered from his defeat in a 1974 race for the U.S.

Poet, Author

World War II General

First Woman U.S. Senator

Founder of Wal-Mart

42nd President of U.S.

House of Representatives and ran successfully for governor in 1979. He then decided to run for the presidency.

Scottie Pippen, a star player of the Chicago Bulls basketball team, was born in Hamburg, Arkansas, in 1965 and attended the University of Central Arkansas. In 1991 the Bulls won their first championship. Pippen sure helped! He made 32 points.

Sam Walton (1918–1992), founder of the Wal-Mart store empire, is one of the great American success stories. He open his first store in Rogers, Arkansas, on July 2, 1962. By the 1980s, he was one of the nation's wealthiest men.

Maya Angelou, poet and author, was raised in Stamps, Arkansas. As a child she helped her grandmother run a small general store. Always filled with the spirit of creativity, she was a professional dancer before she tried her hand at writing. She has been a nominee for the National Book Award, Pulitzer Prize, and the Tony (theater) and Emmy (TV) Awards. She is best known for her autobiographical book *I Know Why the Caged Bird Sings* and for reciting her poem "On the Pulse of Morning" at the 1993 inauguration of President Clinton.

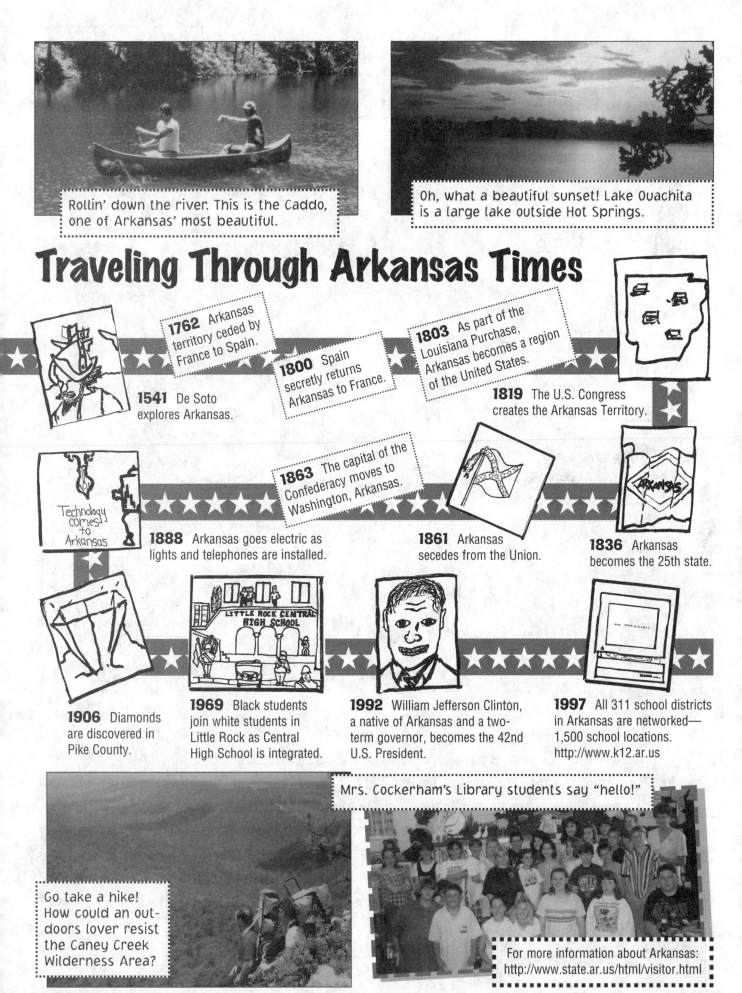

Rollin' down the river. This is the Caddo, one of Arkansas' most beautiful.

Oh, what a beautiful sunset! Lake Ouachita is a large lake outside Hot Springs.

Traveling Through Arkansas Times

1541 De Soto explores Arkansas.

1762 Arkansas territory ceded by France to Spain.

1800 Spain secretly returns Arkansas to France.

1803 As part of the Louisiana Purchase, Arkansas becomes a region of the United States.

1819 The U.S. Congress creates the Arkansas Territory.

Technology comes to Arkansas

1863 The capital of the Confederacy moves to Washington, Arkansas.

1888 Arkansas goes electric as lights and telephones are installed.

1861 Arkansas secedes from the Union.

1836 Arkansas becomes the 25th state.

1906 Diamonds are discovered in Pike County.

1969 Black students join white students in Little Rock as Central High School is integrated.

1992 William Jefferson Clinton, a native of Arkansas and a two-term governor, becomes the 42nd U.S. President.

1997 All 311 school districts in Arkansas are networked—1,500 school locations. http://www.k12.ar.us

Go take a hike! How could an outdoors lover resist the Caney Creek Wilderness Area?

Mrs. Cockerham's Library students say "hello!"

For more information about Arkansas: http://www.state.ar.us/html/visitor.html

California

State Capital
★ **Sacramento**

State Motto
Eureka
(I have found it)

State Flag
Bear Flag

State Fish
Golden Trout

California

The Golden State

State Bird
California Valley Quail

State Seal

To: Kids Everywhere, USA

This is California, where the Gold Rush began in 1849. That's why we're the Golden State! There are a lot of places to have adventures here: Marine World, Africa USA, Disneyland, Water World, and the San Diego Zoo. There's more to California than sunny beaches. We have four distinct regions in our state: the valley, the desert, the mountains, and the coast. We hope you can visit sometime!

Ms. Go's 3rd- & 4th-Grade Class,
Foulks Ranch Elementary, Elk Grove

Famous People and Things They Did in CALIFORNIA

As the first woman to fly her own plane across the Atlantic and Pacific oceans, **AMELIA EARHART** was a natural to try flying around the world on her own. One stop on that journey was Oakland, California. But less than two months later, on July 2, 1937, when she was 39 years old, her plane disappeared from radio contact. Despite a huge search effort, she disappeared forever. Her fate is still a mystery.

Thousands of people work in the farm fields of California, picking crops like lettuce, strawberries, and grapes. The lives of these migrant workers, who move from farm to farm with the seasons, have always been hard. But thanks to the efforts of **CESAR CHAVEZ,** farm workers' conditions have improved. Born in Mexico, Chavez was himself a migrant worker. Starting in the 1960s, he organized a group, the United Farm Workers, to fight for workers' rights.

She's out of this world! **SALLY RIDE,** the astronaut, was born in Los Angeles in 1951 and went to Stanford University in Palo Alto. The second woman in space, she flew aboard the *Challenger* space shuttle in 1983. Sally Ride twice flew in space.

Before he became the 40th president of the United States in 1980, **RONALD REAGAN** was a movie star and then the governor of California.

The name of **JOHN SUTTER** has always been linked with the great Gold Rush that brought thousands of hopeful miners to California. In 1839, the Mexican governor of California gave him a large grant of land in the Sacramento Valley. There he built Sutter's Fort, a trading center and colony for settlers. It was on this land that gold was discovered in 1848.

Traveling Through Time in CALIFORNIA

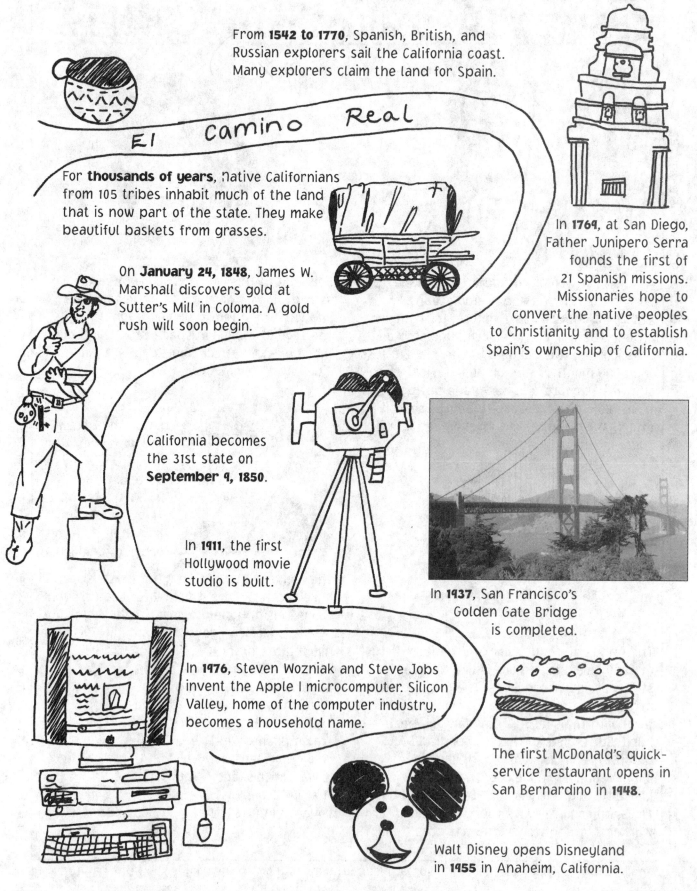

From **1542 to 1770**, Spanish, British, and Russian explorers sail the California coast. Many explorers claim the land for Spain.

El Camino Real

For **thousands of years**, Native Californians from 105 tribes inhabit much of the land that is now part of the state. They make beautiful baskets from grasses.

On **January 24, 1848**, James W. Marshall discovers gold at Sutter's Mill in Coloma. A gold rush will soon begin.

In **1769**, at San Diego, Father Junipero Serra founds the first of 21 Spanish missions. Missionaries hope to convert the native peoples to Christianity and to establish Spain's ownership of California.

California becomes the 31st state on **September 9, 1850**.

In **1911**, the first Hollywood movie studio is built.

In **1937**, San Francisco's Golden Gate Bridge is completed.

In **1976**, Steven Wozniak and Steve Jobs invent the Apple I microcomputer. Silicon Valley, home of the computer industry, becomes a household name.

The first McDonald's quick-service restaurant opens in San Bernardino in **1948**.

Walt Disney opens Disneyland in **1955** in Anaheim, California.

CALIFORNIA Is Way Cool

Drive Through a Tree
Imagine taking your car through the trunk of a tree! You can do that with the General Grant redwood tree, said to be the second-largest living thing on Earth. The tree stands in Grant Grove in Kings Canyon. It is 267 feet high and 107.6 feet wide. The tree was named for Ulysses S. Grant, the Civil War general, and is a shrine to those killed in war.

Death Valley
Death Valley, at 196 feet below sea level, is the largest national park outside of Alaska. During the day, Death Valley has the highest temperatures of any place in California. But at night, temperatures plunge into the 20's. The park in Death Valley is alive with waterfalls, a forest of tall Joshua trees, canyons, mountains, cacti, and springs.

Blue Jeans for Gold Miners
Do you wear Levi's? The blue jeans are named for Levi Strauss, a San Francisco man who was the first to find a wide use for denim fabric. He sold them to gold miners.

Beautiful Yosemite
Camp in Yosemite National Park or hike its 750 miles of trails. Three million people visit there every year. Yosemite was formed thousands of years ago when a glacier melted at the end of the Ice Age. Rushing water formed many incredible natural structures like Half Dome. (photo at right)

The Wonderful California Coast
At every time of the year, the mild coastal climate has plenty of sunshine and a lot of fog. The Pacific Ocean coastline winds along 838 miles. Along it you'll find San Diego, Los Angeles, San Francisco, and Mendocino. Sharks, whales, sea otters, sea lions, fish, octopus, squid, crabs, dolphins, and oysters all live in the coastal waters.

Building a Railroad
Building a railroad across the state and across America in the 1800s depended on good and strong workers. The railroad company sought laborers in China. But it wasn't only the promise of work that encouraged Chinese immigrants to travel to San Francisco. They thought the hills of San Francisco were made of gold and called them "Kum Sham," the golden hills.

Gold Fever
In 1848, James W. Marshall struck gold at Sutter's Mill in Coloma, California. Gold fever, the lure of finding a fortune in gold, caused people to leave their families, homes, and jobs for Sutter's Mill. Because the Gold Rush officially started in 1849, these people were called forty-niners.

For more information:
http://www.state.ca.us

Colorado

Just the Facts...

State Capital
Denver

State Nickname
Centennial State

State Flower
Columbine

State Bird
Lark Bunting

State Fossil
Stegasaurus

Welcome to Colorado where the sun shines 310 days a year! You probably know we have beautiful mountains. Our Rocky Mountains are famous for great hiking, camping, and skiing! In fact, we have 53 mountains that are more than 14,000 feet tall! But you might be surprised to learn we also have rolling plains and rugged plateaus. We also have the tallest sand dunes in all of North America! It's like having a little bit of Egypt in Colorado. We have a lot of old mining towns because there was a gold rush here in 1859. There are even places you can still pan for gold!

Visiting Colorado is like looking through a kaleidoscope. There are endless possibilities of beautiful designs in a kaleidoscope and there are endless possibilites of things to see and do in colorful Colorado! Come visit!

Ms. Burris's and Ms. Pittenger's Third- and Fourth-Grade Class, Slater Elementary, Lakewood

Totally Cool Trivia

Where was the largest silver nugget found? It was found in Aspen, Colorado, in 1835. It was 93% silver! It weighed 1,840 pounds!

What do the two blue stripes and middle white stripe on the Colorado flag represent? The two blue stripes represent skis and the white stripe represents snow. Skiing is big business in Colorado. There are 35 ski resorts in Colorado.

Why do some coins have an uppercase "D" printed on them? Coins with the "D" were printed at the Denver Mint. It is one of only four mints in the U.S. The Denver Mint makes $200,000 worth of coins each day!

Why is Denver called the Mile High City? Denver is 5,280 feet above sea level. One mile equals 5,280 feet.

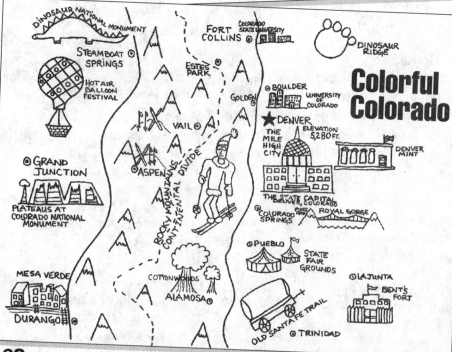

Colorful Colorado

Just the facts... **State Tree:** Blue Spruce
State Insect: Hairstreak Butterfly
State Animal: Rocky Mountain Long Horn Sheep

Major League Sports Teams: Football—Denver Broncos; Basketball—Colorado Nuggets; Hockey—Colorado Avalanche; Baseball—Colorado Rockies

❖ **More information about Colorado is available on the internet: www.state.co.us/colorado.html** ❖

FAMOUS COLORADANS

John Colter was a fur trapper in the 1800s. He wanted to trade with the Blackfeet Indians. They didn't want to because he traded with their enemies the Crow. So  they stripped him naked, gave him a head start, and the warriors told him to run for his life. He escaped by outrunning them and hiding in a beaver lodge.

Molly Brown struck it rich in the silver mines of Colorado. She was on the *Titanic*, a luxurious ocean liner that was supposed to be  unsinkable. On its maiden voyage in 1912, it hit an iceberg and sank. Molly was one of the few survivors. She also saved seven people. Now she is known as "the Unsinkable Molly Brown."

Baby Doe Tabor (1854–1935) got rich from silver mined in Leadville. She was so rich that she enjoyed watching her husband throw silver dollars 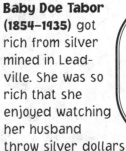 into crowds of people! In 1893 silver became as worthless as dirt and she became very poor. She lived in a shack and guarded the Matchless Silver Mine for 35 years, hoping that silver would become valuable again.

 **Byron White (1917–)** was a justice on the U.S. Supreme Court. He served on the court from 1962–1993. He went to the University of Colorado. He played football at C. U. He earned the nickname "Whizzer" by running and weaving past opponents.

 **Scott Carpenter (1925–)** was one of the first U.S. astronauts in space. He orbited Earth three times in the spaceship *Mercury*. There is a park in Boulder named in his honor.

Justina Ford (1871–1952) was the first African-American woman doctor in Colorado. She delivered 7,000 babies in her 50-year career. Most were from poor families. If they couldn't pay her $15 fee, she would accept clothes, food, or anything they could spare as payment.

Amy Van Dyken (1973–) is an Olympic swimmer. She overcame asthma and won four gold medals in the 1996 Summer Olympic Games. That's more than any U.S. woman has ever won in one Olympics! Amy knows sign language and hopes to work with deaf children in the future.

PIKES PEAK OR BUST

In 1858 gold was discovered in Colorado. In one year 100,000 people headed west hoping to strike it rich! Wagons painted with the slogan "Pikes Peak or Bust" rushed into Colorado. The first way people tried to get rich was by panning for gold in Colorado's rivers. Then the miners started searching inside the earth for gold with picks, hammers, and dynamite. This type of mining is called hard rock mining and it's dangerous, but the miners had gold fever! Cave-ins were common, and many miners died.

Many miners believed that the miners killed in the mines came back as tommy-knockers. Tommy-knockers are small elf-like creatures with old wrinkled faces and long arms like an ape. They wear colorful shirts and tiny miners' boots. Tommy-knockers knock on the mine walls and lead miners to gold. They also warn the miners of cave-ins. Sometimes the tommy-knockers like to play tricks on the miners, and so they spill their lunch buckets and hide their tools.

Colorado Time Traveler Game

Dinosaurs, Indians, explorers, cowboys, silver, and gold—Colorado's history is exciting and bold!
Learn about Colorado's exciting past as you play the Colorado Time Traveler Game.

Players: 2–6

Materials: die, place markers

1. Players take turns rolling the die and moving that number of spaces.

2. Players read the words on the space and do what they say.

3. The winner is the first one to reach the gold dome of the Colorado Capitol. We bet that you will arrive there knowing a lot about Colorado history.

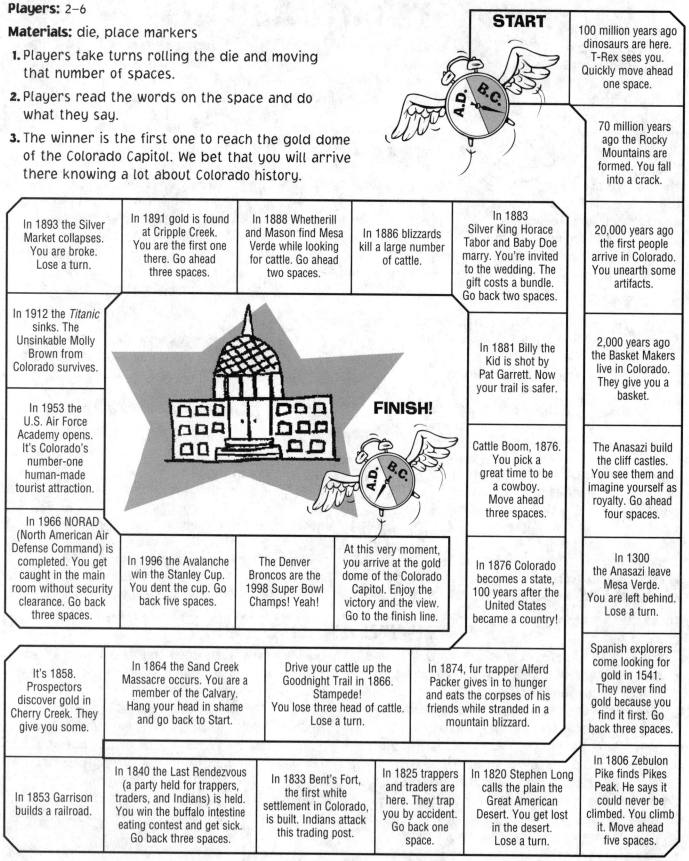

START

100 million years ago dinosaurs are here. T-Rex sees you. Quickly move ahead one space.

70 million years ago the Rocky Mountains are formed. You fall into a crack.

In 1893 the Silver Market collapses. You are broke. Lose a turn.

In 1891 gold is found at Cripple Creek. You are the first one there. Go ahead three spaces.

In 1888 Wetherill and Mason find Mesa Verde while looking for cattle. Go ahead two spaces.

In 1886 blizzards kill a large number of cattle.

In 1883 Silver King Horace Tabor and Baby Doe marry. You're invited to the wedding. The gift costs a bundle. Go back two spaces.

20,000 years ago the first people arrive in Colorado. You unearth some artifacts.

In 1912 the *Titanic* sinks. The Unsinkable Molly Brown from Colorado survives.

In 1881 Billy the Kid is shot by Pat Garrett. Now your trail is safer.

2,000 years ago the Basket Makers live in Colorado. They give you a basket.

In 1953 the U.S. Air Force Academy opens. It's Colorado's number-one human-made tourist attraction.

FINISH!

Cattle Boom, 1876. You pick a great time to be a cowboy. Move ahead three spaces.

The Anasazi build the cliff castles. You see them and imagine yourself as royalty. Go ahead four spaces.

In 1966 NORAD (North American Air Defense Command) is completed. You get caught in the main room without security clearance. Go back three spaces.

In 1996 the Avalanche win the Stanley Cup. You dent the cup. Go back five spaces.

The Denver Broncos are the 1998 Super Bowl Champs! Yeah!

At this very moment, you arrive at the gold dome of the Colorado Capitol. Enjoy the victory and the view. Go to the finish line.

In 1876 Colorado becomes a state, 100 years after the United States became a country!

In 1300 the Anasazi leave Mesa Verde. You are left behind. Lose a turn.

It's 1858. Prospectors discover gold in Cherry Creek. They give you some.

In 1864 the Sand Creek Massacre occurs. You are a member of the Calvary. Hang your head in shame and go back to Start.

Drive your cattle up the Goodnight Trail in 1866. Stampede! You lose three head of cattle. Lose a turn.

In 1874, fur trapper Alferd Packer gives in to hunger and eats the corpses of his friends while stranded in a mountain blizzard.

Spanish explorers come looking for gold in 1541. They never find gold because you find it first. Go back three spaces.

In 1853 Garrison builds a railroad.

In 1840 the Last Rendezvous (a party held for trappers, traders, and Indians) is held. You win the buffalo intestine eating contest and get sick. Go back three spaces.

In 1833 Bent's Fort, the first white settlement in Colorado, is built. Indians attack this trading post.

In 1825 trappers and traders are here. They trap you by accident. Go back one space.

In 1820 Stephen Long calls the plain the Great American Desert. You get lost in the desert. Lose a turn.

In 1806 Zebulon Pike finds Pikes Peak. He says it could never be climbed. You climb it. Move ahead five spaces.

Here we are on the steps of our **Mile High Capitol!**

Dinosaurs used to live in Colorado! Here's proof!

⬛ Colorado ⬛

Colorado, Colorado, the Centennial State,
For many reasons it is great.

The Rockies were formed 70 million years ago.
The dinosaurs were extinct and couldn't watch the show!

The first Coloradans roamed far and wide,
Hunting woolly Mammoth with their thick hides.

The basket makers were definitely not fools.
Archaeologists have found their wonderful tools

Anasazis are known as "the Ancient Ones."
Why did they leave their cliff homes? Where did they go?

Majestic Indian tribes on the plains lived and died.
They used super horsemanship as after buffalo they did ride.

Trappers and traders in the mountains did abide,
Catching fox and beavers, and taking their hides.

Pike and Long were explorers brave.
Mistakes they made were indeed grave.

1858 Gold, Gold, Gold was found.
Prospectors rushed west to dig in rivers and mine underground.

Cattle grazed on prairies fine,
As cowboys rode and kept them in line.

Modern Colorado boasts of NORAD, the Air Force Academy with
    cadets, defenders of the free,
The Broncos, the Rockies, and pristine slopes where we can ski.

Colorado, Colorado, the Centennial State.
And these are the reasons it is great!

The **Anasazi** built the first apartments in the cliffs of southwest Colorado.

Eureka! We're panning for **gold**!

The **sand mountains** are a sight to see.

Connecticut

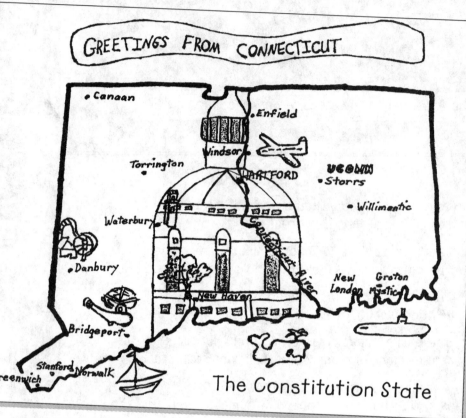

State Nickname
The Constitution State

Connecticut's first laws formed a model for the United States Constitution. Connecticut is also known as the Nutmeg State. Yankee peddlers, whose specialty was nutmeg, traveled the countryside selling imported spices and products made in the state.

State Capital

Hartford

State Bird
Robin
The robin, first named by colonists, became the state bird in 1943.

State Flower
Mountain Laurel
Mountain laurel grows on the rocky slopes and sandy soil of Connecticut.

State Animal
Sperm Whale
Whaling was an important industry in Connecticut in the 1800s.

State Insect
Praying Mantis
The praying mantis can be found throughout the state from early May until cold weather sets in.

GREETINGS FROM CONNECTICUT

The Constitution State

Hi Everyone!
Connecticut has lots of interesting places to visit from aquariums to museums. You can learn about animals, about writers and about history.
Just look at all the construction going on and you'll see how fast we're growing. Roads are being paved so that more and more people can and visit our great state. If you come, you'll enjoy shopping, visiting interesting attractions, and staying at nice hotels.
Mrs. Ricci's Fifth-Grade Class,
St. Mary's School, Waterbury

State Flag
The three grape vines on this flag stand for the three original settlements of the Connecticut Colony: Windsor, Hartford, and Wethersfield. The state motto is *Qui Transtulit Sustinet*, which means "He who brought us over will sustain us."

THOMAS HOOKER is known as the Father of Connecticut. He was a Puritan minister whose sermon led to the writing of the Fundamental Orders, the first written Constitution.

MARK TWAIN, the pen name of Samuel L. Clemens, was a famous artist and humorist. *Tom Sawyer* is one book he wrote. He wrote many other famous books while living in Hartford.

NATHAN HALE was hanged by the British as a spy in 1776. Born in Coventry, he was 21 years old when he died. He said, "I regret that I have but one life to give for my country."

P. T. BARNUM was born in 1810 in Bethel. He began putting on shows in 1836. In 1880, he and J. A. Bailey formed Barnum and Bailey's Circus, "the Greatest Show on Earth."

PRUDENCE CRANDALL opened the first school for African-American women in 1833. She was put on trial for this, and her school closed. She is remembered for having the courage to take a stand against prejudice.

THOMAS GALLAUDET was a teacher. In 1817 he opened the first free public school for the deaf. It is in Hartford and is now called the American School for the Deaf.

Connecticut's Web Site:
http://www. town.usa.com/Connecticut

Connecticut's Division of Tourism
865 Brook Street
Rocky Hill, CT 06067
1-800-282-6863

Many well-known actors, authors, and illustrators come from or live in Connecticut. Here, some share their thoughts about Connecticut.

"Connecticut is the backdrop for several of my historical novels and the subject of all my scholarly works," says **Christopher Collier**, author of *My Brother Sam Is Dead.*

Maurice Sendak, author of *Chicken Soup With Rice* and *Where the Wild Things Are*, says, "The sheer beauty, the silence, the ability to walk through the woods, to anticipate seasons (even winter sometimes)" are the things he likes best about Connecticut.

Steven Kellogg, author and illustrator of *Best Friends, Can I Keep Him?, Pinkerton,* and *Behave*, likes Connecticut because "it is a very beautiful state. I think it helped inspire me to be an artist."

Bridgewater is the favorite town of **Hila Colman**, author of *Claudia, Where Are You?* "It's a wonderful town with interesting people and a great sense of community."

"The friendly people and excellent libraries of Connecticut" are what **Thomas Gunning**, author of *Strange Mysteries*, likes best.

There's no mystery to **Madeleine L'Engle**'s reasons. The author of *A Wrinkle in Time, A Swiftly Tilting Planet,* and *A Wind in the Door,* says, "The northwest corner of the state is one of the most beautiful parts of the world. The Litchfield Hills bring peace and perspective."

Paula Feder, author of *Where Does the Teacher Live?* says, "When I moved to Connecticut 20 years ago, I was able to combine city and country and enjoy the best of both."

Connecticut Has a Lot of History

Before 1614 Native Americans live in Connecticut.

1614 Dutch explorer, Adraien Block, explores the Connecticut River.

1636 Wethersfield, Windsor, and Hartford unite to become Connecticut Colony.

1639 Fundamental Orders, the first written Constitution, is adopted.

1622 John Winthrop receives a charter from King Charles II of England.

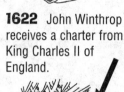

1784 The first American law school is established in Litchfield.

1776 Samuel Huntington, Roger Sherman, William Williams, and Oliver Wolcott sign the Declaration of Independence.

1764 *The Hartford Courant*, the longest-published newspaper in the U.S., begins publication.

1701 Yale College, then called Collegiate School, is founded.

1687 The Charter Oak hides the Charter from the new royal governor, Sir Edmund Andros.

1787 The Connecticut Compromise is adopted by the Constitutional Convention.

1788 Connecticut is the fifth state to join the Union.

1793 Eli Whitney invents the cotton gin.

1807 Noah Webster publishes the first American English dictionary.

1836 Samuel Colt invents the revolver.

1910 United States Coast Guard Academy moves to New London.

1900 First U.S. Navy submarine is built in Groton by Electric Boat Company.

1875 Hartford becomes the only state capital after sharing duties with New Haven since 1701.

1846 Elias Howe invents the sewing machine.

1839 Charles Goodyear develops the vulcanization process for rubber.

  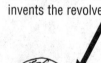

1939 Igor Sikorsky designs the first helicopter in Stratford.

1954 USS *Nautilus*, the world's first atom-powered submarine, is launched at Groton.

1966 Dinosaur tracks are found at Rocky Hill.

1974 Ella Grasso becomes the first woman governor elected on her own, without following her husband in office.

1996 First presidential debate between Bill Clinton and Bob Dole held in Hartford.

  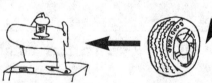 

How did the white oak become Connecticut's state tree?

These events took place in 1687, while Sir Edmund Andros was royal governor of Connecticut and New England.

"Give me the charter, Sir," Andros demanded. He and other people in the room were standing around a table lit by candles.

The charter was just about to be handed over when all became dark. The candles were blown out. When they were relit, the charter was missing. Someone had sneaked out of the building with it. The charter was hidden in a hollow oak tree. The provisions of the charter were restored when a new king came to the throne in England. The oak tree that hid the charter lived until 1856. It was blown down during a storm.

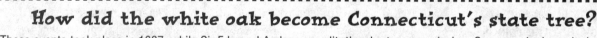

Connecticut Sights and Sounds

Attention!
The United States Coast Guard Academy in New London trains men and women to be U.S. Coast Guard officers. It was established in 1876.

No Bars
During the Revolutionary War, Old Newgate was the colonies' first prison. Now you can visit it.

Underwater
USS *Nautilus*,  the world's first nuclear submarine, is on display at the U.S. Naval Submarine Base in Groton. When you go to see it, stop by the museum to learn more about submarines.

Build a Boat
You can learn to build a boat at the Norwalk Maritime Aquarium by Long Island Sound.

What a Sight!
Connecticut's capitol is a National Historic Landmark. The Legislative Office Building is the most modern state office building in the United States. You can go between it and the capitol by using a tunnel.

Coast Guard Academy
Old Newgate Prison
Nuclear Submarine Base Home of Nautilus
Norwalk Maritime Aquarium
Eli Whitney Museum
Capitol in Hartford
The Peabody Museum
Indian Archaeological Institute
Clock and Watch Museum
U-CONN and its Huskies
The Mattatuck Museum

Still Standing
Find out more about the inventor of the cotton gin at the Eli Whitney Museum. It includes the remaining buildings of Whitneyville, a factory he built to produce firearms using mass production.

Famous Fossils
The Peabody Museum in New Haven is one of the largest museums of natural history in our country. It has a world-famous collection of dinosaur fossils.

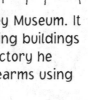

Native Life
If you're interested in the life of Native Americans, the Institute for American Indian Studies is the place to go. It's in Washington, Connecticut.

Full of Brass
The Mattatuck Museum in Waterbury is filled with fascinating facts about the brass industry. Included are displays about Eli Terry and Seth Thomas who began the clock-making industry in Connecticut.

Our Pride
We call the state University of Connecticut, U-CONN. It has about 11,000 students enrolled. The school's mascot is a husky dog. Three woofs for U-CONN.

Tick Tock!
The American Clock and Watch Museum in Bristol salutes the Connecticut clock industry. The museum has old clocks from the late 1700s that have wooden movements as well as modern clocks and watches.

What's in a Name?
Did you know that the name *Connecticut* came from the Algonquian language? It means "at the long tidal river." Many other places in Connecticut also have Native American names.

Native Americans were very sensible in the names they chose. For example, Quinnipiac, which means "long water land," is what Algonquians called the place where New Haven, a major port, now sits. Many cities, rivers, ponds, and beaches have Indian names, like Housatonic, Quassapaug, and Mattatuck.

Even the name "Yankee" is a gift from the Native Americans. It is what they called the English who first came to their shores in the 1600s.

Mrs. Ricci's Fifth-Grade Class

Delaware

State Capital
☆ Dover

Delaware, the state that fits so much into so tiny a space!

State Nickname
The First State

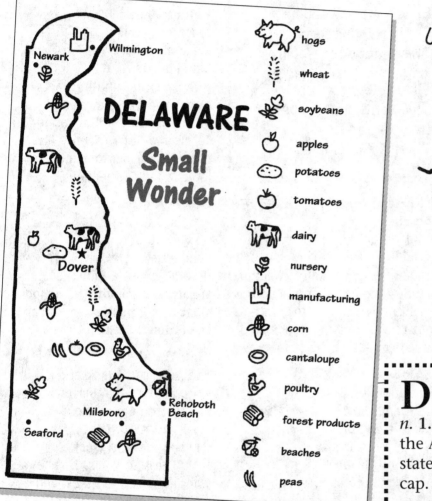

DELAWARE
Small Wonder

- hogs
- wheat
- soybeans
- apples
- potatoes
- tomatoes
- dairy
- nursery
- manufacturing
- corn
- cantaloupe
- poultry
- forest products
- beaches
- peas

Newark • Wilmington
Dover
Milsboro • Rehoboth Beach
Seaford

Delaware, FIRST STATE, the first to join the United States of America!

State Insect
Ladybug

State Flower
Peach Blossom

Del-a-ware

n. **1.** eastern state of the U.S., on the Atlantic: one of the 13 original states; 2,489 sq. mi.; pop.717,000; cap. Dover; abbr. Del., DE

Dear Readers,
   Delaware may be small, but we have a lot to offer! Don't try to see and do everything in a week. We think that the spring and summer are the best times to visit our state because of the beaches.The warm sand and cool breezes call to you. WOW! What a way to spend summer vacation.You can see a variety of things in Delaware from peach orchards to historical sites. Look us up when you get to the northeast.
   Mrs. Tingle and Mrs. Wright's Fourth-Grade Class, Frederick Douglass Intermediate School, Seaford

State Tree
American Holly

Delaware's Finest

Felix Darley
(1822–1888) Lived in Claymont
Have you seen his illustrations in *Legend of Sleepy Hollow* and *Rip Van Winkle*? (They won't put you to sleep!)

Howard Pyle
(1853–1911) Born in Wilmington
An art teacher, he often painted colonial scenes. He's best known for the 15 children's books that he wrote and illustrated. Among them are *The Merry Adventures of Robin Hood* and *Modern Aladdin*.

Richard Allen
(1760–1831) Raised on a plantation near Dover
Born into slavery, he bought his freedom and became a religious leader. His church was a station on the Underground Railroad.

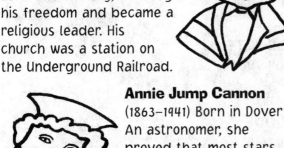

Annie Jump Cannon
(1863–1941) Born in Dover
An astronomer, she proved that most stars can be grouped according to color. She discovered five new stars and classified more than 375,000 stars. She was certainly someone to look up to!

Henry Jay Heimlich
(1920–) Native of Wilmington
If you ever choke on food, you'll be grateful for the Heimlich maneuver. Within 12 years, this technique saved more than 10,000 people.

Edward Robinson Squibb
(1819–1900) Native of Wilmington
As a naval surgeon, convinced the U.S. Navy to build its own drug factory. You may recognize the name of the company he founded: Squibb Pharmaceuticals

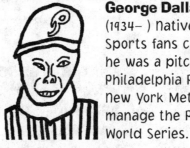

George Dallas Green, Jr.
(1934–) Native of Newport
Sports fans cheered him when he was a pitcher for the Philadelphia Phillies and the New York Mets. He went on to manage the Phillies in the 1980 World Series.

Valerie Bertinelli
(1960–) Born in Wilmington
Among this actress's movies are *Aladdin and His Wonderful Lamp* and *C.H.O.M.P.S.*

Judge Reinhold
(1958–) Born in Wilmington
Have you seen the movies in which he's acted, *Beverly Hills Cop* and *Ruthless People*?

Through the Years in DELA...WHERE??? (aka DELAWARE)

1609....Henry Hudson explores Delaware Bay

1631....Dutch establish Zwaanendael (first European settlement)

1638....Swedes build Fort Christina (now Wilmington)

1682....Duke of York gives William Penn the Delaware Counties

1776....Delaware delegates sign the Declaration of Independence

1787....FIRST STATE IN THE UNION! Hooray for Delaware!

1802....E. I. Du Pont founds Powder Mill on Brandywine Creek

1829....Delaware Canal opens

1861-1865....Ft. Delaware holds Confederate prisoners during Civil War

1917....State Highway Department instituted in Delaware

1939....Du Pont plant, where nylon was first made, opens in Seaford

1951....Delaware Memorial Bridge links Delaware and New Jersey

1957....State gives money for needy to attend University of Delaware

A DELAWARE CALENDAR

August	September	October
Watermelon Festival (Laurel)	Delaware 500 Stock Car Races (Dover) — Nanticoke Indian PowWow (Millsboro)	Sea Witch Festival (Rehoboth Beach) — Coast Day (Lewes)
November	**December**	**January**
Bombay Hook Field Day (Smyrna)	Candelight Tours, Hagley Museum (Wilmington)	Festival for Youth (Seaford)
February	**March**	**April**
Happy Valentine's Day We Love Delaware	Delaware Gem & Mineral Show (Claymont)	Great Delaware Kite Festival (Lewes) — Delmarva Hot Air Balloon Festival (Milton)
May	**June**	**July**
Dover Air Force Base Air Show Old Dover Days World Weakfish Tournament (Milford)	Congratulations, Graduates	Delaware State Fair (Harrington)

Get to Know Delaware

NATURAL RESOURCES
magnesium, sand and gravel, brandywine blue granite

AGRICULTURAL PRODUCTS
chickens, milk, hogs, soybeans, corn, barley, wheat, peas, potatoes, apples, flowers, shrubs

MANUFACTURED GOODS
drugs, industrial chemicals, plastics, nylon, gelatin, pudding, packaged chicken, canned vegetables, fish products, soft drinks, cars, paper products

AREA 2,489 Square Miles

POPULATION 717,197 (1995)

Here's where we work:

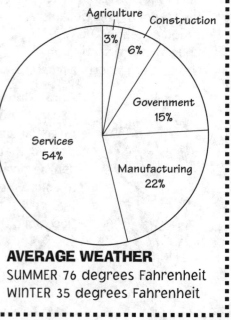

Agriculture 3%
Construction 6%
Government 15%
Manufacturing 22%
Services 54%

AVERAGE WEATHER
SUMMER 76 degrees Fahrenheit
WINTER 35 degrees Fahrenheit

DELAWARE ALMANAC

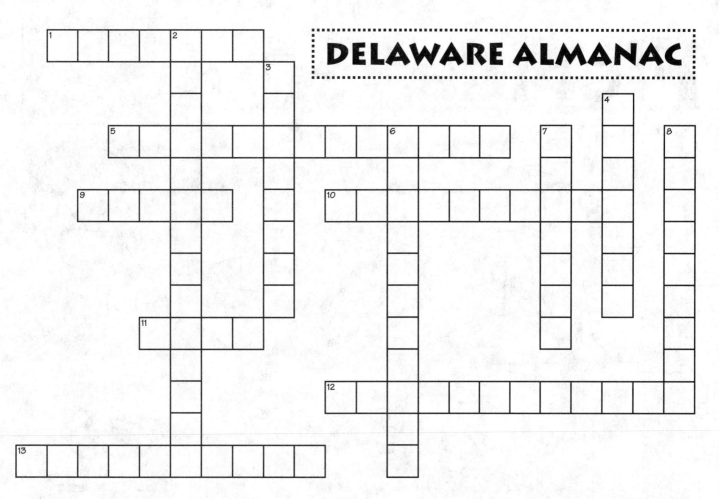

ACROSS

1. State insect
5. State tree
9. Capital
10. Delaware's nickname
11. State beverage
12. State flower
13. Many chemical companies here

DOWN

2. State bird
3. Month U.S. Constitution ratified
4. ___ and Independence (state motto)
6. State song
7. Home of Frederick Douglass Intermediate School
8. Natural resource

WORD BOX

PEACH BLOSSOM
AMERICAN HOLLY
FIRST STATE
DOVER
MAGNESIUM
LIBERTY
SEAFORD

WILMINGTON
MILK
BLUE HEN CHICKEN
LADYBUG
OUR DELAWARE
DECEMBER

Mrs. Tingle and Mrs. Wright's
Fourth-Grade Class
Frederick Douglass Intermediate School
Seaford, Delaware

Delaware Tourism Office
Post Office Box 1401, Dept. R
Dover, Delaware 19903
(800) 441-8846

http://www.state.de.us

Florida

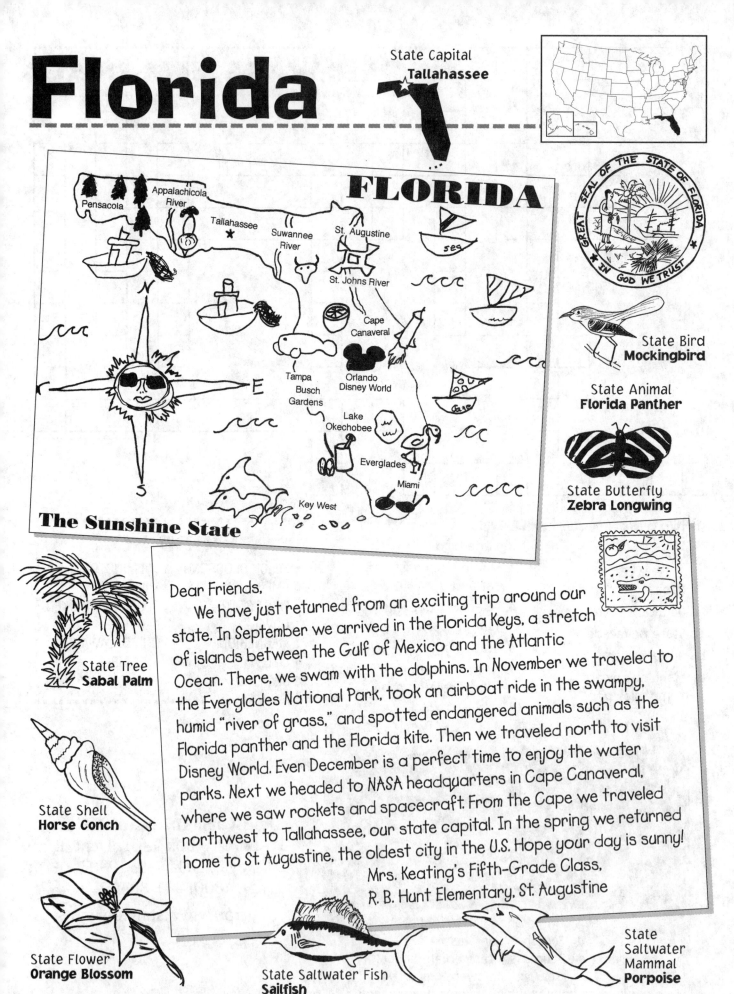

State Capital
Tallahassee

FLORIDA

The Sunshine State

Pensacola
Appalachicola River
Tallahassee
Suwannee River
St. Augustine
St. Johns River
Tampa Busch Gardens
Cape Canaveral
Orlando Disney World
Lake Okechobee
Everglades
Miami
Key West

GREAT SEAL OF THE STATE OF FLORIDA · IN GOD WE TRUST

State Bird
Mockingbird

State Animal
Florida Panther

State Butterfly
Zebra Longwing

State Tree
Sabal Palm

State Shell
Horse Conch

State Flower
Orange Blossom

State Saltwater Fish
Sailfish

State Saltwater Mammal
Porpoise

Dear Friends,
   We have just returned from an exciting trip around our state. In September we arrived in the Florida Keys, a stretch of islands between the Gulf of Mexico and the Atlantic Ocean. There, we swam with the dolphins. In November we traveled to the Everglades National Park, took an airboat ride in the swampy, humid "river of grass," and spotted endangered animals such as the Florida panther and the Florida kite. Then we traveled north to visit Disney World. Even December is a perfect time to enjoy the water parks. Next we headed to NASA headquarters in Cape Canaveral, where we saw rockets and spacecraft. From the Cape we traveled northwest to Tallahassee, our state capital. In the spring we returned home to St. Augustine, the oldest city in the U.S. Hope your day is sunny!
   Mrs. Keating's Fifth-Grade Class,
   R. B. Hunt Elementary, St. Augustine

A Place in the Florida Sun

JUAN PONCE DE LEON (1460–1521) first explored Florida in 1513. In Spanish, the name means "Land of Flowers."

OSCEOLA (1803–1838) was a famous Seminole Indian leader. He led the Seminoles against the white soldiers in the Seminole Wars. He was captured in 1837 and died six months later.

HENRY MORRISON FLAGLER (1830–1913) built railroad lines along Florida's east coast from Jacksonville to Miami. Eventually his railroad lines stretched across bridges connecting the Florida Keys.

MARY MCLEOD BETHUNE (1875–1955) was born in South Carolina and moved to Daytona Beach in 1904. She was the first of her brothers and sisters to go to school. In 1904 she used all the money she had to build a school for black girls. That school became Bethune-Cookman College.

MARJORIE KINNAN RAWLINGS (1896–1952), an award-winning writer, moved to a tiny village in Florida named Cross Creek. She won a Pulitzer prize for *The Yearling*, the story of a Florida boy and his pet fawn.

JANET RENO (1938–) was born in Miami, Florida. She served as Florida's attorney general from 1978 until 1993. That's when she was appointed by President Clinton to be the first female attorney general in U.S. history.

The Secret River
by Marjorie Kinnan Rawlings

This fantastic book is about a girl named Calpurnia and her dog Buggy-horse. Calpurnia's father owns a small fish market but can't seem to catch any fish. Calpurnia hears about a secret river and decides to find it. After a while she and Buggie-horse happen upon the river. They fish there most of the day and catch lots of catfish. On the way home, they meet different creatures of the river and give away some of their fish. But in the end, there is enough for her father to sell.

—*Ryan McDevitt-Galles, reviewer*

Get to Know Florida

Population 14,399,985 (1996)

Major Industry Tourism

Climate Subtropical to tropical, warm and humid

Major Crops Oranges, grapefruit, and tangerines

Fin-tastic Facts

Here's why Florida is full of fun. It has...

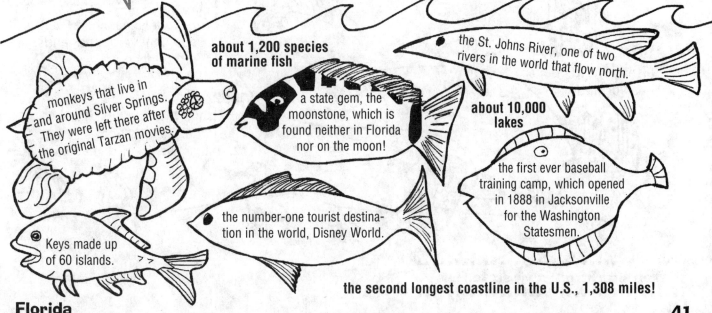

monkeys that live in and around Silver Springs. They were left there after the original Tarzan movies.

about 1,200 species of marine fish

a state gem, the moonstone, which is found neither in Florida nor on the moon!

the St. Johns River, one of two rivers in the world that flow north.

about 10,000 lakes

the first ever baseball training camp, which opened in 1888 in Jacksonville for the Washington Statesmen.

the number-one tourist destination in the world, Disney World.

Keys made up of 60 islands.

the second longest coastline in the U.S., 1,308 miles!

From Sailing Ships To Rocketships . . .
Traveling the Florida Waters of Time

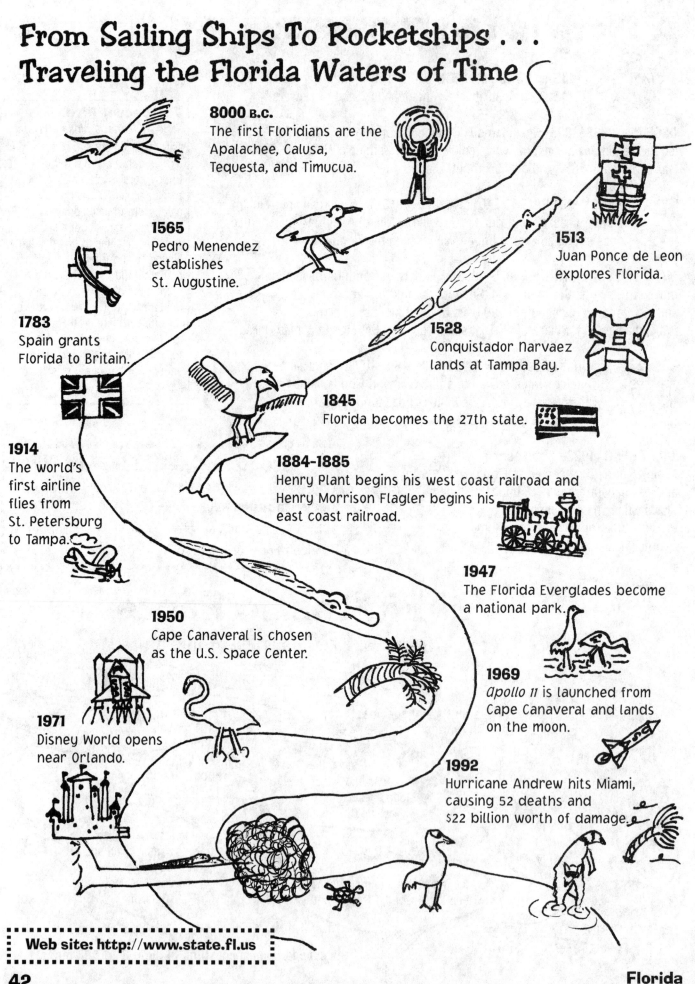

8000 B.C.
The first Floridians are the Apalachee, Calusa, Tequesta, and Timucua.

1565
Pedro Menendez establishes St. Augustine.

1513
Juan Ponce de Leon explores Florida.

1783
Spain grants Florida to Britain.

1528
Conquistador Narvaez lands at Tampa Bay.

1845
Florida becomes the 27th state.

1914
The world's first airline flies from St. Petersburg to Tampa.

1884-1885
Henry Plant begins his west coast railroad and Henry Morrison Flagler begins his east coast railroad.

1947
The Florida Everglades become a national park.

1950
Cape Canaveral is chosen as the U.S. Space Center.

1969
Apollo 11 is launched from Cape Canaveral and lands on the moon.

1971
Disney World opens near Orlando.

1992
Hurricane Andrew hits Miami, causing 52 deaths and $22 billion worth of damage.

Web site: http://www.state.fl.us

Florida Photo File

Don't get wet! In Florida's **Everglades National Park**, we can skim the surface in an airboat.

Ahoy, there! In the Florida Keys you'll see **Alligator Reef Lighthouse**, one of a string of reef lighthouses anchored in south Florida waters.

Every season's the best of all. No matter what the season, we always enjoy Florida's **coastline**.

They're baaack! We encounter **alligators** throughout the state even though they were once on the endangered species list.

M-i-c-k-e-y Mouse entertains us at **Disney World**.

Florida Department of Commerce/Division of Tourism

A beautiful space shuttle launch! We're in touch with our future at the **Kennedy Space Center** at Cape Canaveral.

Robert Overton

See the brown **pelican** flying above you or diving for fish at the beach. These friendly Florida residents of the coastline were once endangered.

Fabulous Florida Key Lime Pie
1 can condensed milk
4 eggs, separated
½ cup key lime juice
6 Tb. sugar
½ tsp. cream of tartar
1 baked pie shell

We're **Mrs. Keating's fifth-grade class**, a group of talented authors and illustrators. We never tire of exploring Florida and having fun in the Sunshine State.

Preheat the oven to 350 degrees. Beat egg yolks, milk, and juice until blended. Beat one egg white until stiff and fold into the mixture. Beat the other egg whites, adding sugar and cream of tartar. Pour filling into the baked pie shell and frost with egg whites. Bake until egg whites are light brown.

Georgia

State Capital
★ **Atlanta**

Peaches and Peanuts

We're known as the Goober State. What's a goober? It's a peanut, one of our most important crops. Sometimes we're known as the Peach State. That's because the peach is our state fruit.

State Flag

State Fruit
Peach

State Song
"Georgia on My Mind"

Have Fun Seeing the Run

The Peachtree Road Race is a fun run to do. This race is on the Fourth of July. The distance is 10 kilometers or 6.2 miles long. Every year, more than twenty-five thousand people come from all over the world to run this race.

Historic Hundredth

The world watched us when Atlanta hosted the 1996 Centennial Olympic Games and the Paralympics (for people with disabilities) in 1996. It was an exciting time for the entire state. Atlanta spent every minute it had to get ready for the Olympics. Events were even held on the Atlanta Hawks basketball court and the Atlanta Falcons football dome.

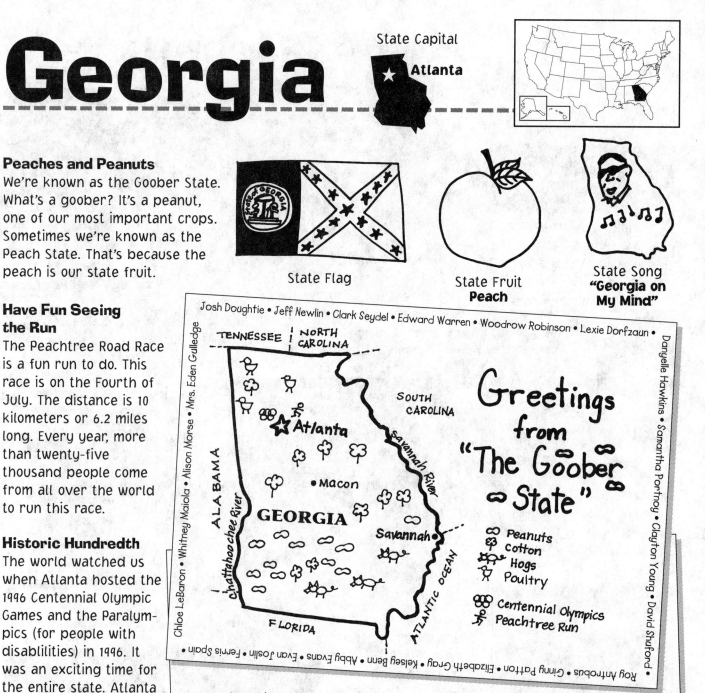

Josh Doughtie • Jeff Newlin • Clark Seydel • Edward Warren • Woodrow Robinson • Lexie Dorfzaun •

Danyelle Hawkins • Samantha Portnoy • Clayton Young • David Shuford •

Chloe LeBaron • Whitney Maiola • Alison Morse • Mrs. Eden Gulledge

Roy Anthrobus • Ginny Patton • Elizabeth Gray • Kelsey Benn • Abby Evans • Evan Joslin • Ferris Spain •

TENNESSEE | NORTH CAROLINA

SOUTH CAROLINA

★ Atlanta

• Macon

GEORGIA

ALABAMA

Chattahoochee River

Savannah River

Savannah •

ATLANTIC OCEAN

FLORIDA

Greetings from "The Goober State"

∞ Peanuts
✿ cotton
Hogs
Poultry

Centennial Olympics
Peachtree Run

Dear Readers,

Georgia is great because it has so many places to visit. While you are traveling through our state, watch for the historical markers that tell you that history happened in various places during the Civil War. The Olympic Games, which were held in Atlanta in 1996, have become part of our history, too. These games were the 100th Olympics to be held. We hope you enjoy your visit to the Goober State.

From Ms. Gulledge's Fifth Grade, The Schenck School, Atlanta

State Tree
Live Oak

State Bird
Brown Thrasher

Famous Georgians

Juliette Low (1860–1927) founded the Girl Scouts of America. She became deaf from poor health, but that didn't keep her from being a great sculptor.

Martin Luther King, Jr. (1929–1968) led nonviolent protests to gain civil rights for black people. He was a Baptist minister and was killed by an assassin. "I Have a Dream," the speech he gave in Washington, DC, has inspired people the world over.

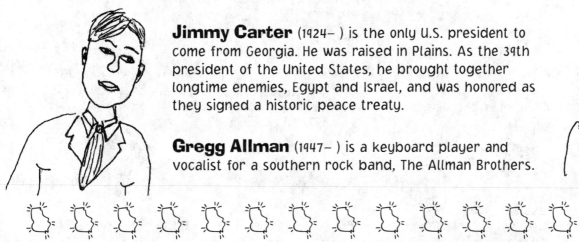

Jimmy Carter (1924–) is the only U.S. president to come from Georgia. He was raised in Plains. As the 39th president of the United States, he brought together longtime enemies, Egypt and Israel, and was honored as they signed a historic peace treaty.

Gregg Allman (1947–) is a keyboard player and vocalist for a southern rock band, The Allman Brothers.

The Georgia Team

Can you match the famous Georgians on the left with the reason they're famous?

1. Maynard Jackson
2. James Brown
3. Sam Nunn
4. Flannery O'Connor
5. Evander Holyfield
6. Jackie Robinson
7. Jeff Foxworthy
8. Joanne Woodward
9. B-52's
10. Indigo Girls
11. Ray Charles
12. Julia Roberts
13. Marquis Grissom
14. Margaret Mitchell
15. Ted Turner

a. former Mayor of Atlanta
b. first African American to play major league baseball
c. Georgia tycoon
d. U.S. senator for 24 years
e. center fielder for the Atlanta Braves
f. wrote *Gone With the Wind*
g. wrote *A Good Man Is Hard to Find*
h. sang "Georgia on My Mind" when it was made the state song
i. sing folk-type songs
j. world-famous stage and film actress
k. known for being a "pretty woman" in the movies
l. boxing champ
m. comedian
n. popular music group
o. sang "I Feel Good"

Peachy Facts

- Georgia's other names are the Peach State, Goober State, Cracker State, Empire State of the South, New York of the South. And that's not peanuts!
- Big. . .bigger. . . biggest state east of the Mississippi River—that's Georgia.
- Sidney Lanier, a well-known poet, lived in Georgia.
- Georgia's first inhabitants were the Creek and Cherokee Indians.
- A Georgian honored around the world, Martin Luther King, Jr. won the Nobel Peace Prize.
- Three cheers for Atlanta! It became the capital of Georgia in 1868.
- **For More Information:**
  285 Peachtree Center Ave., NE
  Suites 1000 and 1100
  Atlanta, GA 30303
  http://trade@itt.state.ga.us

ANSWERS: 1.a 2.o 3.d 4.g 5.l 6.b 7. m 8. j 9. n 10. i 11. h 12. k 13. e 14. f 15.

The Beginnings of Georgia

Georgia, which was named for King George II of Britain in 1732, was one of the original 13 colonies. James Oglethorpe, an early settler, brought 114 debtors to Georgia In 1733. They became the first official residents of Georgia.

Georgia served as a buffer between South Carolina and the Spanish settlers living in Florida. But King George took control of Georgia in 1752 because he felt that James Oglethorpe was not doing a good job.

Many years later . . . On June 27, 1864, the Confederate army won the Battle of Kennesaw Mountain. In the same year, General William Tecumseh Sherman, a northern general, burned Atlanta on his way to Savannah. It is said that a young lady who was admired by General Sherman lived in Savannah. She wrote to him and pleaded that he not burn her beautiful city. According to one story, Sherman arrived in the city and liked Savannah so much that he decided not to burn it.

Georgia's Times

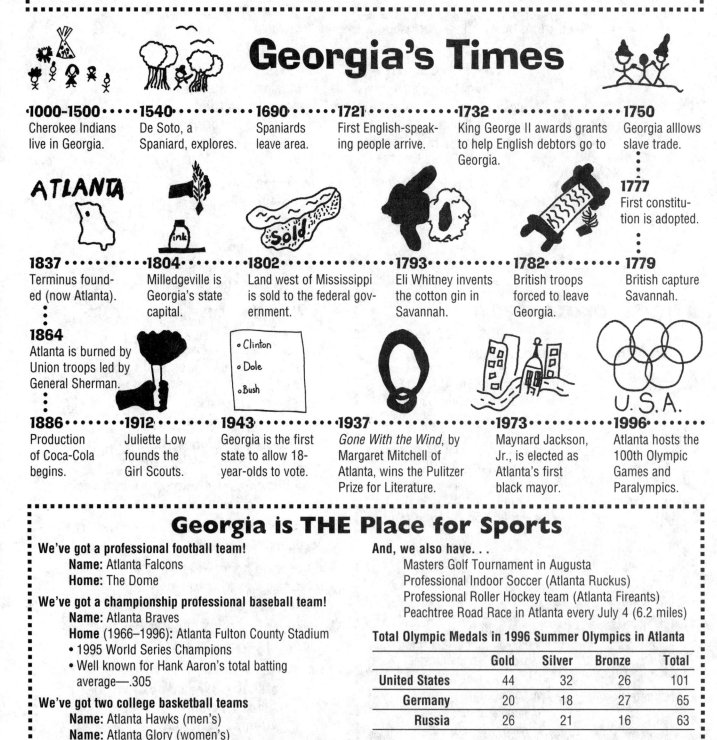

1000-1500 Cherokee Indians live in Georgia.

1540 De Soto, a Spaniard, explores.

1690 Spaniards leave area.

1721 First English-speaking people arrive.

1732 King George II awards grants to help English debtors go to Georgia.

1750 Georgia alllows slave trade.

1777 First constitution is adopted.

1837 Terminus founded (now Atlanta).

1804 Milledgeville is Georgia's state capital.

1802 Land west of Mississippi is sold to the federal government.

1793 Eli Whitney invents the cotton gin in Savannah.

1782 British troops forced to leave Georgia.

1779 British capture Savannah.

1864 Atlanta is burned by Union troops led by General Sherman.

1886 Production of Coca-Cola begins.

1912 Juliette Low founds the Girl Scouts.

1943 Georgia is the first state to allow 18-year-olds to vote.

1937 *Gone With the Wind*, by Margaret Mitchell of Atlanta, wins the Pulitzer Prize for Literature.

1973 Maynard Jackson, Jr., is elected as Atlanta's first black mayor.

1996 Atlanta hosts the 100th Olympic Games and Paralympics.

Georgia is THE Place for Sports

We've got a professional football team!
   Name: Atlanta Falcons
   Home: The Dome

We've got a championship professional baseball team!
   Name: Atlanta Braves
   Home (1966–1996): Atlanta Fulton County Stadium
   • 1995 World Series Champions
   • Well known for Hank Aaron's total batting average—.305

We've got two college basketball teams
   Name: Atlanta Hawks (men's)
   Name: Atlanta Glory (women's)
   Home: University of Georgia Institute of Technology

And, we also have. . .
   Masters Golf Tournament in Augusta
   Professional Indoor Soccer (Atlanta Ruckus)
   Professional Roller Hockey team (Atlanta Fireants)
   Peachtree Road Race in Atlanta every July 4 (6.2 miles)

Total Olympic Medals in 1996 Summer Olympics in Atlanta

	Gold	Silver	Bronze	Total
United States	44	32	26	101
Germany	20	18	27	65
Russia	26	21	16	63

What to See in Georgia

Jekyll Island is one of the famous places in Georgia. Jekyll was once owned by a club of millionaires. Now it is a wonderful public park.

Do you want to know more about parts of the Civil War? Then visit the **Cyclorama**, a huge diorama, which is in a circular building.

Yum! Would you like to eat a "dog walking through the garden"? You can, if you go to the **Varsity**! You can eat there before you go to a Georgia Tech game or any time. Get a chili dog, a hamburger, and a soda. There you can try a "dog walking through the garden," which is a hot dog with cole slaw on it. How about a "chili dog with snow"? That's a chili dog with onions.

Quick! Where was the **first Gold Rush** in the United States? It took place in Dahlonega, Georgia. The gold found there was used to make more than $36 million in gold coins. Benjamin Parks was the one who first discovered gold in Dahlonega. One day, he went hunting and turned over a rock. Surprise! It was laced with gold.

The **Big Chicken** was built in 1963. If you visit it in Marietta, you'll see it's something to cluck about.

Come visit us at the Schenck School.

Hawai'i

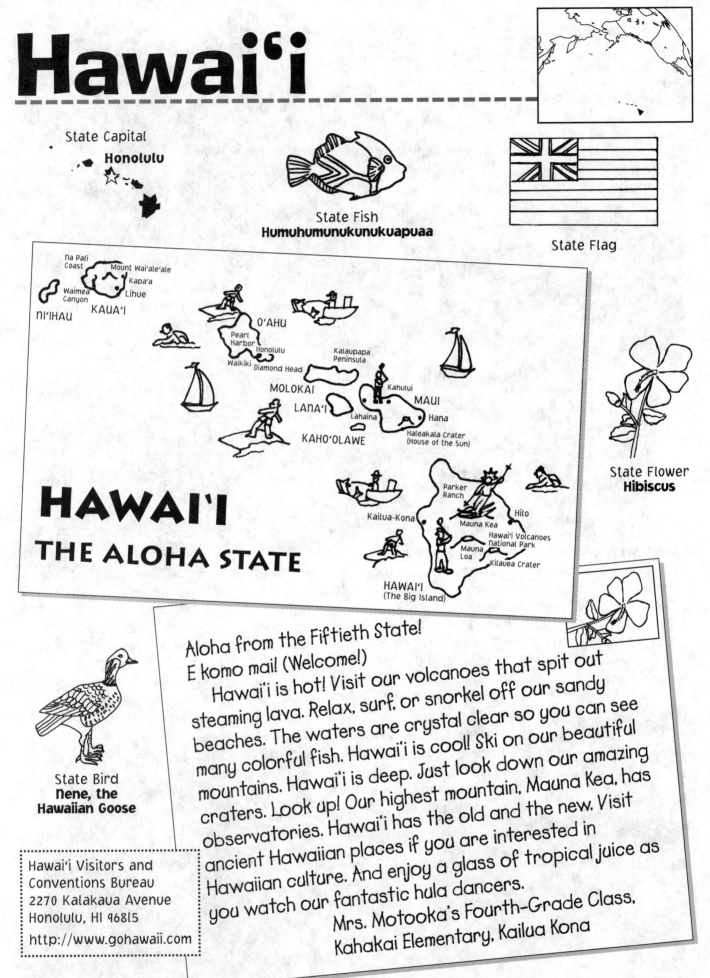

State Capital

Honolulu

State Fish
Humuhumunukunukuapuaa

State Flag

Na Pali Coast
Mount Wai'ale'ale
Kapa'a
Waimea Canyon
Lihue
NI'IHAU
KAUA'I

O'AHU
Pearl Harbor
Honolulu
Waikiki
Diamond Head

Kalaupapa Peninsula

MOLOKAI

LANA'I

Kahului

MAUI

Lahaina
Hana

KAHO'OLAWE
Haleakala Crater
(House of the Sun)

Parker Ranch
Kailua-Kona
Hilo
Mauna Kea
Hawai'i Volcanoes National Park
Mauna Loa
Kilauea Crater
HAWAI'I
(The Big Island)

HAWAI'I
THE ALOHA STATE

State Flower
Hibiscus

State Bird
Nene, the Hawaiian Goose

Hawai'i Visitors and
Conventions Bureau
2270 Kalakaua Avenue
Honolulu, HI 96815
http://www.gohawaii.com

Aloha from the Fiftieth State!
E komo mai! (Welcome!)
   Hawai'i is hot! Visit our volcanoes that spit out steaming lava. Relax, surf, or snorkel off our sandy beaches. The waters are crystal clear so you can see many colorful fish. Hawai'i is cool! Ski on our beautiful mountains. Hawai'i is deep. Just look down our amazing craters. Look up! Our highest mountain, Mauna Kea, has observatories. Hawai'i has the old and the new. Visit ancient Hawaiian places if you are interested in Hawaiian culture. And enjoy a glass of tropical juice as you watch our fantastic hula dancers.
   Mrs. Motooka's Fourth-Grade Class,
   Kahakai Elementary, Kailua Kona

HONORED BY HAWAI'I

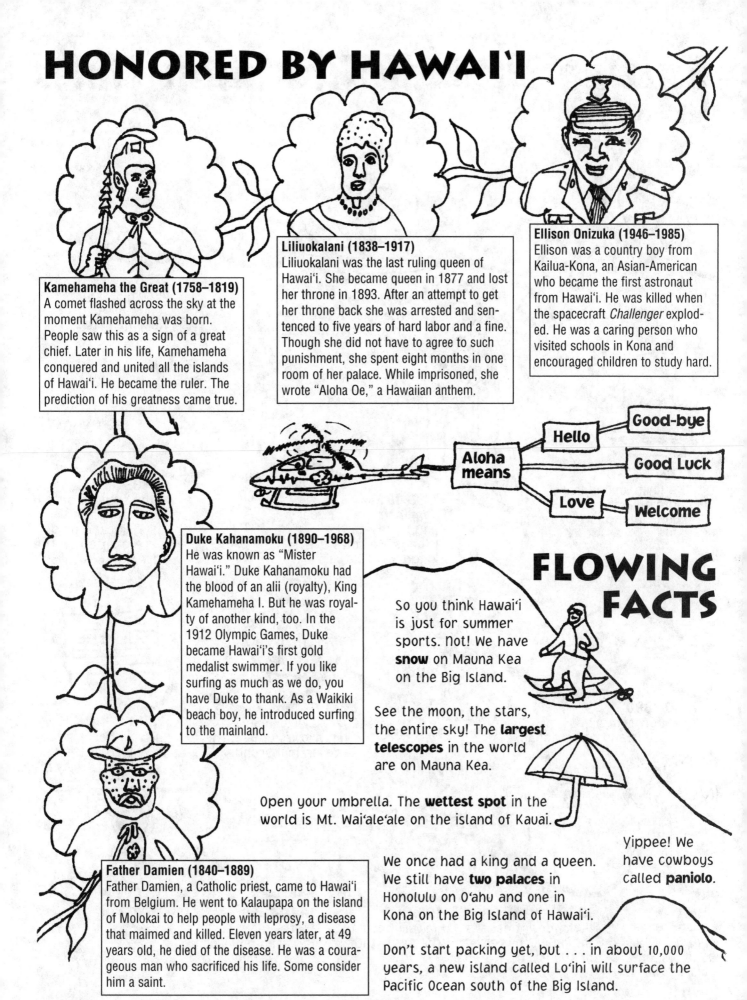

Kamehameha the Great (1758–1819)
A comet flashed across the sky at the moment Kamehameha was born. People saw this as a sign of a great chief. Later in his life, Kamehameha conquered and united all the islands of Hawai'i. He became the ruler. The prediction of his greatness came true.

Liliuokalani (1838–1917)
Liliuokalani was the last ruling queen of Hawai'i. She became queen in 1877 and lost her throne in 1893. After an attempt to get her throne back she was arrested and sentenced to five years of hard labor and a fine. Though she did not have to agree to such punishment, she spent eight months in one room of her palace. While imprisoned, she wrote "Aloha Oe," a Hawaiian anthem.

Ellison Onizuka (1946–1985)
Ellison was a country boy from Kailua-Kona, an Asian-American who became the first astronaut from Hawai'i. He was killed when the spacecraft *Challenger* exploded. He was a caring person who visited schools in Kona and encouraged children to study hard.

Duke Kahanamoku (1890–1968)
He was known as "Mister Hawai'i." Duke Kahanamoku had the blood of an alii (royalty), King Kamehameha I. But he was royalty of another kind, too. In the 1912 Olympic Games, Duke became Hawai'i's first gold medalist swimmer. If you like surfing as much as we do, you have Duke to thank. As a Waikiki beach boy, he introduced surfing to the mainland.

Aloha means
- Hello
- Good-bye
- Good Luck
- Love
- Welcome

FLOWING FACTS

So you think Hawai'i is just for summer sports. Not! We have **snow** on Mauna Kea on the Big Island.

See the moon, the stars, the entire sky! The **largest telescopes** in the world are on Mauna Kea.

Open your umbrella. The **wettest spot** in the world is Mt. Wai'ale'ale on the island of Kauai.

We once had a king and a queen. We still have **two palaces** in Honolulu on O'ahu and one in Kona on the Big Island of Hawai'i.

Yippee! We have cowboys called **paniolo**.

Don't start packing yet, but . . . in about 10,000 years, a new island called Lo'ihi will surface the Pacific Ocean south of the Big Island.

Father Damien (1840–1889)
Father Damien, a Catholic priest, came to Hawai'i from Belgium. He went to Kalaupapa on the island of Molokai to help people with leprosy, a disease that maimed and killed. Eleven years later, at 49 years old, he died of the disease. He was a courageous man who sacrificed his life. Some consider him a saint.

Surfing Through Hawaiian Times

500-750
The first settlers—from the Marquesas—arrive.

1758
A comet signals the birth of the great Kamehameha.

1778
The first European, Captain James Cook from England, arrives.

1790-1810
Kamehameha conquers and unites all the islands. He rules the kingdom of Hawai'i.

1820
Missionaries from Boston, Massachusetts, arrive.

1835
The sugar industry starts as the first sugar cane fields are planted on the island of Kaua'i.

1840-1860
Whaling boom helps increase islands' population.

1850-1907
Immigrants arrive to work in the sugarcane fields.

1893
Queen Liliu'okalani is overthrown, ending the Hawaiian monarchy.

1900
Hawai'i becomes a territory of the U.S.

1941
Japan bombs Pearl Harbor. The U.S. enters World War II.

1949
Punchbowl becomes National Cemetery of the Pacific.

1959
Hawai'i becomes the 50th state.

1988-1996
State elects first Hawaiian governor: John Waihee.

Heidi is sitting on a former **lava flow** at a beach on the Big Island. On this island at times lava still flows to the sea.

Offerings of food to Pele, goddess of the volcano, are made at **Halema'uma'u Fire Pit** in Kilauea Crater on the Big Island.

ALOHA

Waimea Canyon on Kaua'i is the "Grand Canyon of the Pacific."

Aloha from Mrs. Motooka's fourth-grade class of Kahakai School. *Kahakai* means "at the sea." Our school is located about a block from the ocean.

Michael goes boogie boarding at Hapuna Beach, one of the **few sandy beaches** on the Big Island, our youngest island.

Chantelle is suffering from **altitude sickness** and doesn't seem to be enjoying what's left of the snow. The altitude of Mauna Kea is 13,796 feet.

Snow-capped **Mauna Kea** on the Big Island of Hawai'i. Mauna Kea is the highest mountain in our state.

Janver at South Point on the Big Island where fishing is popular. **South Point** is the southernmost point of the United States.

Ty is sitting by a blossoming **coffee tree**. Hawai'i is the only state with a coffee industry.

Idaho

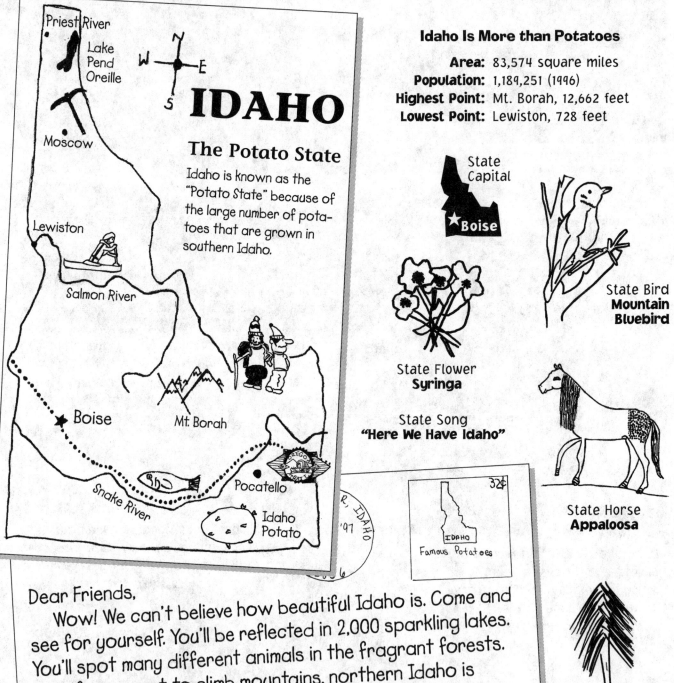

Priest River

Lake Pend Oreille

Moscow

Lewiston

Salmon River

Boise

Mt. Borah

Snake River

Pocatello

Idaho Potato

IDAHO

The Potato State

Idaho is known as the "Potato State" because of the large number of potatoes that are grown in southern Idaho.

Idaho Is More than Potatoes

Area: 83,574 square miles
Population: 1,189,251 (1996)
Highest Point: Mt. Borah, 12,662 feet
Lowest Point: Lewiston, 728 feet

State Capital
★ Boise

State Flower
Syringa

State Song
"Here We Have Idaho"

State Bird
Mountain Bluebird

State Horse
Appaloosa

State Tree
Western White Pine

Famous Potatoes

Dear Friends,
   Wow! We can't believe how beautiful Idaho is. Come and see for yourself. You'll be reflected in 2,000 sparkling lakes. You'll spot many different animals in the fragrant forests. And, if you want to climb mountains, northern Idaho is famous for high hills covered with wild huckleberries. Are you hungry for a super-healthful food? You'll find potato fields in southern Idaho.
                    Ms. Gaudet's Fourth-Grade Class,
                    Priest River School, Priest River

Fabulous People from Idaho

Way up on Mount Rushmore, **Gutzon Borglum** carved the faces of U.S. presidents into the rocks. His father had started the sculptures and on his death, in 1927, Gutzon took over. When he died in 1941, his son completed the world-famous work. Gutzon Borglum was born in St. Charles, Idaho, in 1867. He became known as the "Sculptor with Dynamite." He was certainly a dynamite sculptor!

The only woman to design a state seal was Idaho's own **Emma Edward Green**. The seal is a round picture with different pictures that symbolize objects important to Idaho.

In 1836, **Henry Spalding** and his wife became the first white settlers in Lapwai, Idaho. They built the first flour mill, the first school, the first church, and had the first printing press in the area.

Born in Idaho around 1840, **Chief Joseph** was the chief of the Nez Percé Indians. He tried to keep peace between his tribe and the white settlers, but failed. He almost defeated the U.S. Army in 1877. Rather than be forced to live on a reservation, he decided to flee with his people. He surrendered after a battle in Montana.

Imagine life without television. Not a pretty picture! But thanks to **Philo Farnsworth**, that's not a problem. He was born in 1906 and died in 1971. In 1922, he invented a television camera while attending Rigby High School. He followed that with more than 150 TV-related inventions. He was honored in 1983 with a postage stamp that had his picture and the words "First Television Camera." Surprisingly, Idaho did not get its first television station until 1953.

What to Know About IDAHO

- Whoa! Did you know that the state horse was chosen by a sixth-grade class at Eagle Elementary School?

- Lucky number. Idaho is the 13th largest state.

- Deep, deeper, deepest. Lake Pend Oreille is 189 square miles in area and more than 1,000 feet deep. The U.S. Navy uses the lake to test submarines.

- Idaho is only 45 miles wide at its northern border, but is 310 miles wide at the south.

- Animals must like Idaho. Here are the many kinds that make the state their home: White-tail deer, elk, bear, moose, cougars, caribou, sheep, mountain goats, squirrels, beaver, mink, muskrats, otter, grouse, raccoon, bobcat. In our lakes, you'll find trout, steelhead, salmon, and bass.

Our Class Looks at a Special Book:

Bonanza Girl
by Patricia Beatty

This special book is about Ann Kate and her brother Jemmy. They move to the Idaho territory in the 1880s. The book takes you through Rathdrum, Coeur d'Alene, and Wallace, Idaho. You learn about what it was like to live and survive in a gold and silver mine camp. The book is well written and easy to read at the fourth-grade level. The author makes you feel and understand what Ann Kate had to go through. Our entire class enjoyed reading the book.

Travel Through Idaho Time

1819
Spain gives up its claim to all of its territory west of the Rocky Mountains, including Idaho.

1805
Explorers Meriwether Lewis and William Clark are the first white men to pass through the Idaho region.

1810
Fort Henry is built by a Missouri fur company.

1834
Fort Hall is built by Nathaniel Wyeth.

1836
Henry H. Spalding and his wife, Presbyterian missionaries, are the first white settlers in Idaho. They establish the Lapwai Mission Station near Lewiston.

1863
Idaho becomes a territory on March 4. Lewiston becomes the capital and William Wallace the governor.

1862
Rich gold deposits are found in the Salmon and Boise rivers.

1837
The first school is built to teach Indian children.

1884
The Coeur d'Alene lead and silver deposits are found.

1848
The Cataldo Mission is established.

1890
Idaho becomes a state on July 3. The capital is changed to Boise. The governor is George L. Shoup.

1910
Forest fires burn 3,000 acres in two days in northern Idaho.

1962
The cities of Pocatello and Alameda merge.

1972
A fire at the Sunshine Silver Mine in Wallace kills 91 miners.

Sunshine Silver Mine Monument

1912
The dam at Salmon and Falls Creek is finished.

1915
Lewiston is linked to the Pacific Ocean by the Snake and Columbia rivers.

1936
Sun Valley Resort opens.

1976
The Teton Dam on the Teton river bursts, destroying several farming communities and causing at least 11 deaths.

The Couch Potatoes

Who's your favorite basketball player?

Definitely "Spud" Web!

1984
Almost all of Idaho's interstate highway systems are complete.

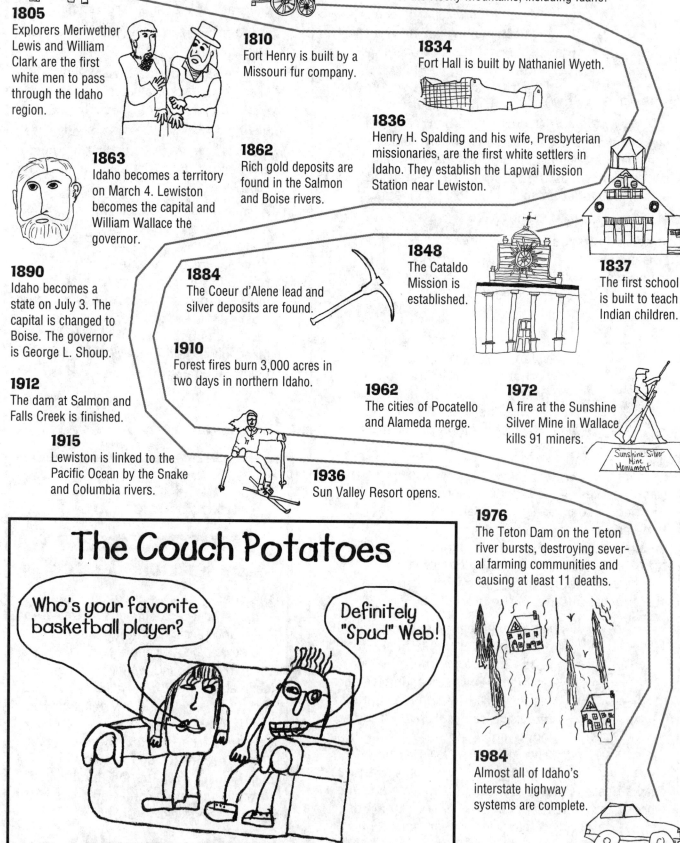

Special "Spud" Spots

An excellent way to spend a day: Sailing is popular on **Lake Coeur d'Alene**.

The **state capitol** is in Boise. The building was completed in 1920.

What's for dinner? Something yummy and fishy, for sure. **Fishing** is just one of the pastimes we enjoy in Idaho. That's because our state has so many rivers and lakes that are suitable for fly-fishing or cast-and-reel fishing. Some of the most popular fish to catch are trout, kamloops, and kokanee.

Can you spot the **moose**? He makes his home in northern Idaho by the Pack River near Lake Pend Oreille.

Ms. Gaudet's fourth-grade class is from Priest River.

For more information on Idaho write to:

Idaho Travel Council
700 W. State St.
Boise, ID 83720

http://www.state.id.us/index.html

Illinois

The Land of Lincoln

State Capitol

State Flag

State Bird
Cardinal

Jeremy Aeilts • Kari Albsmeyer • Brittany Beebe • Kyle Bent • Austin Bruns • Craig Davis • Jer

Welcome to Illinois the Prairie State!

Rockford •

Lake Michigan

Chicago •

Peoria •

Golden •

Illinois River

Quincy •

⊙ Springfield

Mississippi River

East St. Louis •

Ohio River

Mrs. Jan Stanley • Tiffani Wilson • Jeremy Welty • Jessica Tangerose • Jodi Stodgel • Steven Short • Nickie Schoelen • Prunty •

emy Davis • Lauren Flesner • Casey Hamann • Terry Harscher • Wes Heinecke • Jon Hunsaker • Melanie Jackson • Scott Leasman • Beth Leenerts • Monica Lewis • Kyle Mable • Brittany Main • Ashley Peters • Joel Post • Whitn

Dear Readers,

We're so lucky to have great weather. The summers are hot so we can go swimming. But in the winter, brrr! It gets cold so we can go sledding.

Many different people live in Illinois, but they have one thing in common. They enjoy watching all kinds of sports. Their favorite is watching the championship basketball team, the Chicago Bulls.

Chicago is the third-largest city in the U.S. The Sears Tower, located in Chicago, is one of the tallest buildings in the world.

Illinois has two nicknames. It is called the "Prairie State" because prairie grass was growing here when pioneers settled in Illinois. Abraham Lincoln was our most famous citizen so Illinois is also called the "Land of Lincoln."

Mrs. Stanley's Fifth-Grade Class,
Central Middle School, Golden, Illinois

State Flower
Violet

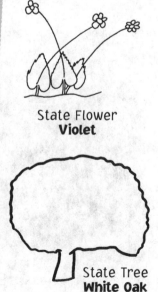

State Tree
White Oak

We're Proud of these Illinoisans

Walt Disney was born in Chicago in 1901. In 1923 he began to produce animated motion pictures with his brother Roy. His most popular cartoon character is Mickey Mouse, who first appeared in *Steamboat Willie*, the first animated cartoon with sound. His cartoon movies include *Cinderella, Snow White and the Seven Dwarfs,* and *Fantasia*.

Ulysses S. Grant was the 18th president of the U.S. He lived from 1822 to 1885. He was a popular Union general in the Civil War. He was modest and unassuming and found it hard to believe that others were not equally honest.

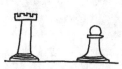

Bobby Fischer became the first American chess player to win the world championship. He was champion from 1972 to 1975. He learned to play chess when he was six. Bobby was the youngest international grand-master in chess. He won the U.S. championship eight times. Bobby was born in Chicago.

Ernest Hemingway won a Pulitzer Prize for his novel *The Old Man and the Sea* in 1925. Hemingway was born in Oak Park in 1899. After high school, he worked as a reporter for the Kansas City *Star*. In 1918 he served as a Red Cross volunteer ambulance driver in Italy. One of his best novels is *For Whom the Bell Tolls*.

Michael Jordan is a famous Chicago Bulls basketball star. He plays more exciting basketball than anyone else. He says that, though he gets paid, he would play for free because he loves the game so much. He sure cam slam dunk! He was born February 17, 1963, in Brooklyn, New York. He grew up in Wilmington, North Carolina.

Carl Sandburg, born in 1878, is a world-reknowned poet and author from Galesburg. One of the books he wrote was *Abe Lincoln Grows Up*. He also wrote *Abraham Lincoln: The Prairie Years*. Sandburg wrote many poems and later became an editorial writer for the Chicago *Daily News*.

John Deere was born in Rutland, Vermont, in 1804. Deere opened his own blacksmith shop in Illinois. He invented the first steel plow. Within 10 years he and his partner were producing 1,000 plows a year. Deere started a new company in Moline, Illinois, which today ranks as one of the largest U.S. industrial corporations.

Hillary Rodham Clinton was born on October 26, 1947, in Park Ridge, Illinois. She married Bill Clinton in 1974. A lawyer, she became first lady in 1993 when her husband was elected president of the U.S.

Jackie Joyner-Kersee is a track and field athlete, two-time Olympic gold medalist, and world champion. Born in 1962 in East St. Louis, Illinois, she won her first national pentathlon at the age of 14. In 1986 she set two world records within one month. She has been called the world's greatest woman athlete.

Abraham Lincoln was born in Kentucky in 1809. With his family, he moved to Indiana and then to Illinois. He had a fine sense of justice, which helped him to be a good lawyer, a great debater, a spellbinding speaker, an excellent writer, and a memorable 16th president. He guided the U.S. through the Civil War. In 1865, he spoke of the end of the war and asked that there be "malice toward none; with charity toward all."

Find the words hidden in this puzzle. The words go up, down, across, backward, and on the diagonal. Some letters are used more than once. The leftover letters spell the last name of an Illinois sports hero.
(See answer on page 58.)

```
P C A R D I N A L
I H O G O F J A I
O I O R T D K O N
N C U B S E A T C
E A W H E A T E O
E G K E W G O L L
R O A R D A M O N
S I O N I L L I O
A F A R M N A V N
```

The leftover letters spell ___ ___ ___ ___ ___ ___ ___.

Watching Time Go By

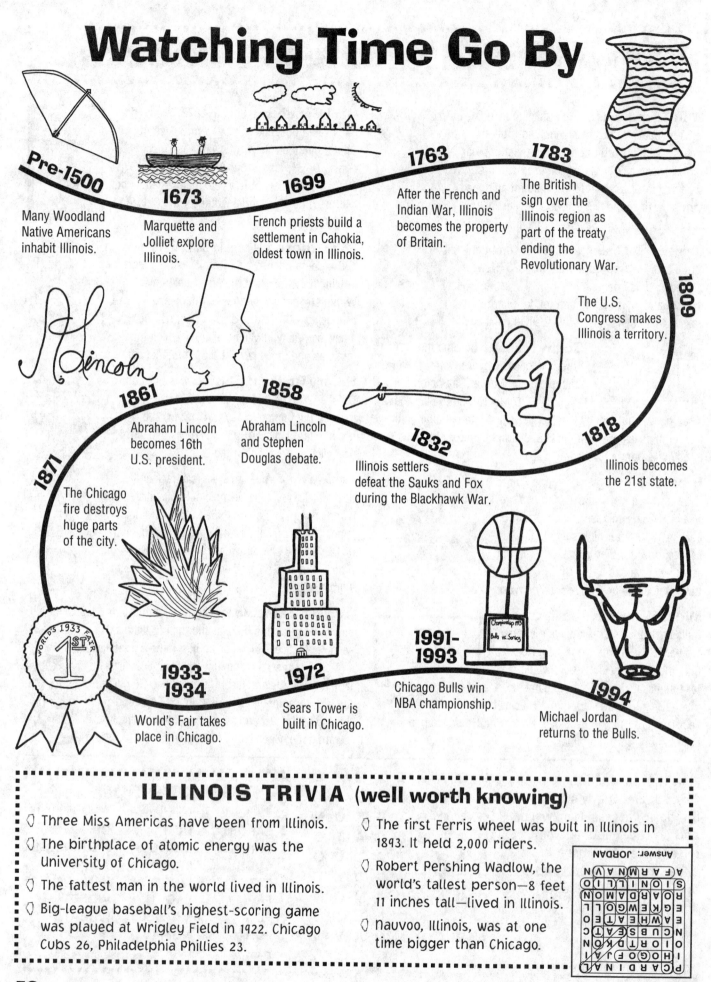

Pre-1500 — Many Woodland Native Americans inhabit Illinois.

1673 — Marquette and Jolliet explore Illinois.

1699 — French priests build a settlement in Cahokia, oldest town in Illinois.

1763 — After the French and Indian War, Illinois becomes the property of Britain.

1783 — The British sign over the Illinois region as part of the treaty ending the Revolutionary War.

1809 — The U.S. Congress makes Illinois a territory.

1818 — Illinois becomes the 21st state.

1832 — Illinois settlers defeat the Sauks and Fox during the Blackhawk War.

1858 — Abraham Lincoln and Stephen Douglas debate.

1861 — Abraham Lincoln becomes 16th U.S. president.

1871 — The Chicago fire destroys huge parts of the city.

1933–1934 — World's Fair takes place in Chicago.

1972 — Sears Tower is built in Chicago.

1991–1993 — Chicago Bulls win NBA championship.

1994 — Michael Jordan returns to the Bulls.

ILLINOIS TRIVIA (well worth knowing)

- Three Miss Americas have been from Illinois.
- The birthplace of atomic energy was the University of Chicago.
- The fattest man in the world lived in Illinois.
- Big-league baseball's highest-scoring game was played at Wrigley Field in 1922. Chicago Cubs 26, Philadelphia Phillies 23.
- The first Ferris wheel was built in Illinois in 1893. It held 2,000 riders.
- Robert Pershing Wadlow, the world's tallest person—8 feet 11 inches tall—lived in Illinois.
- Nauvoo, Illinois, was at one time bigger than Chicago.

Answer: JORDAN

Here in the Land of Lincoln

Watch the sun set over the **golden prairies** of Illinois. This scene is in rural Golden, Illinois. Off in the distance, you can spot a tractor.

Splish, splash! Illinois has great fishing in farm **ponds, rivers, and lakes**. People also like to relax by just watching the ducks in the water.

Visit our state capitol in **Springfield**. This city is our state's third capital. State senators and representatives make Illinois laws here.

Illinois has many **wonderful parks** for hiking, picnicking, boating, and camping. Southern Illinois boasts hills, valleys, forests, lakes, and rivers. Wild animals love Illinois parks, too. Visitors might see blue herons, quails, wild turkeys, Canada geese, deer, squirrels, raccoons, opossums, skunks, badgers, and coyotes. This beautiful scene is Fall Creek Park in Adams County, Illinois.

Lake Michigan is important to Chicago. Many ships come into the harbor to bring supplies. Lake Michigan is also a good place for recreation. People like to come here to swim, boat, sail, or just sit in the sun.

Downtown **Chicago** is filled with skyscrapers, businesspeople, and tourists. Skyscrapers were first built in Chicago because of the high cost of land. So the buildings went up! Many highways and railroads pass through Chicago. O'Hare Field is one of the world's busiest airports. Chicago is the banking center of the Midwest.

Mrs. Stanley's fifth-grade class, Central Middle School, Golden, Illinois

Tourism Offices
Illinois Department of Commerce
  and Community Affairs, Division of Tourism
620 East Adams Street
Springfield, Illinois 62701   http://www.state.il.us

Indiana

State Capital
Indianapolis

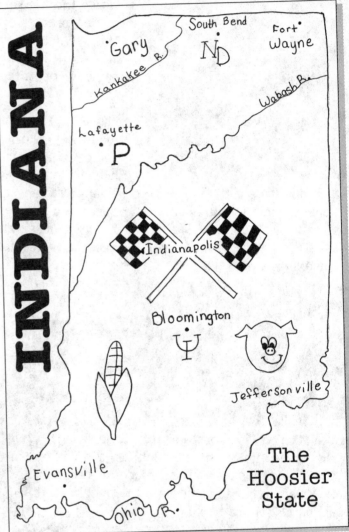

Howdy from the Hoosier State!

INDIANA
The Crossroads of America

Wow! The Hoosier State, Indiana, is a spectacular place. We spent the summer waterskiing on Lake Michigan and "sledding" down the sand dunes! And autumn is unforgettable here. The trees turn the richest shades of orange, red, and yellow. The Hoosier people made us feel right a home while we spent most of the winter watching basketball and eating lots of popcorn. But the best month is May. We go to the Indianapolis 500 car race and get to be part of the world's biggest spectator sport. You won't find a "racier" or more beautiful state. You'll love it here. We do!

Julie Kaiser's Fourth-Grade Class, Morgan Elementary, Palmyra

INDIANA

Gary • • South Bend • Fort Wayne
Kankakee R. N D
Lafayette • P
Wabash R.
Indianapolis
Bloomington •
Jeffersonville •
Evansville •
Ohio R.

The Hoosier State

Awesome Emblems of Indiana

State Flag
1816

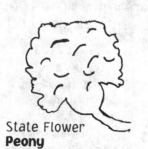

State Flower
Peony

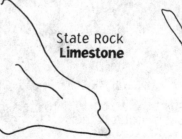

State Rock
Limestone

State Bird
Cardinal

Hoosiers are warm, fun-loving people who live for hospitality, farming, car racing, and basketball.

7 Special Hoosiers
(11, if you count all the Jackson brothers)

Number 7!
His creation, Garfield, makes us smile. That's **Jim Davis** on the left.

Number 6!
The third American to explore outer space, **Virgil "Gus" Grissom** made us proud to be from the same state.

Number 5!
Rock along with **John Mellancamp**, a cool neighbor.

Number 4!
Larry Bird is with the Boston Celtics basketball team, but we're sure his heart is still in Indiana.

Number 3!
What's happening in the big, wide world? Indiana native **Jane Pauley** knows her news.

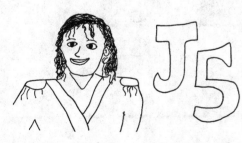

Number 2!
Michael Jackson and his brothers were a group called the **Jackson 5**. Do you know their names?

Number 1!
And first, but not least, here's the king of funny lists, Indiana's very own **David Letterman**, totally fab TV host.

- Do you know where the word *Hoosier* may have come from? One story is that, when settlers first came to this area, people said "Who's your daddy?" Of course it's hard to hear through thick wooden doors, so many thought they said, "Who's 'ere"? or Hoosier! Folks, we couldn't make that up!

- Holiday World (aka Santa Claus Land) was the world's first theme park.

- Indiana is the basketball capital of the world.

- The Empire State building in NYC and many government buildings in DC are made of Indiana limestone. It was carried east by covered wagons.

- The Indy 500 is the world's largest sporting event.

Racing Through Time

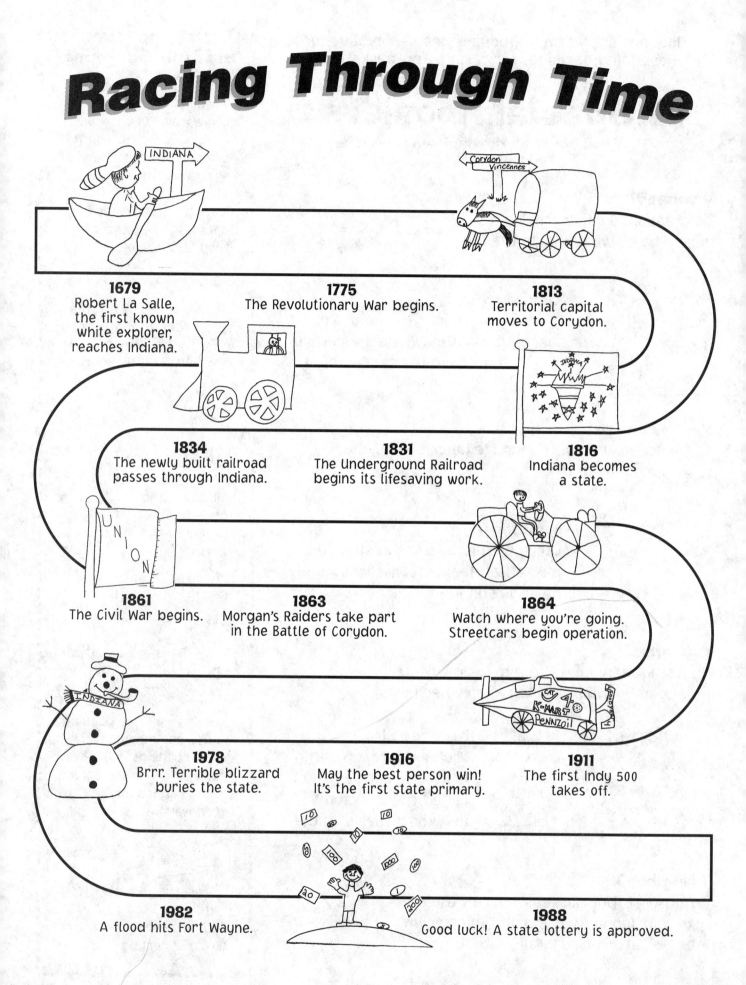

1679
Robert La Salle, the first known white explorer, reaches Indiana.

1775
The Revolutionary War begins.

1813
Territorial capital moves to Corydon.

1834
The newly built railroad passes through Indiana.

1831
The Underground Railroad begins its lifesaving work.

1816
Indiana becomes a state.

1861
The Civil War begins.

1863
Morgan's Raiders take part in the Battle of Corydon.

1864
Watch where you're going. Streetcars begin operation.

1978
Brrr. Terrible blizzard buries the state.

1916
May the best person win! It's the first state primary.

1911
The first Indy 500 takes off.

1982
A flood hits Fort Wayne.

1988
Good luck! A state lottery is approved.

Indiana Scrapbook

Indiana is the leading state in **popcorn**. We grow 1,632,200,000 pounds or 22.9 percent of all the popcorn grown in the U.S. in one year.

Holiday World is in Santa Claus, Indiana. It has rides, a petting zoo, and water park. The roller coaster, the Raven, was voted Ride of the Year.

This is our **first state capitol** building in Corydon.

Glaciers once covered three quarters of Indiana. This is where they stopped.

Find out more about us:
Indiana Department of Commerce & Tourism Development Division
1 North Capital
Indianapolis, IN 46204

http://www.ai.org/index.html

Lee Hamilton, **congressman** from Indiana, visited fourth graders at Morgan Elementary in Palmyra.

Iowa

State Nickname
The Hawkeye State
This nickname honors Chief Black Hawk, a famous Iowa Indian.

State Flower
Wild Rose

State Rock
Geode

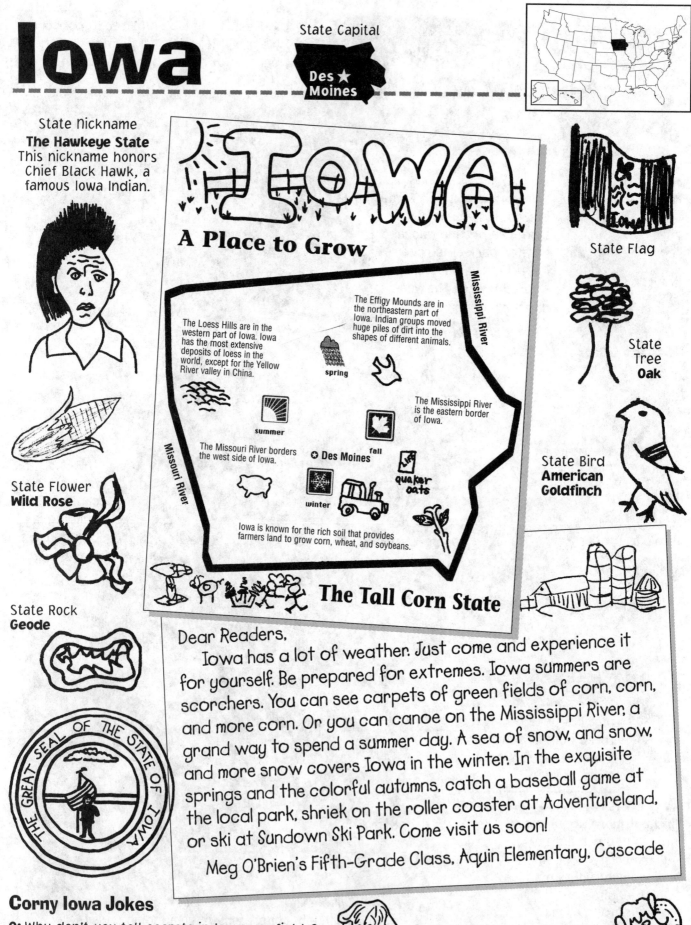

IOWA

A Place to Grow

The Loess Hills are in the western part of Iowa. Iowa has the most extensive deposits of loess in the world, except for the Yellow River valley in China.

The Effigy Mounds are in the northeastern part of Iowa. Indian groups moved huge piles of dirt into the shapes of different animals.

spring

The Mississippi River is the eastern border of Iowa.

Mississippi River

The Missouri River borders the west side of Iowa.

Missouri River

summer

☩ Des Moines

fall

quaker oats

winter

Iowa is known for the rich soil that provides farmers land to grow corn, wheat, and soybeans.

The Tall Corn State

State Flag

State Tree
Oak

State Bird
American Goldfinch

Dear Readers,
   Iowa has a lot of weather. Just come and experience it for yourself. Be prepared for extremes. Iowa summers are scorchers. You can see carpets of green fields of corn, corn, and more corn. Or you can canoe on the Mississippi River, a grand way to spend a summer day. A sea of snow, and snow, and more snow covers Iowa in the winter. In the exquisite springs and the colorful autumns, catch a baseball game at the local park, shriek on the roller coaster at Adventureland, or ski at Sundown Ski Park. Come visit us soon!

Meg O'Brien's Fifth-Grade Class, Aquin Elementary, Cascade

Corny Iowa Jokes

Q: Why don't you tell secrets in Iowa cornfields?
A: Because corn has ears!

Q: What does corn do well?
A: It husk-les! (hustles)

People We Shared With the World

Iowa Actor
★ He was one of Hollywood's finest. But he was ours first! **JOHN WAYNE** (1907–1979), an actor who made western movies his own, was born in Winterset. Fans can visit the John Wayne Birthplace and Museum.

Iowa Musicians
★ **GREG BROWN** is a singer and songwriter from Iowa. He has written more than 100 songs about Iowa alone, including "Iowa Waltz."

In the days before and during World War II, the music of **GLENN MILLER** cheered people far beyond his hometown of Clarinda. He was a band leader, arranger, and trombonist, most popular from 1939 to 1942. A movie was made about his life.

Iowa President
★ **HERBERT HOOVER**, 31st U.S. president from West Branch, Iowa, did not get paid as president of the United States. (He wouldn't accept a salary for his work.)

Iowa Author
★ In the far corner of northeast Iowa, you will find the village of Burr Oak. In 1876, Laura Ingalls Wilder and her family arrived in town. *The Little House in the Big Woods* is the first book in her *Little House* series. One of America's most beloved writers, she lived from 1867–1957.

Iowa Artist
★ **GRANT WOOD**'s most famous painting is "American Gothic." It shows a midwestern farm couple. Have you seen it? Grant Wood was born in Stone City in 1892 and died in 1942. You can read about him in *Artist in Overalls: The Life of Grant Wood* by John Duggleby.

Iowa Actor
★ **DONNA REED** was a famous movie star from Denison. She starred in more than 40 movies! But she became even more well known as the star of her own TV show. She played TV's idea of a perfect mother. Donna Reed died in 1996.

Interesting Iowa Inventions

Christian Nelson from Onawa invented the **Eskimo Pie**.

Fred Maytag invented his first **clothes washer** in Newton in 1907.

The **red delicious apple** was developed by Jesse Hiatt near East Peru. Lightning struck an apple tree. The next day a neighbor came over and tried one of the apples. He said it tasted great!

Incredible Iowa Info

☐ 88% of Iowa students graduate from high school compared to the nation's 71%.

☐ In 1881, Barnum & Bailey's Circus stopped in Cedar Rapids and displayed the first electric lights seen in Iowa.

☐ The Iowa Old Capitol in Iowa City has a golden dome, a beautiful winding staircase, and 27 fireplaces.

☐ The first McDonald's restaurant in Iowa opened in Davenport in 1958.

All Aboard the Iowa Express

1846
The state of Iowa is admitted to the United States. Iowa City is the capital. Ansel Briggs is the first governor of Iowa.

1854
First state fair is held at Fairfield.

1857
The capital of the state of Iowa moves to Des Moines.

1867
First railroad across Iowa is ready to roll.

1873
Near Adair, outlaw Jesse James commits the first train robbery.

1928
The only U.S. President from Iowa, Herbert Hoover, wins election.

1939
John Atanasoff and Clifford Berry build the world's first automatic, electronic computer.

1950
Iowa's first TV broadcast from station WOI-TV in Ames.

1970
"Iowa a Place to Grow" becomes state theme.

1958
Dr. James Van Allen leads a team of scientists gathering information about the earth's magnetic field. The Van Allen radiation belt is discovered.

1986
Linda K. Newman is the first woman appointed to Iowa's Supreme Court.

1996
Iowa celebrates its 150th birthday with celebrations across the state.

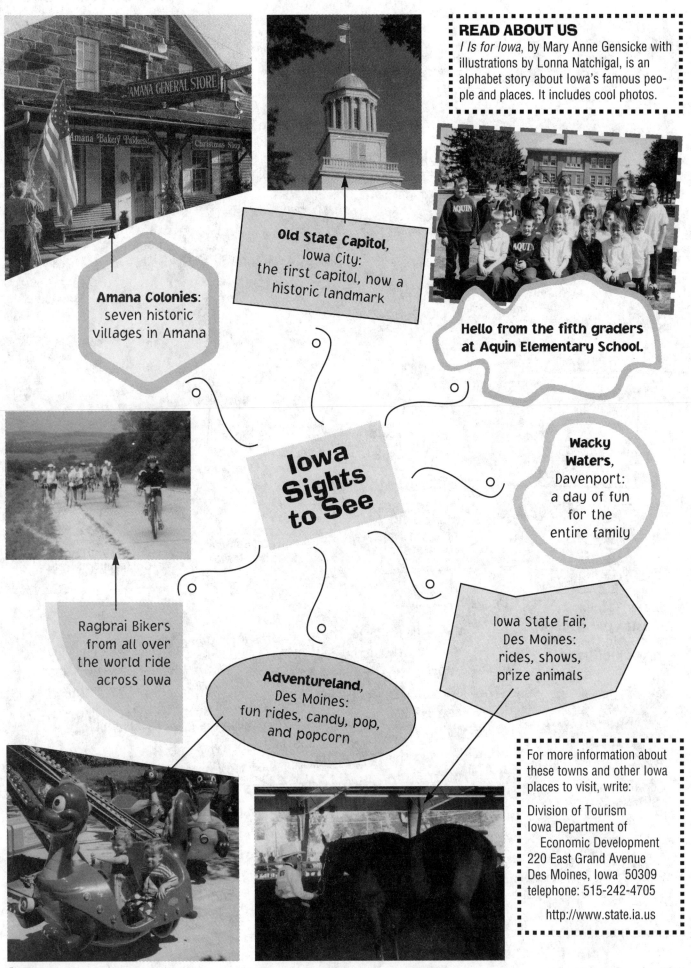

READ ABOUT US
I Is for Iowa, by Mary Anne Gensicke with illustrations by Lonna Natchigal, is an alphabet story about Iowa's famous people and places. It includes cool photos.

Amana Colonies: seven historic villages in Amana

Old State Capitol, Iowa City: the first capitol, now a historic landmark

Hello from the fifth graders at Aquin Elementary School.

Iowa Sights to See

Wacky Waters, Davenport: a day of fun for the entire family

Ragbrai Bikers from all over the world ride across Iowa

Adventureland, Des Moines: fun rides, candy, pop, and popcorn

Iowa State Fair, Des Moines: rides, shows, prize animals

For more information about these towns and other Iowa places to visit, write:

Division of Tourism
Iowa Department of
   Economic Development
220 East Grand Avenue
Des Moines, Iowa 50309
telephone: 515-242-4705

http://www.state.ia.us

Kansas

State Capital
Topeka ★

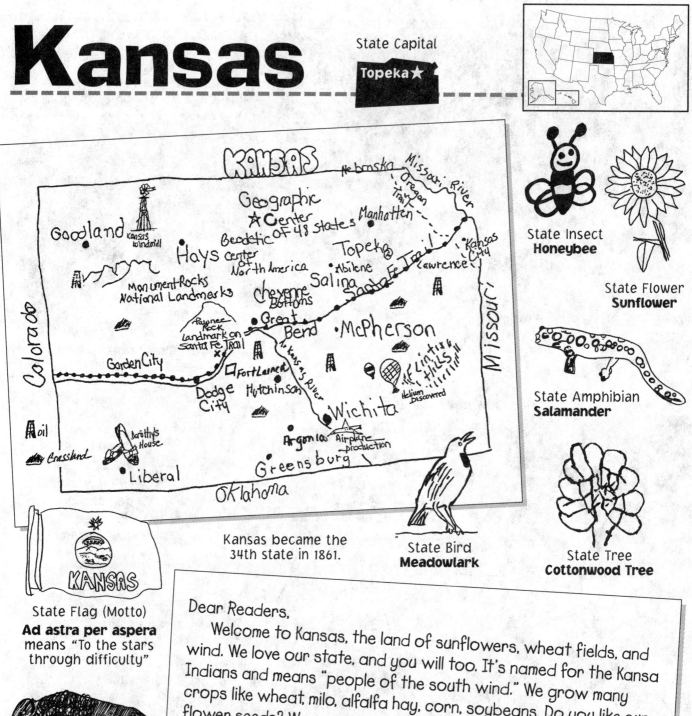

State Insect
Honeybee

State Flower
Sunflower

State Amphibian
Salamander

State Bird
Meadowlark

State Tree
Cottonwood Tree

Kansas became the
34th state in 1861.

State Flag (Motto)
Ad astra per aspera
means "To the stars
through difficulty"

State Animal
Buffalo (Bison)

State Reptile
Ornate Box Turtle

Dear Readers,

Welcome to Kansas, the land of sunflowers, wheat fields, and wind. We love our state, and you will too. It's named for the Kansa Indians and means "people of the south wind." We grow many crops like wheat, milo, alfalfa hay, corn, soybeans, Do you like sunflower seeds? We grow our own! Maybe you like basketball or football. Our University of Kansas Jayhawks are the 1997 #1 basketball team in the USA, and Kansas State University has a football team that goes to a bowl game almost every year. You'll love our sunsets and our weather too with its mild winters, hot summers, and some of Dorothy's favorite storms too, TORNADOES!! You can even visit Dorothy's House in Liberal while you're here. If you don't have time to drive to Kansas, maybe you could just fly on one of those big jets made right here in Wichita.

Mrs. Reed's Fourth-Grade Class,
Park Elementary, Great Bend

68

Famous Kansans

Robert "Bob" Dole was born July 22, 1923, in Russell, Kansas. He was elected to the Kansas House of Representatives for three terms and served in the Senate from 1968 to 1996. He ran for president of the United States in 1996.

Bob Dole

JAMES A. Naismith

James A. Naismith (1861–1939) was born in Canada. He invented basketball as an alternative to gymnastics while teaching physical education in Massachusetts. In 1891, he coached the first game using peach baskets for the goals and a soccer ball. The basic rules Naismith published in 1892 are still in use today. He was a coach at the University of Kansas.

Amelia Earhart (1897–1937) was born in Atchinson, Kansas. In 1923, she became the first woman to get a pilot's license from NAA. In 1932, she became the first woman to fly solo across the Atlantic Ocean. Her

Amelia Earhart

airplane disappeared in July 1937 as she and her navigator, Frederick J. Noonan, were attempting the first round-the-world flight following the equator.

Dwight D. Eisenhower

Dwight D. Eisenhower

(1890–1969) was born in Denison, Texas. He spent his boyhood years in Abilene, Kansas. Eisenhower had an impressive military career. He was supreme commander of Allied Forces in Europe during World War II. He was elected the 34th president of the United States. He was president for two terms.

Susanna Madora Salter

Susanna Madora Salter

(1860–1961) was the first woman mayor in the United States. She was elected mayor of Argonia, Kansas, in 1887 and served for one year. Susanna Salter lived in a house constructed in 1884 from bricks fired in a kiln near her home.

Great Facts About the Great Plains State

- ☐ **Population:** 2,572,150 (1996)
- ☐ **Area:** 82,282 square miles
- ☐ **Size:** 204 miles wide, 406 miles long (almost a perfect rectangle)
- ☐ **Main Rivers:** Arkansas, Missouri, Kansas
- ☐ **Highest Point:** Mt. Sunflower (4,039 ft.)
- ☐ **Lowest Point:** Verdigris River (680 ft.)
- ☐ **Nicknames:** Sunflower State, Wheat State, Jayhawker State, Bread Basket of America
- ☐ People born in Kansas are called **Jayhawkers**.

More colorful Kansas facts...

In the 1830s gunpowder was taking its toll, but about 40 million buffalo still roamed the grasslands of Kansas.

Kansas grows popcorn, sunflower seeds, and cotton.

The world's largest salt mine (now used for storage) is in Hutchinson.

Sod House

There were no trees to cut down so the pioneers used squares of sod to build their sod houses or "soddies"

Everyone thinks we are a flat state, but really we are a slant-ed state. The elevation drops about eight feet per mile, moving from west to the east.

Pizza Hut was started in Wichita (1958).

Kansas is nicknamed "Tornado Alley."

Many fossils can be found in Kansas.

FOLLOW THE YELLOW BRICK ROAD TO KANSAS

1541
Coronado looks for gold in Kansas.

1830
First wagon trains travel the Oregon Trail.

1860
First railroad reaches Kansas.

1860
The Pony Express starts in Kansas.

Santa Fe Trail

1861
William Becknell opens the Santa Fe Trail. It is one of the longest trails in the U.S. and goes from Independence, Missouri, to Santa Fe, New Mexico.

Yellow Brick Road

Dorothy And Toto

Dorothy and Toto are in *The Wizard of Oz* of course. They are from Kansas too! They landed in magic Munchkin Land during a tornado. Dorothy's house, in Liberal, was built in **1902**. *The Wizard of Oz* movie was made in **1939**.

1867-1872
Cowboys drive 3,000 cattle from Texas to Abilene, Kansas, on the Chisholm Trail.

1930
Clyde Tombaugh, Burdette, Kansas, discovers Pluto.

1947
The biggest tornado ever hits Kansas. It kills 169 persons.

1997
Steve Hawley, astronaut from Salina, went on his fourth space shuttle mission. He operated the robot arm to repair the Hubble Telescope.

Kansas

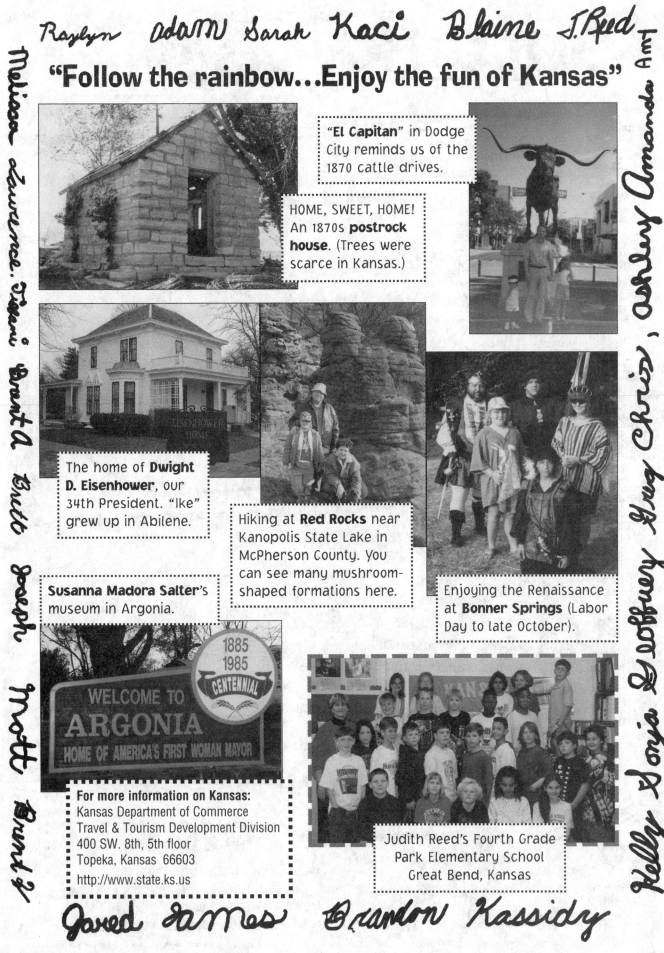

Raylyn adam Sarah Kaci Blaine J.Red

"Follow the rainbow...Enjoy the fun of Kansas"

"**El Capitan**" in Dodge City reminds us of the 1870 cattle drives.

HOME, SWEET, HOME! An 1870s **postrock house**. (Trees were scarce in Kansas.)

The home of **Dwight D. Eisenhower**, our 34th President. "Ike" grew up in Abilene.

Hiking at **Red Rocks** near Kanopolis State Lake in McPherson County. You can see many mushroom-shaped formations here.

Enjoying the Renaissance at **Bonner Springs** (Labor Day to late October).

Susanna Madora Salter's museum in Argonia.

1885 1985 CENTENNIAL

WELCOME TO ARGONIA HOME OF AMERICA'S FIRST WOMAN MAYOR

For more information on Kansas:
Kansas Department of Commerce
Travel & Tourism Development Division
400 SW. 8th, 5th floor
Topeka, Kansas 66603

http://www.state.ks.us

Judith Reed's Fourth Grade Park Elementary School Great Bend, Kansas

Jared James Brandon Kassidy

Melissa Laurence Tiffani Brent A Brett Joseph Matt Brandy

Ashley Amanda Amy Greg Chris Jeffrey Sonja Kelly

Kentucky

State Capital
Frankfort

State Flag

State Motto
**United
We Stand,
Divided
We Fall**

State Flower
Goldenrod

State Tree
**Kentucky
Coffee Tree**

State Bird
Cardinal

State Horse
Thoroughbred

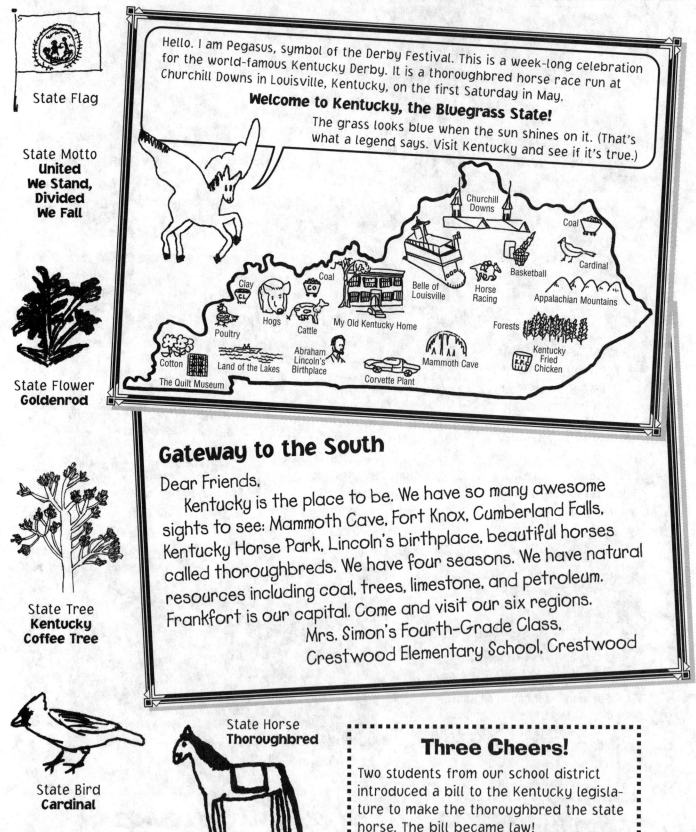

Hello. I am Pegasus, symbol of the Derby Festival. This is a week-long celebration for the world-famous Kentucky Derby. It is a thoroughbred horse race run at Churchill Downs in Louisville, Kentucky, on the first Saturday in May.

Welcome to Kentucky, the Bluegrass State!

The grass looks blue when the sun shines on it. (That's what a legend says. Visit Kentucky and see if it's true.)

Churchill Downs

Coal

Cardinal

Basketball

Horse Racing

Appalachian Mountains

Belle of Louisville

Clay

Coal

Hogs

Cattle

My Old Kentucky Home

Forests

Poultry

Cotton

Land of the Lakes

Abraham Lincoln's Birthplace

Corvette Plant

Mammoth Cave

Kentucky Fried Chicken

The Quilt Museum

Gateway to the South

Dear Friends,
    Kentucky is the place to be. We have so many awesome sights to see: Mammoth Cave, Fort Knox, Cumberland Falls, Kentucky Horse Park, Lincoln's birthplace, beautiful horses called thoroughbreds. We have four seasons. We have natural resources including coal, trees, limestone, and petroleum. Frankfort is our capital. Come and visit our six regions.
        Mrs. Simon's Fourth-Grade Class,
        Crestwood Elementary School, Crestwood

Three Cheers!

Two students from our school district introduced a bill to the Kentucky legislature to make the thoroughbred the state horse. The bill became law!

Read All About Us

ABRAHAM LINCOLN, the 16th president of the U.S., led the United States during the Civil War. He was born near Hodgenville.

DANIEL BOONE was among those who first settled here in 1767. Boone guided pioneers through the mountainous Cumberland Gap and carved out the Wilderness Road.

MUHAMMAD ALI, one of the greatest boxers, was born in Louisville in 1942. He won a gold medal for boxing in the 1960 Olympic Games. In 1964 he became the heavyweight champion of the world.

JESSE STUART, a teacher and principal, is known for the stories he wrote about the mountains of Kentucky. He has also composed poetry for adults and children. He taught his students to love reading and writing, but most of all to cherish their roots.

LORETTA LYNN, a country singer from Butcher Hollow, received a Grammy award and was named "Entertainer of the Decade" in the 1970s.

PEE WEE REESE is in the National Baseball Hall of Fame. He was born in Kentucky and went to New York to played for the Brooklyn Dodgers. He helped his team win the World Series.

COLONEL SANDERS founded Kentucky Fried Chicken (KFC) in 1956. There are now Kentucky Fried Chicken restaurants all over the world.

Get to Know Kentucky

Kentucky has four seasons, with mild winters and warm to hot summers. Average rainfall in Kentucky is 48 inches a year.

Highest Point: 4,154 feet above sea level

Lowest Point: 257 feet above sea level

Kentucky is about 425 miles wide from east to west and 182 miles long from north to south. It is 40 miles wide at its narrowest point. The state has six unique natural land regions: Bluegrass, Knobs, Eastern Mountains, Western Coal Fields, Pennyroyal, and Jackson Purchase.

About Our State

A peaceful group, the **Shakers** came to Kentucky in the 1800s. The men and women lived apart and did not marry or have children. They were called Shakers because, during religious ceremonies, they would become so excited that they would shake uncontrollably. The Shakers invented the washing machine and the wooden clothespin.

Reelfoot Lake was formed by an earthquake in 1818. This caused the Mississippi River to flow backward.

Did you know that there is a **Kentucky Fried Chicken** restaurant in Beijing, China? It seats 500 people at a time.

We're Proud That. . .

The University of Kentucky at Lexington is the home of the 1996 NCAA Basketball Championship.

Transylvania University in Lexington is the oldest college west of the Allegheny Mountains.

The oldest cathedral west of the Allegheny Mountains is St. Joseph's in Bardstown.

Do you like barbecue? Owensboro is famous for its barbecue. You won't find any better anywhere!

Racing Through Time

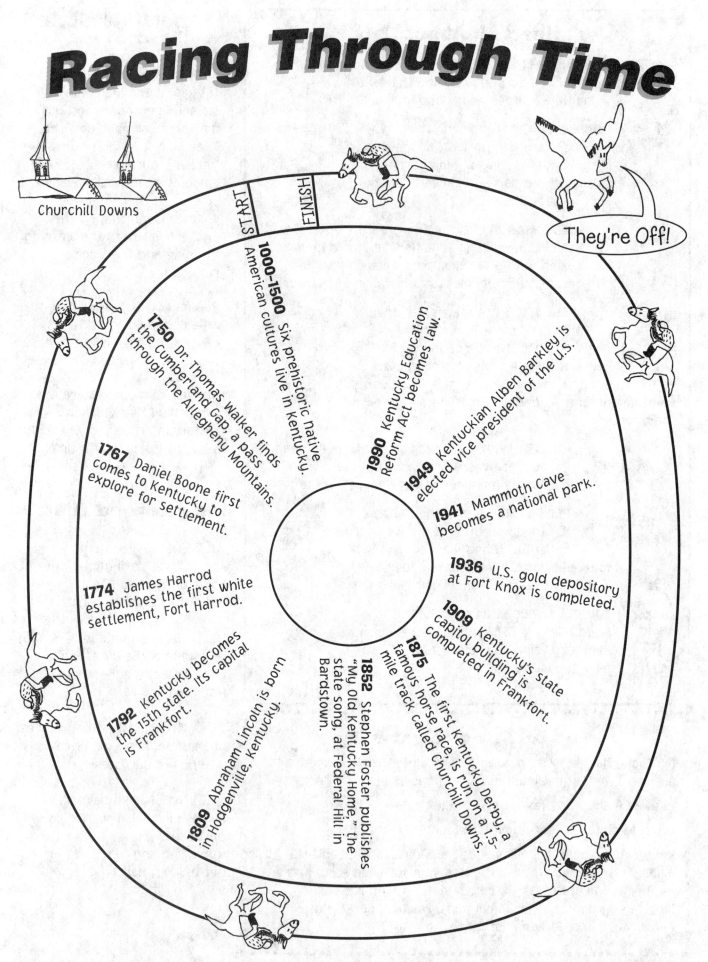

Churchill Downs

They're Off!

START

FINISH

1000-1500 Six prehistoric native American cultures live in Kentucky.

1750 Dr. Thomas Walker finds the Cumberland Gap, a pass through the Allegheny Mountains.

1767 Daniel Boone first comes to Kentucky to explore for settlement.

1774 James Harrod establishes the first white settlement, Fort Harrod.

1792 Kentucky becomes the 15th state. Its capital is Frankfort.

1809 Abraham Lincoln is born in Hodgenville, Kentucky.

1852 Stephen Foster publishes "My Old Kentucky Home," the state song, at Federal Hill in Bardstown.

1875 The first Kentucky Derby, a famous horse race, is run on a 1.5-mile track called Churchill Downs.

1909 Kentucky's state capitol building is completed in Frankfort.

1936 U.S. gold depository at Fort Knox is completed.

1941 Mammoth Cave becomes a national park.

1949 Kentuckian Alben Barkley is elected vice president of the U.S.

1990 Kentucky Education Reform Act becomes law.

Our Splendid State

Mammoth Cave
The world's largest cave system is a natural wonder. It has five levels with two lakes, three rivers, and eight waterfalls.

Cumberland Falls
This gorgeous waterfall is often called the "Niagara of the South." It is one of two places in the world where you can see a moonbow.

Fort Knox
Imagine a place that holds billions of dollars in gold. This is the place! It's bombproof, of course.

Louisville Slugger Museum
Swack! See the world's largest baseball bat.

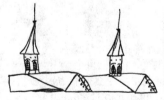

Churchill Downs
Horse racing is the pride of Kentucky. This is our most famous track.

For more information about our splendid state:

Commonwealth of Kentucky
Department of Travel Development
P.O. Box 2011
Frankfort, KY 40601

http://www.state.ky.us

We are very proud to have contributed a chapter to this book.

Louisiana

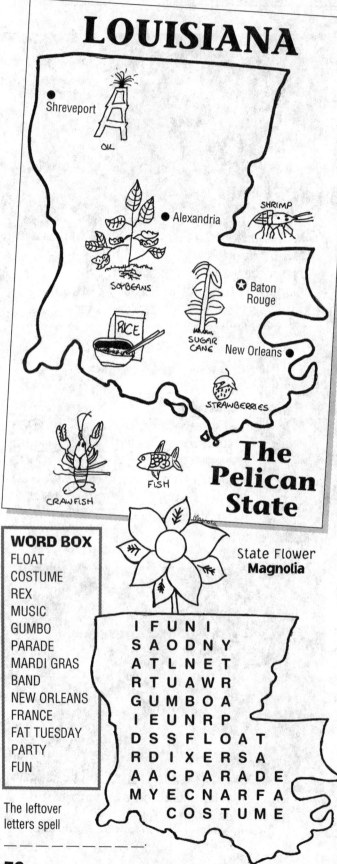

LOUISIANA

Shreveport
OIL

Alexandria

SHRIMP

SOYBEANS

RICE

SUGAR CANE

★ Baton Rouge

New Orleans

STRAWBERRIES

CRAWFISH

FISH

The Pelican State

State Bird
Eastern Brown Pelican

State Capital
Baton Rouge

State Flower
Magnolia

WORD BOX

FLOAT
COSTUME
REX
MUSIC
GUMBO
PARADE
MARDI GRAS
BAND
NEW ORLEANS
FRANCE
FAT TUESDAY
PARTY
FUN

The leftover
letters spell

_ _ _ _ _ _ _ _ _

```
I F U N I
S A O D N Y
A T L N E T
R T U A W R
G U M B O A
I E U N R P
D S S F L O A T
R D I X E R S A
A A C P A R A D E
M Y E C N A R F A
C O S T U M E
```

Dear Readers,

Imagine a place that's filled with music, great food, interesting buildings, and super shops—all with a French accent. That's the French Quarter in New Orleans. But Louisiana is more than New Orleans. Louisiana is swamp tours on which you can see many kinds of animals and plants. Or you could go to Cajun country and learn how to dance at a fais-dodo. (Say *fay dough dough*.) If you want to learn more about our history, take a plantation tour. Up north you can go to Kisatchie National Forest and camp or hike. We hope you will come and see some of these fascinating things!

Ms. Stefanowicz and Fifth-Grade Class at Ronald E. McNair Elementary School, New Orleans

Mardi Gras Seek-'n'-Find

We hold an exciting Mardi Gras festival in Louisiana. It's a custom brought from France. The Mardi Gras (*mardee grah*) includes huge, colorful floats in a big parade held on Fat Tuesday, the day before Ash Wednesday. During Mardi Gras, things are wild. But then comes Lent. It starts on the next day, Ash Wednesday, a serious holy day when some people fast.

Find and circle the Mardi Gras words in the Word Box in the puzzle. They go up, down, and across. Some go backward and some letters are used more than once. The leftover letters spell the name of the most fun state in the country. (See answer on page 77.)

Famous Folks

If you like jazz, **LOUIS ARMSTRONG** is probably one of your heroes. Born in 1900, he lived in New Orleans. As a child he was a street singer. Later he became known as the greatest jazz trumpet player. He played in New York and Chicago and took his fabulous sound all over the world. He died in 1971. Armstrong Park in New Orleans is named after him.

Louis Armstrong

Go, man, go! And **BILL RUSSELL** did. He was born February 2, 1934, in Monroe. He wanted to play in the National Basketball Association (NBA). Lucky NBA. And lucky Bill. After he graduated from college, the legendary Boston Celtics basketball team drafted him. He led the team to two championships. After retiring as a player, he became the first African American to coach an NBA team.

Bill Russell

Sing out, Mahalia. No one who heard **MAHALIA JACKSON** sing could forget her magnificent voice. She was born in 1911 and sang in her daddy's choir when she was three years old. She grew up to became a famous gospel singer. "He's Got the Whole World in His Hands" is one of her songs. She died in 1972, but her music lives on.

JEAN LAFITTE's life was the stuff legends are made of. He was born in the 1700s in Bayonne, France. At the age of nine, he ran away from home and went to sea and the dangerous, hard life of a sailor. He became a pirate, sailing in the Atlantic Ocean and Caribbean Sea, seeking ships to attack. One story claims that Lafitte buried his treasures in one of the many swamps outside of New Orleans. Besides being a pirate, he fought for America in the War of 1812.

Mahalia Jackson

Jean Lafitte

The lives of many Louisiana women were changed for the good by **ELEANOR McMAIN**. She was born on March 2, 1868, in a cottage along Amite River in Louisiana. She had many older brothers. When she grew up she became a teacher and was appointed to the staff at Newcomb College in New Orleans. Later she joined Kingsley College and soon became its leader. She died in 1934 after a lifetime dedicated to helping young women get an education. A school in New Orleans is named for her.

Eleanor McMain

The **MARSALIS FAMILY** has been called "the first family of jazz." **Ellis Marsalis** was born in 1934. He teaches jazz piano. **Branford Marsalis**, Ellis's son, was born in 1960. He plays jazz and rock on the saxophone. **Wynton Marsalis**, Ellis's younger son, was born in 1961. He plays the trumpet and has won eight Grammy Awards for his recordings of classical and jazz music. In 1997 he won the first Pulitzer Prize awarded for Jazz. All three Marsalises were born in New Orleans.

Wynton Marsalis

Answer: LOUISIANA

Louisiana Gumbo: Our History

INGREDIENTS

- **Population:** 4,350,579 (1996)
- **Natural resources:** petroleum, salt, sulfur
- **Agriculture:** sugar, rice
- **Major industries:** chemicals, lumber, electronics
- **Average temperature in January:** 62°F
- **Average temperature in July:** 90°F
- **Average rainfall in one year:** 57 inches
- **Statehood:** 1812 (18th state)
- **State song:** "You Are My Sunshine"
- **State web site:** http://www.state.la.us

INSTRUCTIONS

Start with rich, fertile land and a warm climate. Mix in many different peoples: Native Americans, Spaniards, French, Africans, and Americans. Form a small town along the Mississippi. Stir it up by world events. Add more people: Irish, Italian, and Vietnamese. Let sit until matured. The result is a unique blend of culture like no other place in the world!   Serves: everyone.

INFORMATION: Office of Tourism, P.O. Box 94291, Baton Rouge, LA 70804; tel. 800-334-8626

10 Major Moments in Louisiana History

12,000 years ago
Native Americans arrive in Louisiana.

1541
Hernando de Soto is the first European to sail the Mississippi River.

1760
Cajun French start arriving from Canada.

1800
Napoleon sells Louisiana to the United States.

1815
General Andrew Jackson leads American troops to victory against the British in the Battle of New Orleans.

1865
All the slaves in Louisiana and other southern states win their freedom.

1872
Pinkney Pinchback becomes the first African-American governor.

1901
Oil is discovered in Jennings.

1928
Huey P. Long becomes governor.

1977
Ernest Morial becomes the first African-American mayor of New Orleans.

Six Super Places to Visit

Jackson Square, New Orleans: On Jackson Square you can tour the historic St. Louis Cathedral, shop, or watch street performers play music or put on magic shows.

French Quarter, New Orleans: It has churches, gardens, courtyards, guest houses, hotels, museums, souvenir shops, and restaurants.

Tabasco Sauce Factory, New Iberia: Tour the factory. See how Tabasco is made.

Jean Lafitte National Park, Barataria: Take a nature walk and see many animals, such as alligators, very close up.

Jazz and Heritage Festival (Jazz Fest), New Orleans Fairgrounds: Hear every kind of music from classical to Cajun. Eat hot food and see cool arts and crafts.

Audubon Zoo, New Orleans: See wild and endangered animals. Visit exhibition the African Savanna and the Asian Domain.

FUN-FILLED FESTIVALS

January: Oyster Food Festival, Lafitte
February/March: Mardi Gras, New Orleans
March: Jazz/Rhythm & Blues Festival, Natchitoches
April: Crawfish Festival, Chalmette
May: May Festival, Abbeville
June: Blueberry Festival, Mansfield

July: Seafood Festival, Franklinton
August: Red River Drag Boat Race, Shreveport
September: Sugar Cane Festival, New Iberia
October: Louisiana State Fair, Shreveport
November: Christmas Light Festival, Homer
December: Living Christmas Celebration, Morgan City

Louisiana

Maine

State Capital
Augusta

State Seal

State Bird
Chickadee

State Animal
Moose

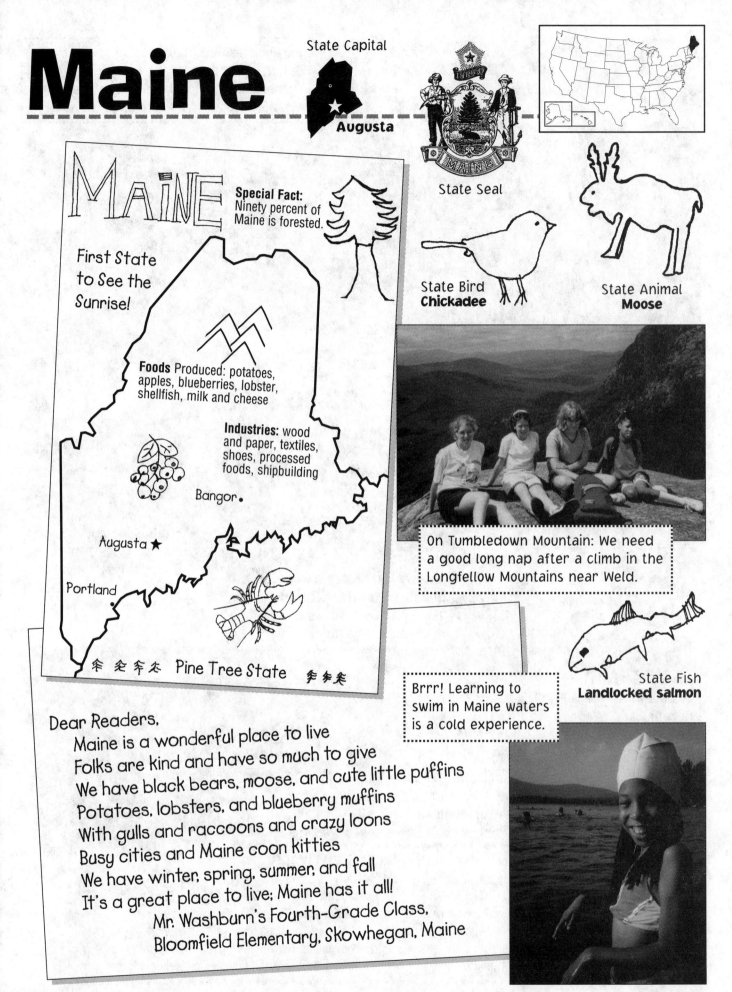

MAINE

Special Fact: Ninety percent of Maine is forested.

First State to See the Sunrise!

Foods Produced: potatoes, apples, blueberries, lobster, shellfish, milk and cheese

Industries: wood and paper, textiles, shoes, processed foods, shipbuilding

Bangor.

Augusta ★

Portland .

Pine Tree State

On Tumbledown Mountain: We need a good long nap after a climb in the Longfellow Mountains near Weld.

State Fish
Landlocked salmon

Brrr! Learning to swim in Maine waters is a cold experience.

Dear Readers,
Maine is a wonderful place to live
Folks are kind and have so much to give
We have black bears, moose, and cute little puffins
Potatoes, lobsters, and blueberry muffins
With gulls and raccoons and crazy loons
Busy cities and Maine coon kitties
We have winter, spring, summer, and fall
It's a great place to live; Maine has it all!
Mr. Washburn's Fourth-Grade Class,
Bloomfield Elementary, Skowhegan, Maine

Just the Maine Facts

- Maine's nickname is Vacationland because so many tourists visit here.
- Earmuffs were invented by Chester Greenwood in Farmington.
- The Aroostook War was fought between Maine and Canada in 1837. The cause was the disputed border between them. No one was hurt or killed, but there was a fistfight in a tavern.
- Maine has no native poisonous creatures.
- Hide your handkerchiefs! It is against the law to publicly blow your nose in Waterville.
- It you want to go to Estcourt, Maine, be sure to take your passport. It can be reached only by driving through Canada.

- The coast of Maine is 3,000 miles long, much longer than California's coast.
- They probably didn't trust those newfangled dial phones. Bryant Pond was the last town in America to use crank telephones.
- Some coastal farmers put their sheep out to pasture on small islands. Baaa.
- Portland Head Light, built in 1787 by order of George Washington, is one of the oldest lighthouses in America.

- One potato…two potatoes…three weeks out of school. That's what children in Aroostook County get every fall so they can help with the potato harvest.
- Be glad you didn't live in Maine in 1816. Every month that year had a killing frost. People call that year "Eighteen-Hundred-and-Froze-to-Death." (Well, at least their sense of humor didn't freeze.)

- Food for thought. Bath has a fancy wooden building called the Chocolate Church. In Kennebunk, there is a fancy house called the Wedding Cake House.
- In 1908, you could take a trolley all the way from Waterville to Boston—more than 180 miles! Today, there are no trolleys left in Maine, except in museums. (They were probably all tuckered out from those long rides.)
- DID YOU KNOW THAT. . . Portland's symbol is the phoenix? The city burned to the ground twice and had to be rebuilt both times.

- Quite a few towns in Maine are named for foreign places: China, Rome, Belgrade, Moscow, Sweden, Denmark, Athens, Madrid, Vienna, Mexico, Naples, Norway, Paris, Peru, Poland, Wales, and Stockholm.
- The most easterly point in the United States is called West Quoddy Head.
- Here's a Maine riddle. What is Moosehead Lake shaped like? (A moose's head. Honest. We wouldn't make that up.)

Famous Mainers

Charlotte, Wilbur, and Stuart Little all came from the imagination of **E. B. White** (1899–1985). He moved to Maine from New York City, where he had written for the *New Yorker* magazine for many years. He is famous for his three classic children's books: *Charlotte's Web, Stuart Little,* and *The Trumpet of the Swan*. Wilbur the Pig's barn still stands in South Brooklin, Maine!

Samantha Smith, a student, was very worried about the possibility of a nuclear war between the U.S. and the former Soviet Union. She wrote a letter to Yuri Andropov, then the premier of the Soviet Union, asking why our countries did not get along better. He wrote back. She was invited to Russia and became an ambassador for peace when she was only 11 years old!

George Bush was our 41st president. Although he lived most of his life in Texas, he has a home in Kennebunkport. It became a vacation White House from 1988 to 1992. Most summers, the former president still fishes and goes boating there.

Margaret Chase Smith (1897–), from Skowhegan, was the first woman to serve in both houses of the U.S. Congress and the first woman to campaign for U.S. president. She is also one of the first people to stand up to Senator Joseph McCarthy during in the 1950s when he was accusing many people of being Communists. She's our Maine heroine.

Maine

Time Flows Along
THE KENNEBEC RIVER

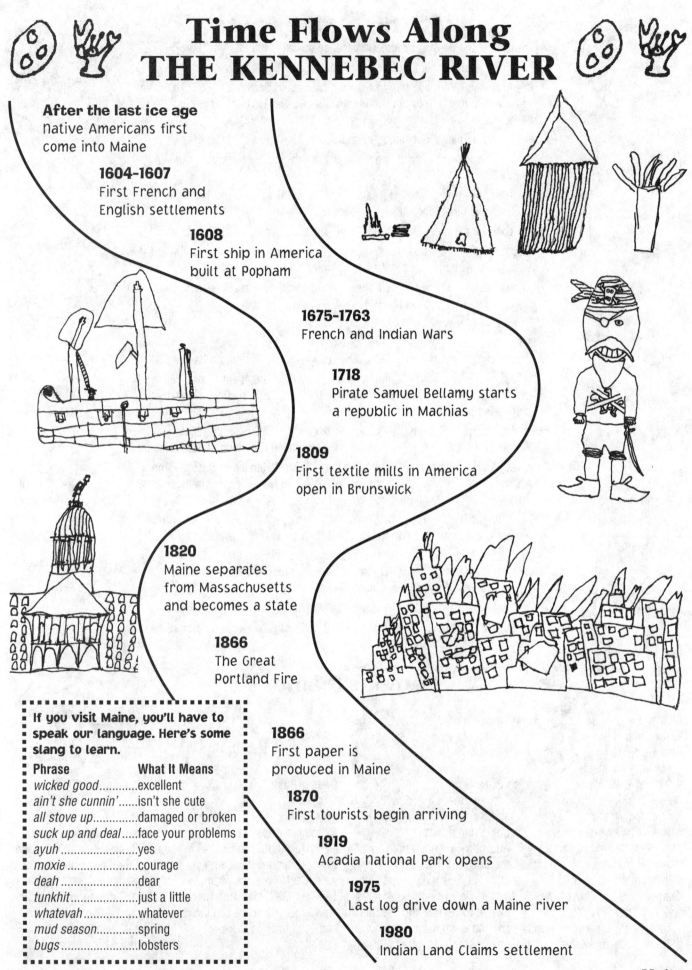

After the last ice age
Native Americans first come into Maine

1604-1607
First French and English settlements

1608
First ship in America built at Popham

1675-1763
French and Indian Wars

1718
Pirate Samuel Bellamy starts a republic in Machias

1809
First textile mills in America open in Brunswick

1820
Maine separates from Massachusetts and becomes a state

1866
The Great Portland Fire

1866
First paper is produced in Maine

1870
First tourists begin arriving

1919
Acadia National Park opens

1975
Last log drive down a Maine river

1980
Indian Land Claims settlement

If you visit Maine, you'll have to speak our language. Here's some slang to learn.

Phrase	What It Means
wicked good	excellent
ain't she cunnin'	isn't she cute
all stove up	damaged or broken
suck up and deal	face your problems
ayuh	yes
moxie	courage
deah	dear
tunkhit	just a little
whatevah	whatever
mud season	spring
bugs	lobsters

Maine

Take a Tour

Ice fishing is cold! Many people in Maine drill holes through the ice in winter and go fishing.

Ski lift at Saddleback ski resort in **Rangeley**. In the 1800s, people took trains to Rangeley to go flyfishing.

Steamed clams and butter go great with corn on the cob and a garden salad.

Slip over still waters, glide over the reflections of the sky and the hills.

For more information, contact:

The Maine Publicity Bureau
PO Box 2300
Hallowell, ME 04347

http://www.visitmaine.com

Many of our beaches are rocky, but the rocks are beautifully rounded by the tumbling surf. The waves make a lovely sound on the pebbles.

Mr. Washburn's Fourth-Grade Class, Bloomfield Elementary, Skowhegan, Maine

Maryland

State Capital

Annapolis

State Bird
Baltimore Oriole

The oriole has the colors of Lord Baltimore, who founded Maryland.

State Flower
Black-eyed Susan

This flower is black and gold, Maryland's state colors. Thirteen petals on the flower can symbolize the 13 original colonies.

PENNSYLVANIA

The National Aquarium, Baltimore

Baltimore •

WEST VIRGINIA

Potomac River

Potomac River

VIRGINIA

Annapolis ★

Chesapeake Bay

DELAWARE

Lighthouses let ships know where they are.

Atlantic Ocean

MARYLAND
The Old Line State

Dear Friends,

Maryland is magnificent and majestic even though it's not very large. Here, you can swim at the beach, ski, play all kinds of sports, fish, or go horseback riding. If you prefer the big indoors, we've got super shopping. And if you're hungry after exercising your body, mind, and eyes, go to world-famous Chesapeake Bay and enjoy delicious crabs and oysters. Hope to see you soon!

Mrs. Phillips's class,
Glenmount Elementary,
Baltimore

State Motto
Fatti maschii, parole femine
"Manly deeds, womanly words"

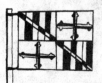

State Flag and Seal
Maryland's flag is on its state seal. Lord Baltimore is shown armed and mounted on the obverse side. The seal, known as Courtesy the State of Maryland, was brought to America in colonial days.

State Tree
White Oak

State Dog
Chesapeake Bay Retriever

The Chesapeake Bay retriever is one of the best hunting dogs and loves the water. In his brown, curly coat, he is friendly and gentle.

ABOUT MARYLAND

Land area: 12,407 square miles

Population: 5,071,604 (1996)

Capital: Annapolis

Lowest point: Along the ocean at sea level

Highest point: Backbone Mountain, 3,360 feet

Major rivers: Patapsco River, Patuxent River, Susquehanna River, Wicomico River

Major bodies of water: Chesapeake Bay, Deep Creek Lake (artificial), Liberty Lake (artificial)

Resources, industries, products: aluminum, copper, steel, coal, stone, chickens, oysters, milk, corn, soybeans, crabs

American Indian groups: Conoy, Delaware, Nanticoke, Powhatan, Shawnee, Susquehanna

How Maryland got its name: Maryland was named for Queen Henrietta Maria, wife of King Charles I of England.

Mighty Marylanders

Harriet Tubman

Cal Ripkin

Because she led people to freedom, **HARRIET TUBMAN** was known as the "Moses of her People." She was born in Dorchester County around 1823. Before the Civil War she went into the Deep South and helped 300 slaves make their way north to become free.

CAL RIPKIN of the Baltimore Orioles won three Golden Glove awards in baseball. Aberdeen has built a nine-foot bronze statue in honor of him.

He was curious about everything around him. What do you think he became when he grew up? **BENJAMIN BANNEKER**, born in Baltimore in 1731, became a great mathematician and astronomer. He helped survey Washington, D.C.

If you're a space buff, you'll recognize the name of **DR. ROBERT H. GODDARD** (1882–1945). He replaced highly explosive gunpowder fuel in rockets with safer liquid fuel. After his death, the Goddard Space Flight Center in Greenbelt was dedicated to him.

A crow caws. A pendulum swings slowly toward a captive man. With exquisite imagery, **EDGAR ALLAN POE** wrote terrifying suspense and horror stories and poetry. He lived from 1809 to 1845. He is buried in Baltimore. You can visit his grave—if you dare!

Benjamin Banneker

Edgar Allan Poe

Incredible Events

1608 Captain John Smith explores Chesapeake Bay.

1694 Capital moves from Saint Mary's City to Annapolis.

1632 Charles I grants a charter to the first Lord Baltimore, George Calvert.

1788 April 28, Maryland becomes the seventh state.

1811 Construction of the first national road begins.

1814 Francis Scott Key writes "The Star-Spangled Banner."

1847 U.S. Naval Academy opens in Annapolis.

1977 Francis Scott Key Bridge opens, completing the beltway around Baltimore.

1952 Chesapeake Bay Bridge is completed.

1904 Over two days in February, a fire destroys much of the city of Baltimore.

1981 A new aquarium, designated by congress to be the National Aquarium, opens in Baltimore.

1995 Cal Ripkin of the Baltimore Orioles breaks Lou Gehrig's long-standing record of playing in 2,130 consecutive baseball games.

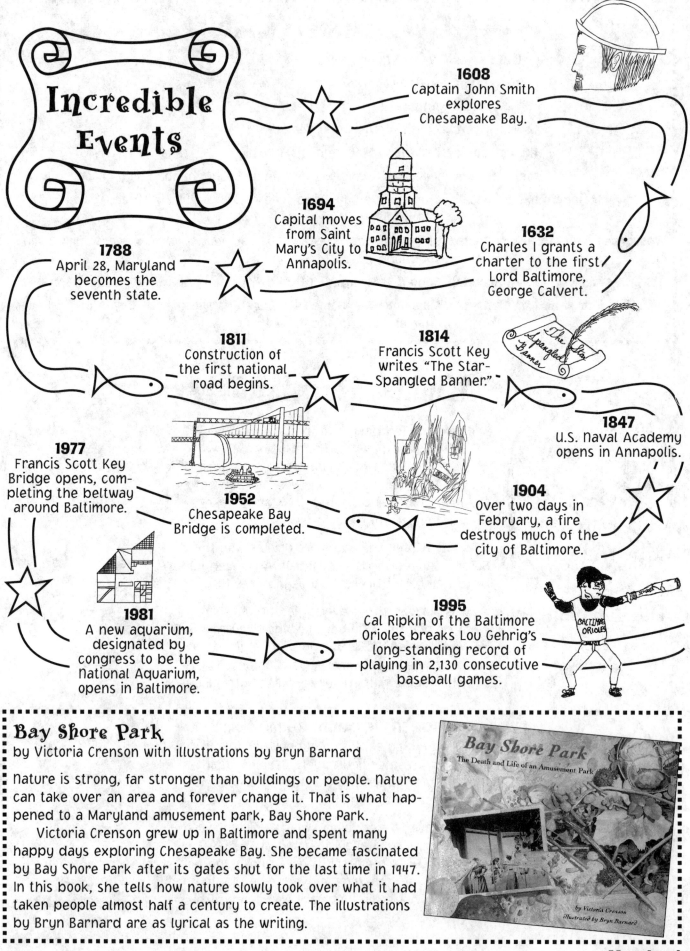

Bay Shore Park
by Victoria Crenson with illustrations by Bryn Barnard

Nature is strong, far stronger than buildings or people. Nature can take over an area and forever change it. That is what happened to a Maryland amusement park, Bay Shore Park.

Victoria Crenson grew up in Baltimore and spent many happy days exploring Chesapeake Bay. She became fascinated by Bay Shore Park after its gates shut for the last time in 1947. In this book, she tells how nature slowly took over what it had taken people almost half a century to create. The illustrations by Bryn Barnard are as lyrical as the writing.

Bay Shore Park
The Death and Life of an Amusement Park

by Victoria Crenson
illustrated by Bryn Barnard

Go to **Fort McHenry** and visit the battleground that inspired Francis Scott Key to write "The Star-Spangled Banner."

Maryland is known for its delicious **crabs** caught in the Chesapeake Bay.

It's a whale of an experience at the **National Aquarium**. Experience the sight of beluga whales, dolphins, and huge tanks full of sea creatures so close you can almost touch them.

Surf the waves, ride the rides. Do it all at **Ocean City** on the Atlantic Ocean. When you leave, it will be like waking from a dream.

Picture This in Maryland

Horseback riding and racing are popular in Maryland. The well-known Preakness race at Pimlico is held every year.

Did you know that the U.S. government pays the tuition, room, and board for all four years of college, for students accepted at the **U.S. Naval College** at Annapolis?

Refresh yourself in **Swallow Falls State Park**. You can hop across rocks or just float in the cool, clear water.

Tourist Information:

Office of Tourism
217 East Redwood Street
Baltimore, MD 21202
800-543-1036

http://www.MDisfun.org

Say "hello" to Mrs. Phillips's class.

Massachusetts

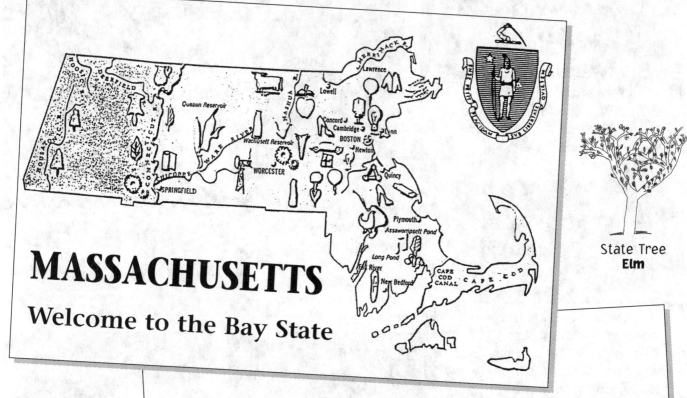

MASSACHUSETTS
Welcome to the Bay State

State Capital
Boston

State Bird
Chickadee

State Flower
Mayflower

State Tree
Elm

Dear Readers,

You'll never get bored in Massachusetts. If you're interested in history, we've got it. Massachusetts was the sixth original colony and played an important role in the history of our country. We're also on the cutting edge of what's happening today. Our hook-shaped state stretches from the sandy beaches of Cape Cod to the rolling hills of the Berkshires. That means you can enjoy hiking, swimming, boating, skating, skiing, and snow-shoeing. Whatever the season, there's a reason to visit our state.

Librarian Carolyn Janssen and the Fifth Graders
at Silvio Conte Community School, Pittsfield

Q: If April showers bring May flowers, what do may flowers bring?

A: Pilgrims

Famous Ship
Mayflower

What Do You Know About Massachusetts?

Quiz yourself. Circle the letter of the right answer. Then find out how you score.

1. Where were the first Ryder golf matches played between the U.S. and England?
   a. Kookamonga
   b. Tottering-on-the-Brink
   c. Worcester Country Club

2. Which city hosted the first World Series?
   a. Miami
   b. San Diego
   c. Boston

3. In which city was volleyball developed?
   a. Rome
   b. Athens
   c. Holyoke

4. Who invented the rocket?
   a. Dr. Goddard
   b. Dr. Seuss
   c. Dr. Frankenstein

5. Which four U.S. presidents were born in our state?
   a. Johnson, Truman, Grant, Washington
   b. Garfield, Lincoln, Adams, Kennedy
   c. John and John Quincy Adams, John F. Kennedy, George Bush

6. Where is the only church in the world without any steps?
   a. Stepford
   b. High Point
   c. St. Joseph's Church, Pittsfield

7. Where was the first state park located?
   a. Las Vegas
   b. Chicago
   c. Elm Street Park, Worcester

ANSWERS: 1.c 2.c 3.c 4.a 5.c 6.c 7.c

 If you got all the answers right, you must live in Massachusetts. Lucky you!

 If you got any of the answers wrong, come to Massachusetts. Learn more about us.

Massachusetts

Some Very Famous People

Students from Silvio O. Conte Community School interviewed one of our senators, **EDWARD KENNEDY**, to find out what he likes best about Massachusetts. The senator said that the four seasons was one of the best things about our state. He enjoys sailboating and fishing. He also likes to visit the Berkshires to go skiing, swimming, and camping. But most important, the Senator feels that Massachusetts is the best place to live because people care about and help one another.

BENJAMIN FRANKLIN was born in Boston in 1706. He was an amazing man—an inventor, publisher, and statesman. He was the U.S. ambassador to France. He invented the lightning rod and proved that lightning is electricity. He published *Poor Richard's Almanack*.

EMILY DICKINSON was born in Amherst in 1830. She was a very private person who wrote about nature from a very personal point of view. Just a few of her poems were published while she was alive. But, after she died, thousands of poems were found in her desk.

We're proud of **SILVIO O. CONTE**—and not just because our school was named for him. Former President Bush called him the Education Congressman because, as our congressman for 32 years, he showed such support for education. Silvio O. Conte was born in Pittsfield in 1921. He represented the people of western Massachusetts for 17 terms. He was a man of spirit who had a great sense of humor. He is fondly remembered by the people of western Massachusetts.

We've always shared the writer known as Dr. Seuss with the world. But **THEODORE SEUSS GEISEL** (his real name) was born in Springfield. This year his wonderful creation, *The Cat in the Hat*, is 40 years old. He won the Pulitzer Prize in 1984. He died in 1991.

SUSAN B. ANTHONY was born in Adams in 1820. She campaigned for women's rights and was the first woman pictured on a U.S. coin.

Time Travel with the Pilgrims and the Patriots

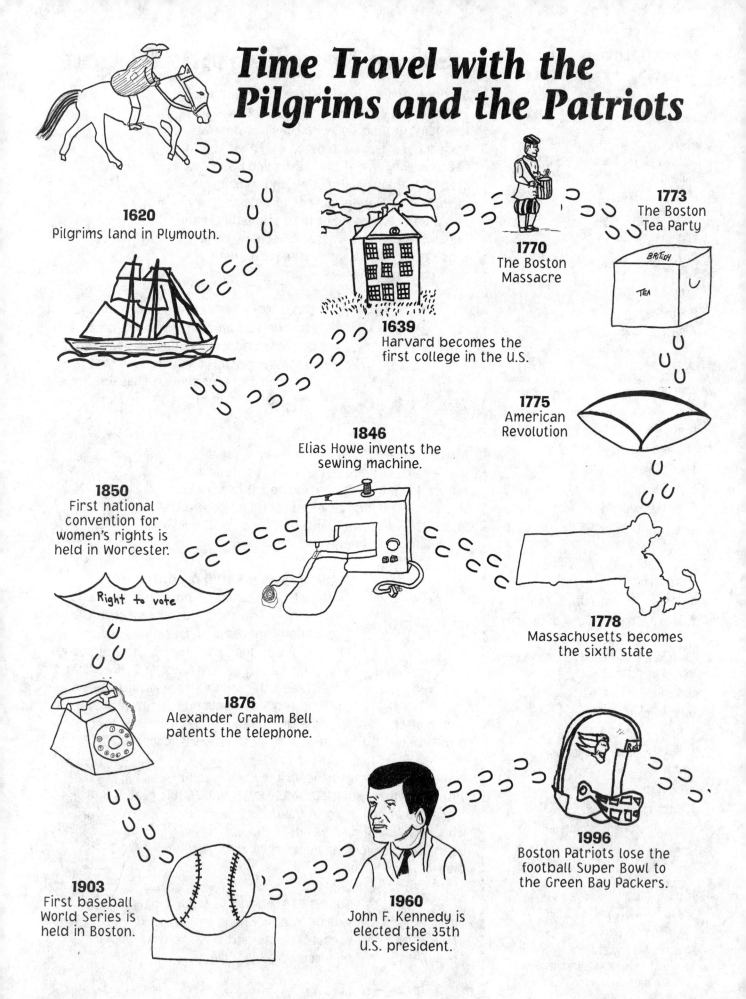

1620
Pilgrims land in Plymouth.

1639
Harvard becomes the first college in the U.S.

1770
The Boston Massacre

1773
The Boston Tea Party

BRITISH
TEA

1775
American Revolution

1846
Elias Howe invents the sewing machine.

1850
First national convention for women's rights is held in Worcester.

Right to vote

1778
Massachusetts becomes the sixth state

1876
Alexander Graham Bell patents the telephone.

1996
Boston Patriots lose the football Super Bowl to the Green Bay Packers.

1903
First baseball World Series is held in Boston.

1960
John F. Kennedy is elected the 35th U.S. president.

Our Great Outdoors

Our **snow** is deep and clean and there's lots of it.

The perfect vacation spot: Come to **Cape Cod**. Join us. What are you waiting for?

Courtesy of Walter H. Scott

Imagine coming to a new land aboard a tiny ship. Hop aboard the *Mayflower II* and experience what being a Pilgrim might have been like.

Mount Greylock is the highest point in our state. At the top—3,491 feet up—there's a monument.

You and the stars and the music. It couldn't be more perfect. Relax on the lawn at **Tanglewood**. You can enjoy a picnic while listening to the Boston Symphony Orchestra.

This chapter was created by the fifth-grade Quad F Team with help from Carolyn Janssen, Kathy Baker, Claire Asselin, and Anne Hynes at Silvio Conte Community School.

Do you like to **boat** or **swim** or **fish** or just **look** at a beautiful river or the wide-open sea? You can do any of that in Massachusetts.

Office of Travel and Tourism
100 Cambridge St., 13th Floor
Boston, MA 02202
(800) 447-6277   http://www.state.ma.us

Michigan

State Capital

Lansing

OUR MICHIGAN

- **Michigan's name** is derived from the Indian words *Michi-Gama* meaning "large lake."
- **Area:** 59,954 square miles of land
  1,573 square miles of inland water
  38,575 square miles of Great Lakes water
- **Number of inland lakes:** 11,037
- **Population:** 9,594,350 (1996)
- **Nickname:** Wolverine State
- Hope you like water. In Michigan you are **never more than six miles** from a lake or a stream.
- Michigan is a **four-season** tourist attraction.
- **Four flags** have flown over Michigan.
- No point in Michigan is more than 85 miles from any one of the **Great Lakes.** Michigan is the only state that borders on four of the five Great Lakes.

State Flag

State Stone
Petoskey Stone

State Motto
If you seek a pleasant peninsula, look about you.

State Bird
American Robin

YES M!CH!GAN

Cooper Harbor

Ironwood

Lake Superior

Alpena

Traverse City

Lake Huron

Lake Michigan

Midland

Grand Haven

Grand Rapids

Holland

Lansing

Detroit

Battle Creek

Lake Erie

Hello from Michigan

The Wolverine State

Dear Readers,
  WE LOVE MICHIGAN!
Michigan is a four-season tourist attraction.
In winter we go sledding down big, snowy hills.
In spring we watch snow melt and beautiful flowers grow.
In summer we swim and fish in our many lakes and rivers.
In fall we rake the colorful leaves and jump into piles of them.
  COME AND VISIT OUR WONDERFUL STATE!
    Barbara Poel's Fourth-Grade Class
    Beach School, Fruitport

State Flower
Apple Blossom

State Reptile
Painted Turtle

State Gem
Isle Royale Greenstone

State Fish   **Brook Trout**

State Tree
White Pine

92

You Might Be From Michigan If...
✔ your summer is three months of bad sledding.
✔ the Big Mac is something you drive across.
✔ you learned to steer a boat before you rode a bicycle.
✔ you've had frostbite and sunburn in the same week.
✔ your favorite holiday is the opening of deer hunting season.
✔ traveling coast to coast means from Lake Huron to Lake Michigan.
✔ some of the change in your pocket is Canadian.
✔ you point to the palm of your hand to show where you live.

Match the names of the SPORTS FAVORITES in the left column with what they did in the right column.

1. Ty Cobb
2. Joe Louis
3. Magic Johnson
4. Gordie Howe

a. World heavyweight boxing champion from Detroit
b. Professional basketball player from Lansing
c. Famous hockey player from Detroit
d. First player in Baseball Hall of Fame

Answers: 1.d 2.a 3.b 4.c

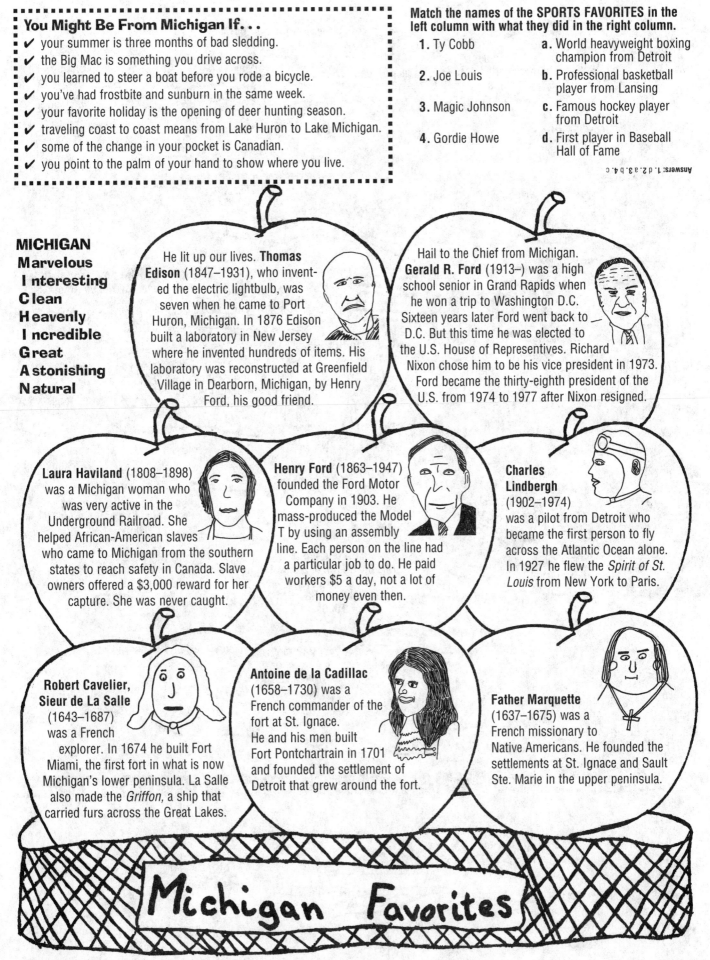

MICHIGAN
M arvelous
I nteresting
C lean
H eavenly
I ncredible
G reat
A stonishing
N atural

He lit up our lives. **Thomas Edison** (1847–1931), who invented the electric lightbulb, was seven when he came to Port Huron, Michigan. In 1876 Edison built a laboratory in New Jersey where he invented hundreds of items. His laboratory was reconstructed at Greenfield Village in Dearborn, Michigan, by Henry Ford, his good friend.

Hail to the Chief from Michigan. **Gerald R. Ford** (1913–) was a high school senior in Grand Rapids when he won a trip to Washington D.C. Sixteen years later Ford went back to D.C. But this time he was elected to the U.S. House of Representatives. Richard Nixon chose him to be his vice president in 1973. Ford became the thirty-eighth president of the U.S. from 1974 to 1977 after Nixon resigned.

Laura Haviland (1808–1898) was a Michigan woman who was very active in the Underground Railroad. She helped African-American slaves who came to Michigan from the southern states to reach safety in Canada. Slave owners offered a $3,000 reward for her capture. She was never caught.

Henry Ford (1863–1947) founded the Ford Motor Company in 1903. He mass-produced the Model T by using an assembly line. Each person on the line had a particular job to do. He paid workers $5 a day, not a lot of money even then.

Charles Lindbergh (1902–1974) was a pilot from Detroit who became the first person to fly across the Atlantic Ocean alone. In 1927 he flew the *Spirit of St. Louis* from New York to Paris.

Robert Cavelier, Sieur de La Salle (1643–1687) was a French explorer. In 1674 he built Fort Miami, the first fort in what is now Michigan's lower peninsula. La Salle also made the *Griffon*, a ship that carried furs across the Great Lakes.

Antoine de la Cadillac (1658–1730) was a French commander of the fort at St. Ignace. He and his men built Fort Pontchartrain in 1701 and founded the settlement of Detroit that grew around the fort.

Father Marquette (1637–1675) was a French missionary to Native Americans. He founded the settlements at St. Ignace and Sault Ste. Marie in the upper peninsula.

Michigan Favorites

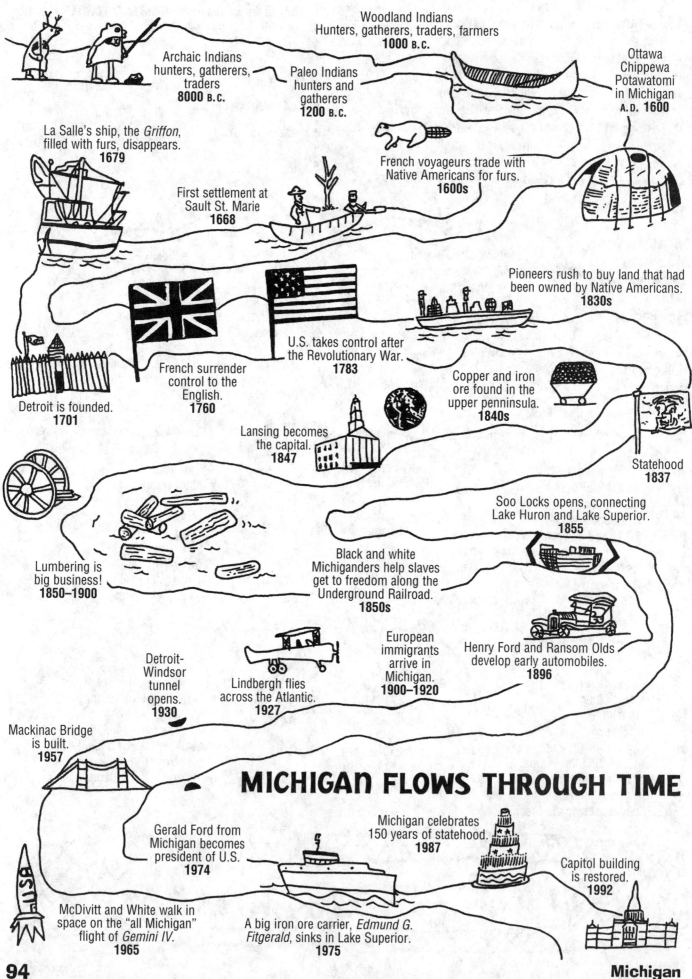

Woodland Indians
Hunters, gatherers, traders, farmers
1000 B.C.

Archaic Indians
hunters, gatherers,
traders
8000 B.C.

Paleo Indians
hunters and
gatherers
1200 B.C.

Ottawa
Chippewa
Potawatomi
in Michigan
A.D. 1600

La Salle's ship, the *Griffon*,
filled with furs, disappears.
1679

First settlement at
Sault St. Marie
1668

French voyageurs trade with
Native Americans for furs.
1600s

Pioneers rush to buy land that had
been owned by Native Americans.
1830s

U.S. takes control after
the Revolutionary War.
1783

French surrender
control to the
English.
1760

Detroit is founded.
1701

Copper and iron
ore found in the
upper penninsula.
1840s

Lansing becomes
the capital.
1847

Statehood
1837

Soo Locks opens, connecting
Lake Huron and Lake Superior.
1855

Lumbering is
big business!
1850–1900

Black and white
Michiganders help slaves
get to freedom along the
Underground Railroad.
1850s

Henry Ford and Ransom Olds
develop early automobiles.
1896

Detroit-
Windsor
tunnel
opens.
1930

Lindbergh flies
across the Atlantic.
1927

European
immigrants
arrive in
Michigan.
1900–1920

Mackinac Bridge
is built.
1957

MICHIGAN FLOWS THROUGH TIME

Gerald Ford from
Michigan becomes
president of U.S.
1974

Michigan celebrates
150 years of statehood.
1987

Capitol building
is restored.
1992

McDivitt and White walk in
space on the "all Michigan"
flight of *Gemini IV.*
1965

A big iron ore carrier, *Edmund G.
Fitgerald*, sinks in Lake Superior.
1975

Isle Royale, in Lake Superior, is Michigan's only national park. It has one of the largest moose herds in the United States.

Tahquamenon Falls in the upper peninsula was the setting of Longfellow's poem "The Song of Hiawatha."

Soo Canals, at Sault Ste. Marie, allow ships to travel between Lake Huron and Lake Superior.

Sleeping Bear Dunes, near Empire, is a 480-foot mound of sand shaped like a sleeping bear.

MAGNIFICENT

The **Mackinac Bridge** crosses the Straits of Mackinac and connects the lower peninsula to the upper peninsula. It is one of the world's longest suspension bridges.

Michigan Travel Bureau
P.O. Box 30226
Lansing, MI 48909
(800) 5432-YES
http://www.traverse.
com/michguides

Tawas Point Lighthouse, built in 1876, is on Lake Huron.

MICHIGAN

The **Hackley-Hume Historic Site** is in Muskegon. It features two mansions built by lumber barons.

Windmill DeZwaan, in Holland, is an authentic operating Dutch windmill.

The **State Capitol** in Lansing was completed in 1879 and rededicated in 1992.

The **Gerald R. Ford Museum** is in Grand Rapids on the banks of the Grand River. It was opened in 1981 to honor the 38th president of the U.S.

Beach School fourth grade visiting the Michigan Historical Museum in Lansing.

Minnesota

State Capital
St. Paul ★

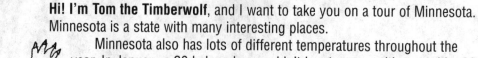

Hi! I'm Tom the Timberwolf, and I want to take you on a tour of Minnesota. Minnesota is a state with many interesting places.

Minnesota also has lots of different temperatures throughout the year. In January a 20 below day wouldn't be strange, neither would a 90 degree day in August!

On a winter day when it's too cold to play outdoors, you can go to the Mall of America. It's the second largest mall in the world. It has many stores and an amusement park inside. It even has an underwater aquarium that has sharks and all kinds of fish. You can walk through a tunnel and look at them.

On one of those hot days in summer you can visit Valleyfair, which is an amusement park. At Valleyfair you can ride on the second largest roller coaster in the world. It's called "Wild Thing."

I hope you enjoyed your tour of Minnesota!

Dear Friends,

It's really fun here in Minnesota. All the lakes and rivers are so peaceful. In one state park you can hear the state bird, the loon, cry at night while you are camping. You can also go canoeing there and see a loon swimming, a bald eagle flying overhead, and two beavers swimming alongside of the boat. Nature is everywhere here in Minnesota! Visit us soon!

Mrs. Gartner's Fifth/Sixth Grade, St. John's in Redwood Falls

MINNESOTA
"Land of the Lakes"

State Flag

State Tree
Norway Pine

State Bird
Common Loon

State Flower
Lady's Slipper

Henry Sibley helped organize the Minnesota territory. When Minnesota became a state in 1858, he was chosen to be its first governor. Four years later he served as a colonel in the Battle of Wood Lake.

In 1819, **Henry Schoolcraft** (1793–1864) identified Lake Itaska as the source of the Mississippi River. From 1822 to 1841, he served as Indian agent to the Ojibwa tribe. He also wrote many books about Native American history.

William Mayo (1819–1911) was an English immigrant. The Mayo Clinic was founded after a tornado hit Rochester in 1907. A group of nuns asked Mr. Mayo to help put together a clinic. Mayo first refused, but then gave in. Today, the Mayo Clinic provides important health care for hundreds of thousands of people each year. It has treated more than four million people since 1907.

Walter Mondale served in Congress from 1963 to 1964 as a senator and from 1964 to 1977 as a representative. Mondale served as a vice president under Jimmy Carter and lost in the presidential race against Ronald Reagan.

Hubert Humphrey (1911–1978) made a name for himself beyond Minnesota. He was mayor of Minneapolis and vice president in the administration of Lyndon B. Johnson. In 1968, he ran for president but lost to Richard Nixon. You may have seen Hubert Humphrey's picture on U.S. stamps in 1991. Minnesota honored him by naming the Hubert H. Humphrey Metrodome in Minneapolis after him. That is where Minnesota sports teams play.

What was it live to be a girl pioneering on the prairie in the 1800s? Thanks to a series of books by **Laura Ingalls Wilder** and a long-running TV series based on her stories, many Americans found out. Among her books are *Little House on the Prairie, On the Banks of Plum Creek,* and *The Long Winter.*

Eugenie Anderson was a founder of the DFL (Democratic-Farmer-Labor Party). She became a U.S. ambassador to Denmark in 1949. Anderson also served as a minister to Bulgaria.

> **Did You Know...?** Minnesota's name comes from the Dakota Sioux and means "cloudy water" or "sky-tinted water." It refers to the Minnesota River.

Minnesota Crossword

You may have to look up some of these answers.

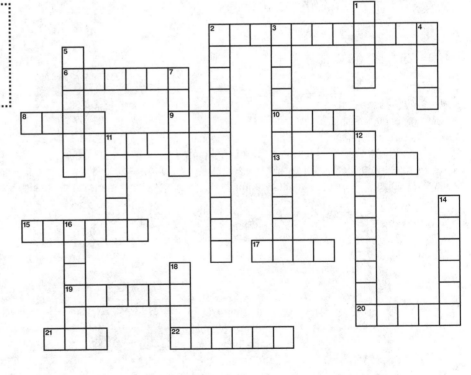

Across

2. This river starts in Minnesota
6. An insect that can ruin farmers
8. State tree
9. Kids go _____ skating
10. State song, "_____, Minnesota"
11. State bird
13. Mall of _____
15. Many trees make up a _____
17. State flower, _____'s slipper
19. Minnesota's first governor
20. _____ Dakota
21. St. Paul's original name was Pig's _____
22. German town in Brown County

Down

1. State grain, wild _____
2. St. Paul and _____.
3. Minnesota's western neighbor
4. Minnesota's southern neighbor
5. Famous in Rochester, Mayo _____
7. Minnesota baseball team
11. Land of 10,000 _____
12. Minnesota's eastern neighbor
14. Important city hub
16. First governor of the territory
18. County that is home to Marshall

Answers on page 98.

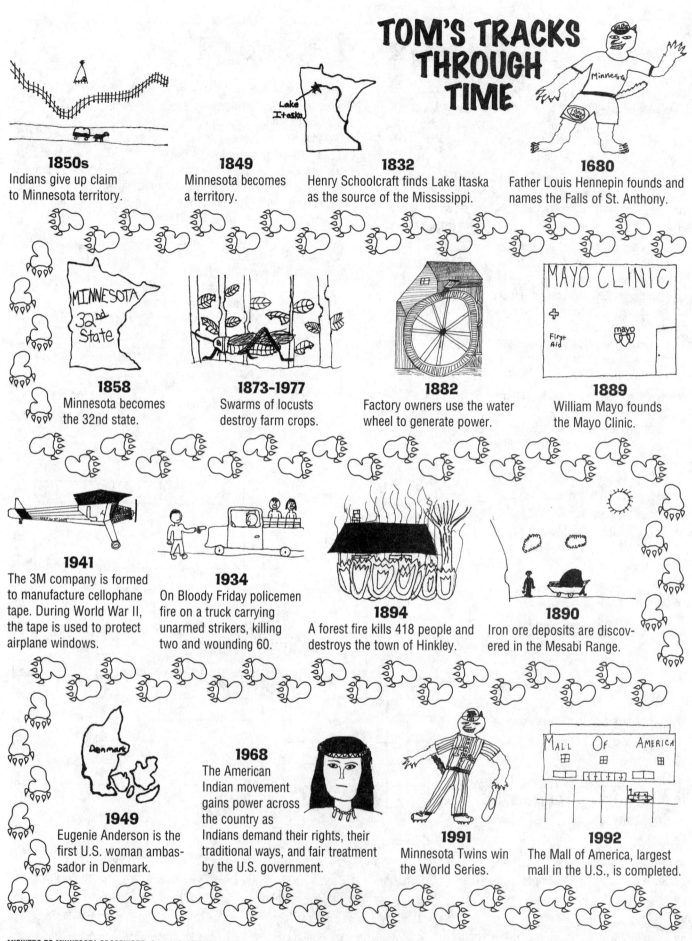

TOM'S TRACKS THROUGH TIME

1850s
Indians give up claim to Minnesota territory.

1849
Minnesota becomes a territory.

1832
Henry Schoolcraft finds Lake Itaska as the source of the Mississippi.

1680
Father Louis Hennepin founds and names the Falls of St. Anthony.

1858
Minnesota becomes the 32nd state.

1873-1977
Swarms of locusts destroy farm crops.

1882
Factory owners use the water wheel to generate power.

1889
William Mayo founds the Mayo Clinic.

1941
The 3M company is formed to manufacture cellophane tape. During World War II, the tape is used to protect airplane windows.

1934
On Bloody Friday policemen fire on a truck carrying unarmed strikers, killing two and wounding 60.

1894
A forest fire kills 418 people and destroys the town of Hinkley.

1890
Iron ore deposits are discovered in the Mesabi Range.

1949
Eugenie Anderson is the first U.S. woman ambassador in Denmark.

1968
The American Indian movement gains power across the country as Indians demand their rights, their traditional ways, and fair treatment by the U.S. government.

1991
Minnesota Twins win the World Series.

1992
The Mall of America, largest mall in the U.S., is completed.

ANSWERS TO MINNESOTA CROSSWORD: Across: 2. Mississippi **6.** locust **8.** pine **9.** ice **10.** Hail **11.** loon **13.** America **15.** forest **17.** lady **19.** Sibley **20.** North **21.** Eye **22.** New Ulm **Down: 1.** rice **2.** Minneapolis **3.** South Dakota **4.** Iowa **5.** Clinic **7.** Twins **11.** Lakes **12.** Wisconsin **14.** Duluth **16.** Ramsey **18.** Lyon

Finding big bucks and does by **Redwood Falls**

Fish big **northern pikes** on McDonald Lake.

Minnesota Moments

Split Rock Lighthouse is fun to see in northern Minnesota.

The Mayo Clinic provides **health care** for thousands of people each year.

Sleigh riding is fun; so is driving horses down the streets of Danube.

Walking the **beautiful trails** of Goodrich

Farming corn and beans is good near Fairfax.

Wiping out while **waterskiing** on one of the 10,000 lakes

For more information about the great state of Minnesota:
Minnesota Tourism Bureau
(800) 657-3700
http://www.state.mn.us

The fifth and sixth grades at St. John's Lutheran School

Mississippi

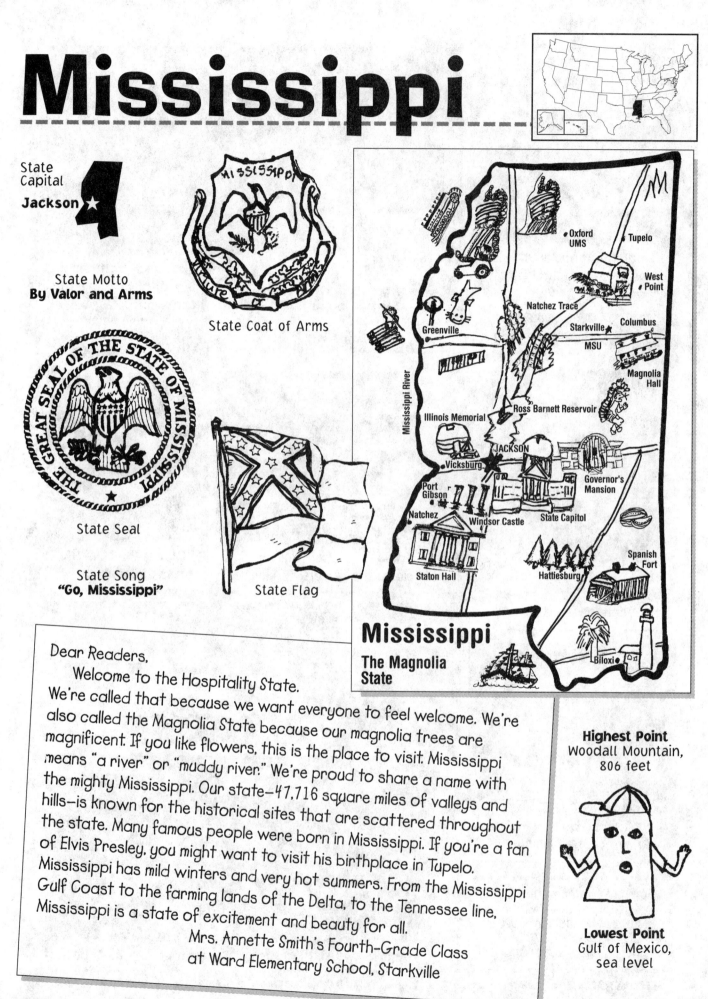

State Capital
Jackson

State Motto
By Valor and Arms

State Coat of Arms

State Seal

State Song
"Go, Mississippi"

State Flag

Mississippi
The Magnolia State

Oxford UMS · Tupelo · West Point · Natchez Trace · Greenville · Starkville · Columbus · MSU · Magnolia Hall · Mississippi River · Ross Barnett Reservoir · Illinois Memorial · JACKSON · Vicksburg · Governor's Mansion · Port Gibson · Natchez · Windsor Castle · State Capitol · Staton Hall · Hattiesburg · Spanish Fort · Biloxi

Dear Readers,
    Welcome to the Hospitality State. We're called that because we want everyone to feel welcome. We're also called the Magnolia State because our magnolia trees are magnificent. If you like flowers, this is the place to visit. Mississippi means "a river" or "muddy river." We're proud to share a name with the mighty Mississippi. Our state—47,716 square miles of valleys and hills—is known for the historical sites that are scattered throughout the state. Many famous people were born in Mississippi. If you're a fan of Elvis Presley, you might want to visit his birthplace in Tupelo. Mississippi has mild winters and very hot summers. From the Mississippi Gulf Coast to the farming lands of the Delta, to the Tennessee line, Mississippi is a state of excitement and beauty for all.
    Mrs. Annette Smith's Fourth-Grade Class
    at Ward Elementary School, Starkville

Highest Point
Woodall Mountain,
806 feet

Lowest Point
Gulf of Mexico,
sea level

Mississippi Is...

☘ the only state that holds a Miss Hospitality pageant.

☘ the home of four Miss Americas: Mary Ann Mobley, Lynda Lee Mead, Cheryl Prewitt, and Susan Diane Akin.

☘ the original home of Coca-Cola.

☘ ranked number one in the production of catfish.

☘ among the top 10 producers of timber, rice, sorghum, sweet potatoes, pecans, and soybeans.

☘ served by 17 railroads.

☘ the home of cotton, its major crop.

READ THIS BOOK!

Everywhere in Mississippi
by Laurie Parker

A dog named Skippy is lost in Mississippi. His owner is worried about him and goes all over the state looking for him. He goes to Scooba, Hot Coffee, Coldwater, and Money looking for his dog. That's the story in Everywhere in Mississippi, published by Quail Ridge Press in Brandon. It is a great book!

Mighty Mississippians

Eudora Welty was born in 1909 in Jackson. She has won many awards, including a Pulitzer Prize in 1975. In *One Writer's Beginnings*, she talks about her life and what it was like to grow up in Mississippi.

Oprah Winfrey, born in Kosciusko in 1954, hosts a television talk show. She is also a successful actress and producer.

What's the number-one best-selling fiction book for adults? Chances are, it's by **John Grisham**. His books have been turned into popular movies.

Every year, **B. B. King** returns to the Delta for the Blues Festival. He is a blues guitarist, singer, and songwriter.

BAKE THIS CAKE!
Mississippi Mud Cake

Cake ingredients:
1 cup cooking oil
1½ cups flour
1¾ cups sugar
4 beaten eggs
3 tsp. vanilla
1 cup nuts
⅓ cup cocoa
1 bag miniature marshmallows

Icing ingredients:
1½ sticks melted margarine
⅓ cup cocoa
1 tsp. vanilla
1 box confectioners' sugar
½ cup evaporated milk
1 cup chopped nuts

Mix the ingredients well.
Bake in floured and greased pan for 30 minutes at 350°F.
Remove from oven. Pour 1 bag miniature marshmallows on top. Return to oven to melt.
Cool cake.
Mix icing and spread on cake.

Tracks Through Time

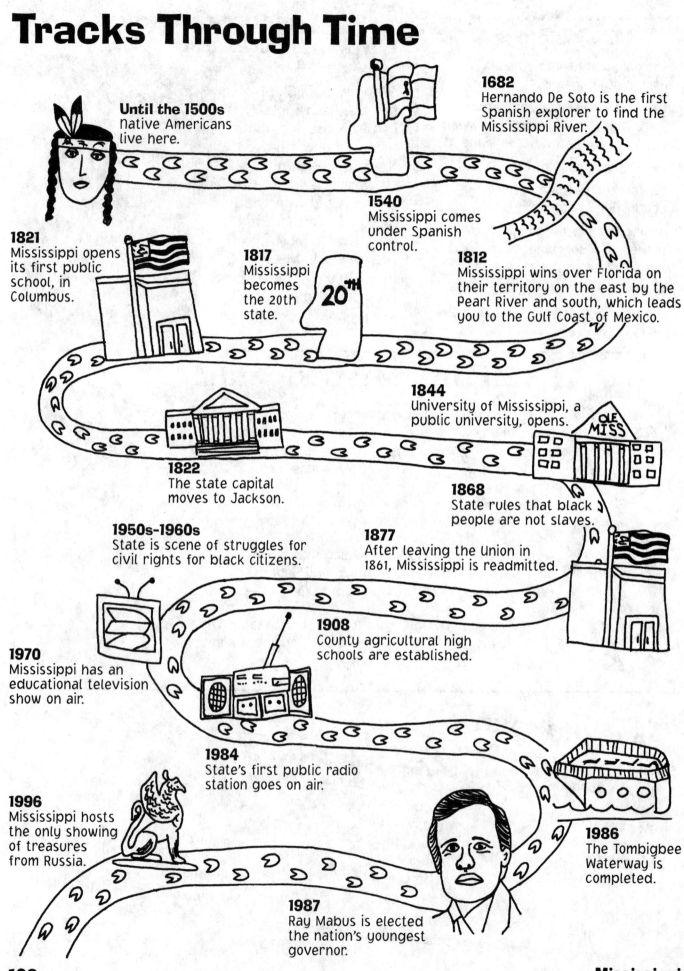

Until the 1500s
Native Americans live here.

1682
Hernando De Soto is the first Spanish explorer to find the Mississippi River.

1540
Mississippi comes under Spanish control.

1821
Mississippi opens its first public school, in Columbus.

1817
Mississippi becomes the 20th state.

1812
Mississippi wins over Florida on their territory on the east by the Pearl River and south, which leads you to the Gulf Coast of Mexico.

1844
University of Mississippi, a public university, opens.

1822
The state capital moves to Jackson.

1868
State rules that black people are not slaves.

1950s-1960s
State is scene of struggles for civil rights for black citizens.

1877
After leaving the Union in 1861, Mississippi is readmitted.

1970
Mississippi has an educational television show on air.

1908
County agricultural high schools are established.

1984
State's first public radio station goes on air.

1996
Mississippi hosts the only showing of treasures from Russia.

1986
The Tombigbee Waterway is completed.

1987
Ray Mabus is elected the nation's youngest governor.

What to See in Mississippi

Antebellum homes tell part of our history in Natchez, Port Gibson, Vicksburg, and Columbus.

The activities—boating, camping, skiing, fishing—and the beauty of the Gulf Coast are never ending. You can also visit **Jefferson Davis's house** (Beauvoire).

Mississippi Division of Tourism
P.O. Box 1705
Ocean Springs, MS 39566-1705
(800) 927-6378
http://www.mississippi.org

Follow our beginnings in **Ocean Springs** (site of Fort Maurepas).

This **lighthouse in Biloxi** has guided many ships for years.

Illinois Memorial in Vicksburg's **Civil War National Park**.

We can't believe it snowed in Starkville! We're the fourth grade at Ward Elementary. Our teacher is Mrs. Annette Smith.

Missouri

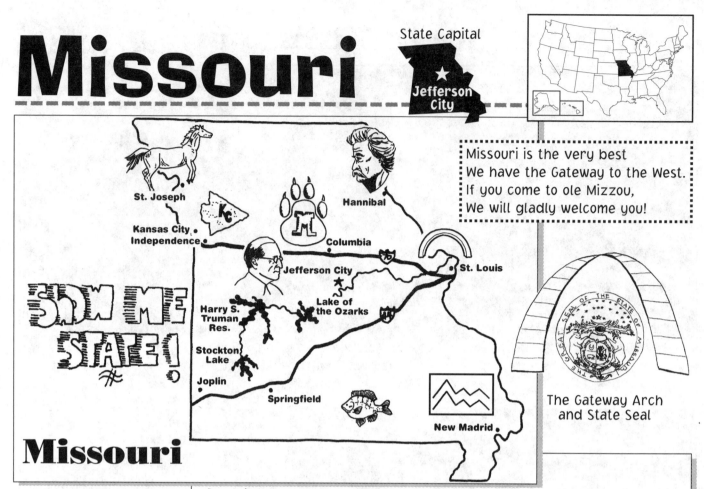

Missouri is the very best
We have the Gateway to the West.
If you come to ole Mizzou,
We will gladly welcome you!

SHOW ME STATE!

Missouri

The Gateway Arch and State Seal

Missouri's Nicknames

"I'm from Missouri, you've got to show me." That comment, given in an 1899 speech by Congressman Willard D. Vandive, gave Missouri the nickname "The Show Me State." The name characterizes Missourians as tough-minded people who demand proof.

"The Gateway to the West" is another nickname for our state. Many pioneers crossed the mighty Mississippi River into "St. Louie." Adventuring pioneers began their wagon journeys to the West on the Santa Fe and Oregon Trails, which started in Missouri.

We are also called the "Cave State." There are 5,000 caves in our southern Ozark hills alone. Tourists visit Mark Twain's cave, where Tom Sawyer and Becky Thatcher were lost in *The Adventures of Tom Sawyer*, Graham Cave, Devil's Icebox, Daniel Boone Cave, Fantastic Caverns, and the Bridal Cave. Meramac Cavern is noted for its use as a stop for escaping slaves on the Underground Railroad.

Dear Readers,

WELCOME TO MISSOURI! Missouri is a lovely place with many famous people. We're home to baseball's *St. Louis Cardinals* and *Kansas City Royals*, football's *Kansas City Chiefs* and *St. Louis Rams*, and hockey's *St. Louis Blues*.

Landmarks and attractions are abundant in Missouri. Six Flags Over Mid America Amusement Park and the Fox Theater are located near *St. Louis*. Our first capital, *St. Charles*, boasts riverfront scenery and shopping, and our second and current capital, *Jefferson City*, offers fine artwork and historical museums.

In the summer, you can spend warm days boating, waterskiing, and swimming at the beautiful Lake of the Ozarks. Enjoy the graceful spring growth on our northern prairies and the vivid splashes of autumn color on the hills of our southern Ozarks region. Winter days in Missouri average 31°F, making for perfect sledding and snowboarding weather. We've got it all, so come and see us!

Team Starburst, Smithton Middle School, Columbia, Missouri

State Tree
Dogwood

State Flower
Hawthorn

State Bird
Bluebird

TRUMAN TRIVIA

⭐ Harry S. Truman served as the 33rd president of the United States from 1945 to 1952.

⭐ He was born in Lamar, Missouri, in 1884; he died in 1972.

⭐ Truman fought in World War I.

⭐ He did not have a middle name, so he chose S for his middle initial as an adult.

⭐ He ran a haberdashery (men's hat and tie shop) in Independence, but it failed.

⭐ Truman served as a judge and a senator.

⭐ His nickname was "Honest Harry."

⭐ He served as vice president for only a few months before he became president due to Franklin D. Roosevelt's death.

⭐ You can visit President Truman's home today in Independence.

Yo! This is Joe!
I'm from the state of MO
Come to MO...
Go to MO...
Just get here by truck, car, or tractor,
but first get done reading this chapter!

Kickin' Around Some Facts

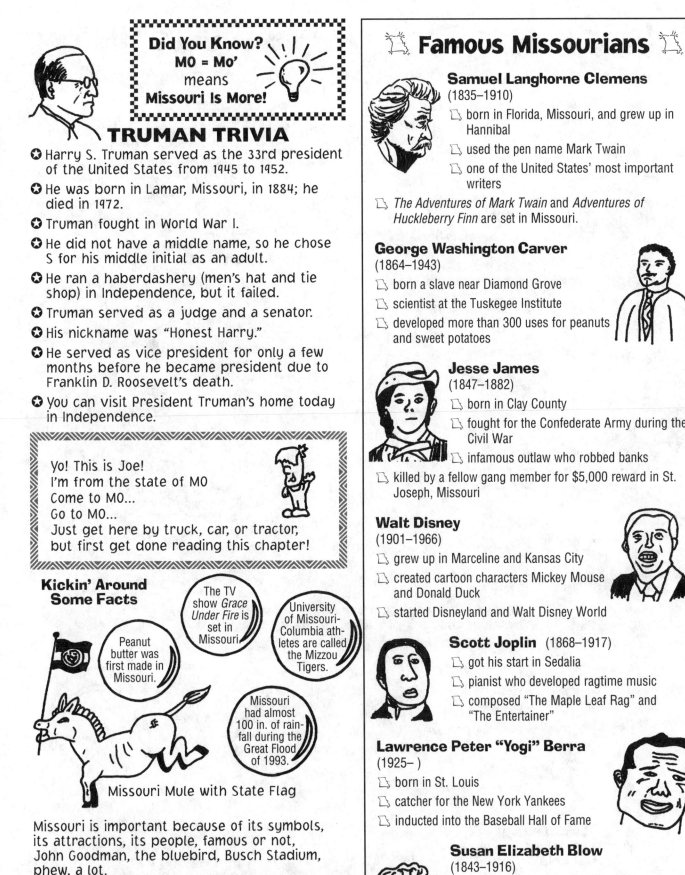

The TV show *Grace Under Fire* is set in Missouri.

University of Missouri-Columbia athletes are called the Mizzou Tigers.

Peanut butter was first made in Missouri.

Missouri had almost 100 in. of rainfall during the Great Flood of 1993.

Missouri Mule with State Flag

Missouri is important because of its symbols, its attractions, its people, famous or not, John Goodman, the bluebird, Busch Stadium, phew, a lot.

Don't forget President Harry Truman, Mark Twain, Laura Ingalls Wilder, the Gateway Arch, the Ozarks, Worlds of Fun, the honeybee, the dogwood, the Missouri mule, oh my, there sure is a lot to see and do in ole Mizzou.

Famous Missourians

Samuel Langhorne Clemens
(1835–1910)

🗋 born in Florida, Missouri, and grew up in Hannibal

🗋 used the pen name Mark Twain

🗋 one of the United States' most important writers

🗋 *The Adventures of Mark Twain* and *Adventures of Huckleberry Finn* are set in Missouri.

George Washington Carver
(1864–1943)

🗋 born a slave near Diamond Grove

🗋 scientist at the Tuskegee Institute

🗋 developed more than 300 uses for peanuts and sweet potatoes

Jesse James
(1847–1882)

🗋 born in Clay County

🗋 fought for the Confederate Army during the Civil War

🗋 infamous outlaw who robbed banks

🗋 killed by a fellow gang member for $5,000 reward in St. Joseph, Missouri

Walt Disney
(1901–1966)

🗋 grew up in Marceline and Kansas City

🗋 created cartoon characters Mickey Mouse and Donald Duck

🗋 started Disneyland and Walt Disney World

Scott Joplin (1868–1917)

🗋 got his start in Sedalia

🗋 pianist who developed ragtime music

🗋 composed "The Maple Leaf Rag" and "The Entertainer"

Lawrence Peter "Yogi" Berra
(1925–)

🗋 born in St. Louis

🗋 catcher for the New York Yankees

🗋 inducted into the Baseball Hall of Fame

Susan Elizabeth Blow
(1843–1916)

🗋 born in St. Louis

🗋 her efforts led to the first kindergarten in the United States, in St. Louis

Ride the Rails Through Missouri's History

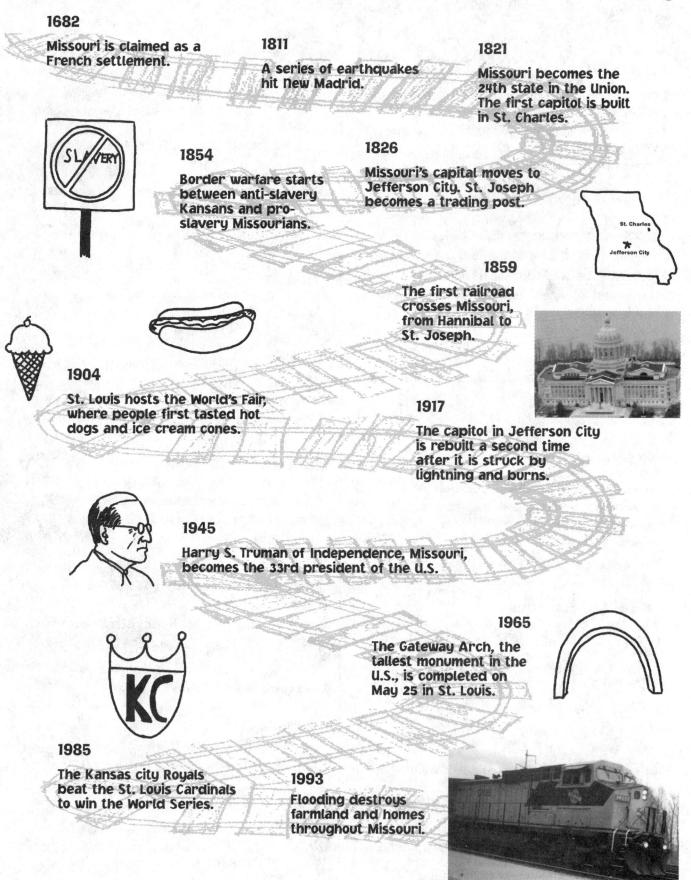

1682
Missouri is claimed as a French settlement.

1811
A series of earthquakes hit New Madrid.

1821
Missouri becomes the 24th state in the Union. The first capitol is built in St. Charles.

1854
Border warfare starts between anti-slavery Kansans and pro-slavery Missourians.

SLAVERY

1826
Missouri's capital moves to Jefferson City. St. Joseph becomes a trading post.

St. Charles
Jefferson City

1859
The first railroad crosses Missouri, from Hannibal to St. Joseph.

1904
St. Louis hosts the World's Fair, where people first tasted hot dogs and ice cream cones.

1917
The capitol in Jefferson City is rebuilt a second time after it is struck by lightning and burns.

1945
Harry S. Truman of Independence, Missouri, becomes the 33rd president of the U.S.

1965
The Gateway Arch, the tallest monument in the U.S., is completed on May 25 in St. Louis.

KC

1985
The Kansas City Royals beat the St. Louis Cardinals to win the World Series.

1993
Flooding destroys farmland and homes throughout Missouri.

Moments and Momentos From Missouri

St. Louis Sites

The **Gateway Arch** is one of the most popular tourist stops In Missouri. Trams crawl through the hollow sides of the tunnel to allow visitors a view of St. Louis from 630 feet up. **The Museum of Westward Expansion** is undergound, below the Arch.

The **Old St. Louis Courthouse**, where it was determined that Dred Scott was still a slave although he had lived in free territories.

Dinosaur Park, outside of the St. Louis Science Center.

Busch Stadium, home of the St. Louis Cardinals.

Branson plays host to many **country-western theaters and music** shows.

A "must see" in southwest Missouri—the **Precious Moments Chapel** outside of Carthage.

The **Missouri State Capitol** in Jefferson City houses a museum and many artifacts and paintings.

Visit the **Missouri State Fair** in Sedalia for exhibits, livestock shows, tractor pulls, and concerts.

The **Winston Churchill Library and Memorial** at Westminister College in Fulton. Churchill, Great Britain's prime minister, gave his famous 1946 "Iron Curtain" speech here.

Memorial Union, on the University of Missouri-Columbia campus, is a tribute to the students who fought in the world wars.

Missouri license plate new in '97!

MISSOURI
000 000
JUL — SHOW ME STATE — 98

Missouri **Lieutenant Governor, Roger Wilson**, speaks to members of Team Starburst during our "Great State of Missouri" Research Day.

For more information on Missouri, contact:
Missouri Division of Tourism
P.O. Box 1055
Jefferson City, MO 65102
888-925-3875 ext. 124
http://www.ecodev.state.mo.us/tourism

TEAM STARBURST
Smithton Middle School, Columbia, Missouri

The Great Flood of 1993

The flood of '93 was long-lasting and tragic. The Mississippi and Missouri rivers flooded and destroyed nearly everything within two miles of their banks. Towns and areas such as Hartsburg, Rocheport, Boonville, and Howard County, Missouri, were flooded.

Volunteer sandbaggers came from around the state to help block the flood. Often, the levees and sandbag walls couldn't hold back the rising water. The flood destroyed highways and thousands of homes and businesses. Property damage was estimated at 2.7 billion dollars, just in Missouri. The flood claimed three lives in 1993, and Missourians were again affected by flooding in 1995.

The Missouri River on a calm day.

Normally this area is farmland.

The remains of a flooded-out home in St. Genevieve.

Montana

State Capital

★ Helena

State Motto
Oro y Plata
(Gold and Silver)

State Tree
Ponderosa Pine

Map of Montana

Glacier National Park

Milk River

oil

wheat

coal

Missouri River

Great Falls

Yellowstone River

Forestry

★ Helena

wheat

oil

• Butte

Metal Products

oil

cattle

Mining

The Big Sky Country

MONTANA

Dear Readers,
   The sky is so big here it seems like it never stops. That's why we are called the Big Sky Country. Montana is a state of contrasts—from the beauty of the high, cool western Rockies to the semi-arid eastern plains. The wilderness comes tumbling down to the edge of modern cities. Business and industry try to keep a balance with nature.
   Come and visit our beautiful land!
      From All of Us at Easter Seals Career Designs,
      Sponsor Jodi Brown, Great Falls

State Bird
Western Meadowlark

UNOFFICIAL STATE SAYING

If you don't like the weather in Montana . . . Wait a minute!

On one day in 1916, the temperature ranged from 44 degrees above zero to 56 degrees below zero. (It must have been hard to decide what to wear that day!)

State Flower
Bitterroot

MONTANA

M is for our majestic mountains

O is for the open plains

N is for the natural resources

T is for the trees that cover one quarter of the land

A is for agriculture, a major source of income

N is for our natural environment

A is for the varied animals that make it their home.

Put them all together and they spell **MONTANA**, the greatest state in the land!

People We're Proud Of

FIRST CITIZENS

Montana has been the home of many Indian tribes and has seven reservations. Among the tribes that live here are the **Blackfoot, Crow, Sioux, Assiniboine,** and **Cheyenne**.

ACTRESS

Myrna Loy (1905–1993) was an actress born in Helena. She starred in many movies. Two of her most famous films are *Cheaper by the Dozen* and *The Best Years of Our Lives*. She played strong, intelligent women and was as talented in drama roles as she was in comedy. Many of her movies are on video—and they're worth seeing.

FAMOUS DOG

Shep, a sheepdog, was one of historic Fort Benton's most famous citizens. He greeted incoming trains for many years, waiting for his deceased master to return from a trip.

ARTIST

Charles M. Russel (1865–1926) was a famous painter and sculptor. He moved to Montana when he was 16 years old because he wanted-ed to paint pictures of the West. You can see his work in many museums around the country.

LAWMAKER

Jeannette Rankin (1880–1973) was the first woman elected to the U.S. House of Representatives. She was a leader who worked hard for women's right to vote. She hated war so much that, before both world wars, she was the only member of the U.S. Congress to vote against our nation taking part.

Big Facts About Big Sky Country

Thirty-seven states the size of Rhode Island would fit in Montana.

Although Montana is the fourth largest state in the U.S., it ranks 44th in population.

For every square mile in our state, there are fewer than six people.

Montana is the birthplace of the Missouri River. It starts in Three Forks, Montana.

Fort Peck is one of the world's largest earthen dams. It forms a lake bigger than the whole city of Chicago.

Our state has 10 national forests, Glacier National Park, and 41 state parks.

People here know snow. In 1958, Kings Hills had almost 407 inches of the white stuff.

Meandering Through Montana History

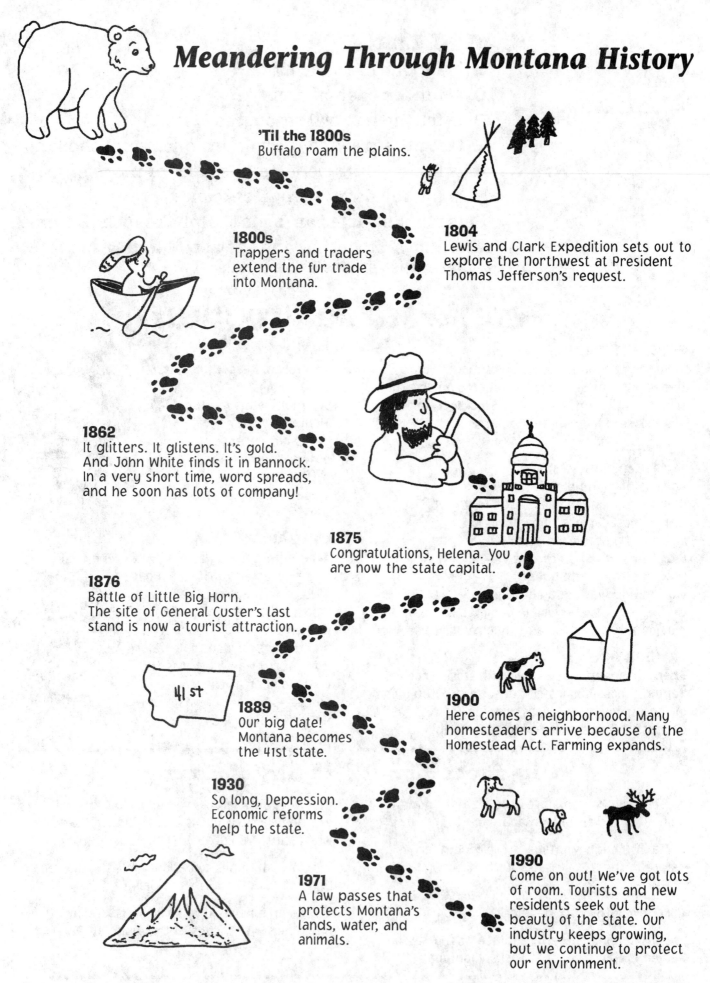

'Til the 1800s
Buffalo roam the plains.

1804
Lewis and Clark Expedition sets out to explore the Northwest at President Thomas Jefferson's request.

1800s
Trappers and traders extend the fur trade into Montana.

1862
It glitters. It glistens. It's gold. And John White finds it in Bannock. In a very short time, word spreads, and he soon has lots of company!

1875
Congratulations, Helena. You are now the state capital.

1876
Battle of Little Big Horn. The site of General Custer's last stand is now a tourist attraction.

1889
Our big date! Montana becomes the 41st state.

1900
Here comes a neighborhood. Many homesteaders arrive because of the Homestead Act. Farming expands.

1930
So long, Depression. Economic reforms help the state.

1971
A law passes that protects Montana's lands, water, and animals.

1990
Come on out! We've got lots of room. Tourists and new residents seek out the beauty of the state. Our industry keeps growing, but we continue to protect our environment.

Montana in a Flash

Bobcat kitten at Hardy Creek
Montana, a great place to grow up.

Black Bear
"Bearly" speaking—
you'll love Montana.

Orphaned Fawn
Communicating with nature and loving it.

White Tail and Mule Deer Fawns
Make "deer" friends in Montana.

Montana section prepared by
Easter Seals Career Designs,
Great Falls, Montana

Tourism Information:

Travel Montana
P.O. Box 200533
Helena, MT 59620-0533
800-VISIT-MT

http://www.mt.gov

Nebraska

The name Nebraska comes from the Otto Indian word *Nebrathka*, which means "flat water."

State Nickname

Lil' Red is the Nebraska mascot that entertains the fans at half-time. He is inflatable, but a real person makes him move.

State Capital

Lincoln ★

State Tree
Cottonwood

State Bird
Western Meadowlark

State Fossil
Mammoth

State Flower
Goldenrod

Niobrara River
Missouri River
Elkorn River
Morman Trail
North Platte River
Omaha
Kearny
Grand Island
Lincoln

Nebraska   **The Cornhusker State**

Dear Friends,
Greetings from Nebraska's diverse climates and seasons. Fall offers a crispy, cool climate to go to see football games, whooping crane migration in Kearney, and the snow geese in Desota Bend. Winter is wonderful too, even though it's cold and snowy, for hunting deer, antelope, and pheasant. Snow sledding and cross-country skiing are enjoyed. Spring is a lovely time to plant flowers and vegetable gardens. Farmers plant crops of corn, wheat, beans, and soybeans. Summer brings the College World Series at Rosenblatt Stadium, visits to the Henry Doorly Zoo, indoor rain forest, and aquarium. If you want to see a change in weather, spend a few minutes in Nebraska.
        Go, Cornhuskers,
        Mrs. Pavel's class, King Science Center, Omaha

State Song
"Beautiful Nebraska"

State Gem
Blue Agate

State Motto
Equality before the law

Statehood
March 1, 1867
37th state

112

They Came from

Nebraska!

BUFFALO BILL was the nickname of Frederick William Cody. He was born in 1846. He was known not only as a scout in the U.S. army but also as an actor in a wild west act that he took on tour.

MALCOLM X was born May 18, 1925, with the name Malcolm Little. He is remembered for leading other black people in the fight for equal rights. He was assassinated on February 21, 1965, while addressing a meeting in Harlem, New York.

HENRY FONDA, the actor, was born in Grand Island in 1905 and died in 1982. During his 40-year career, Fonda appeared in 87 films and won two Academy Awards.

CRAZY HORSE was a Sioux chief whose tribe joined the Cheyenne against General Custer's troops in the Battle of Little Big Horn in 1876. Crazy Horse's tribe was captured and moved to a reservation. He was killed in 1877 while resisting arrest.

In January 1803, the U.S. Congress approved money for exploring the Louisiana Purchase. President Thomas Jefferson's secretary, **MERIWETHER LEWIS**, and Captain **WILLIAM CLARK** led the expedition.

Almost 200 years ago, **STANDING BEAR** was chief of the Ponca. White officials moved the Ponca to a reservation in Oklahoma. After his son died, Standing Bear asked to bury him in Nebraska, 300 miles away. He was finally given permission. He lived peacefully into old age.

WILLA SIBERT CATHER was born in 1873 in Virginia, but she grew up in Nebraska. She worked as a journalist, editor, and fiction writer. In 1895, Cather gradu-

Test Your Star I.Q.

Try answering these questions before you read the biographies that follow.

1. Which author was a Pulitzer Prize winner for the book *One of Ours*?
2. Who was the chief of the Ponca tribe?
3. Which star hosted his own late night TV show from 1962 to 1992?
4. Which two men were sent by Thomas Jefferson to explore the Louisiana Purchase?
5. Which civil rights leader helped fight for the freedom of African Americans?

ated from the University of Nebraska. Many of her books were about Nebraska. One of her most famous books was the award-winning *One of Ours*. Willa Cather died on April 24, 1947.

ROBERT KERREY has been a U.S. senator since 1989. He received a medal for bravery in the Vietnam War.

JAY STERLING MORTON was born on April 22, 1832, and died in 1902. He loved trees and, in 1885, started Arbor Day to honor them. That year Nebraskans planted one million trees. More than 200 kinds of trees are planted at his former Nebraska home.

JOHNNY CARSON was born on October 23, 1925. For 30 years, he hosted televsion's *Tonight Show*. Johnny's dry sense of humor and laid-back style helped his show make history for its long run. He first practiced his skills using a mail order kit.

DOROTHY MCGUIRE performed with Henry Fonda at the Omaha Community Playhouse in 1930. She went on to become a Hollywood star known for her gentle and dignified manner.

RED CLOUD was chief of the Oglala Sioux tribe. He was born in 1822 and died in 1909. In 1868, after many bloody battles, Red Cloud signed a peace treaty with the whites. He agreed to live in peace on the desolate Pine Ridge Reservation. Some history books say he was the only American Indian to win a war against the U.S.

NEBRASKA HISTORY TRAIL

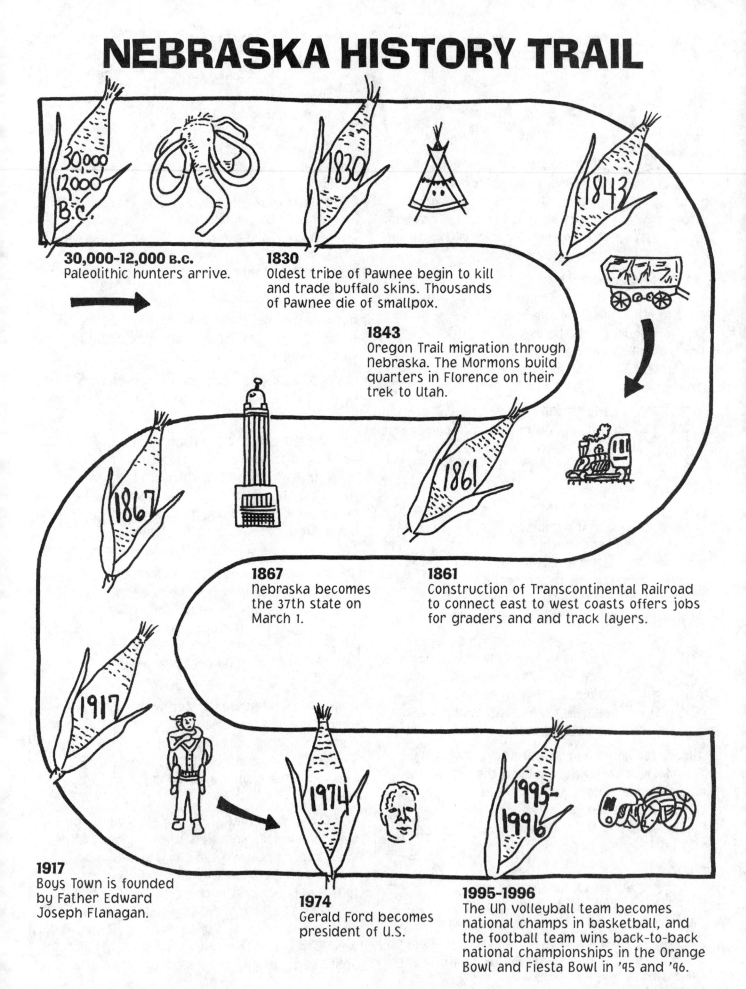

30,000–12,000 B.C.
Paleolithic hunters arrive.

1830
Oldest tribe of Pawnee begin to kill and trade buffalo skins. Thousands of Pawnee die of smallpox.

1843
Oregon Trail migration through Nebraska. The Mormons build quarters in Florence on their trek to Utah.

1867
Nebraska becomes the 37th state on March 1.

1861
Construction of Transcontinental Railroad to connect east to west coasts offers jobs for graders and and track layers.

1917
Boys Town is founded by Father Edward Joseph Flanagan.

1974
Gerald Ford becomes president of U.S.

1995–1996
The UN volleyball team becomes national champs in basketball, and the football team wins back-to-back national championships in the Orange Bowl and Fiesta Bowl in '95 and '96.

What Sites to See!

The rock that gives the **Chimney Rock Trail** its name rises over the North Platte and is a landmark visible for 30 miles.

Visit Smith Falls along the **Niobrara River.**

Tourist Information:
Omaha Convention and Visitors Bureau
6800 Mercy Road, Suite 202
Omaha, NE 68106
(402) 444-4660
http://www.state.ne.us

Boys Town, near Omaha, is the home for boys and girls from all over the world.

Henry Doorly Zoo has a wild rain forest. Come on in!

We're Mrs. Pavel's sixth-grade class at the King Science Center in Omaha.

Nebraska

Nevada

State Capital
★ Carson City

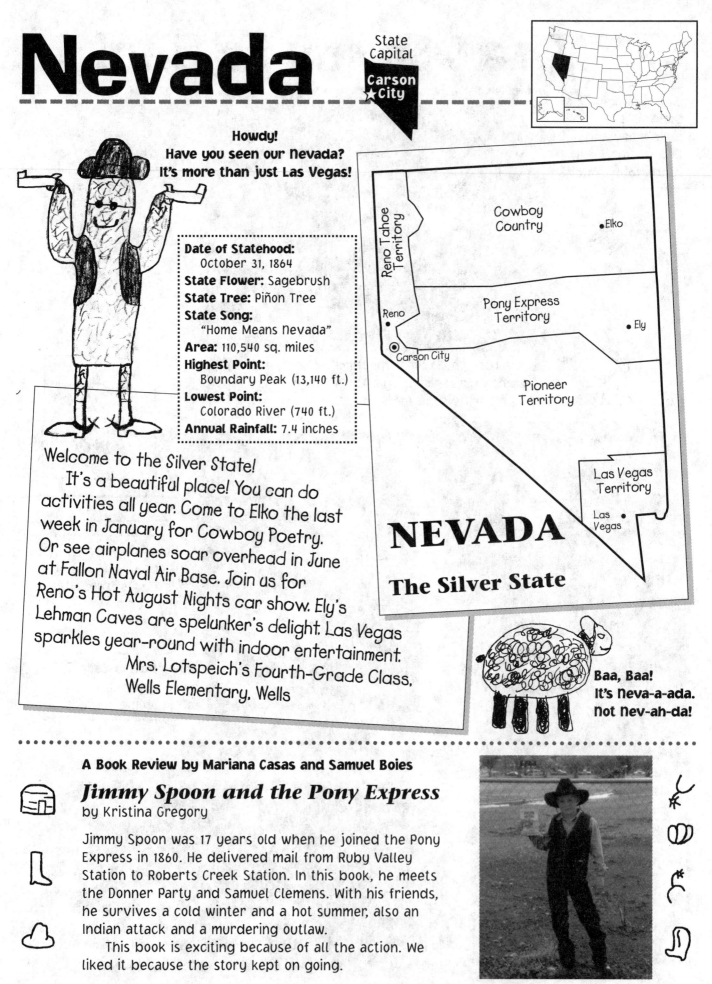

**Howdy!
Have you seen our Nevada?
It's more than just Las Vegas!**

Date of Statehood:
    October 31, 1864
State Flower: Sagebrush
State Tree: Piñon Tree
State Song:
    "Home Means Nevada"
Area: 110,540 sq. miles
Highest Point:
    Boundary Peak (13,140 ft.)
Lowest Point:
    Colorado River (740 ft.)
Annual Rainfall: 7.4 inches

Cowboy Country
• Elko

Reno Tahoe Territory

Pony Express Territory

Reno •

⊙ Carson City

• Ely

Pioneer Territory

Las Vegas Territory

Las Vegas •

NEVADA

The Silver State

Welcome to the Silver State!
    It's a beautiful place! You can do activities all year. Come to Elko the last week in January for Cowboy Poetry. Or see airplanes soar overhead in June at Fallon Naval Air Base. Join us for Reno's Hot August Nights car show. Ely's Lehman Caves are spelunker's delight. Las Vegas sparkles year-round with indoor entertainment.
    Mrs. Lotspeich's Fourth-Grade Class,
    Wells Elementary, Wells

**Baa, Baa!
It's Neva-a-ada.
Not Nev-ah-da!**

A Book Review by Mariana Casas and Samuel Boies

Jimmy Spoon and the Pony Express
by Kristina Gregory

Jimmy Spoon was 17 years old when he joined the Pony Express in 1860. He delivered mail from Ruby Valley Station to Roberts Creek Station. In this book, he meets the Donner Party and Samuel Clemens. With his friends, he survives a cold winter and a hot summer, also an Indian attack and a murdering outlaw.
    This book is exciting because of all the action. We liked it because the story kept on going.

Did You Know...?

One of Nevada's mining towns, Virginia City, was once so rich that the streets were paved with silver!

The oldest living tree in the world is the bristlecone pine tree.

The first railroad was built across Nevada in 1868.

Nevada is the seventh biggest state.

Nevada is one of only three states that allow legal gambling.

Nevada Game

To play, get a die and some markers. See how much you know about Nevada.

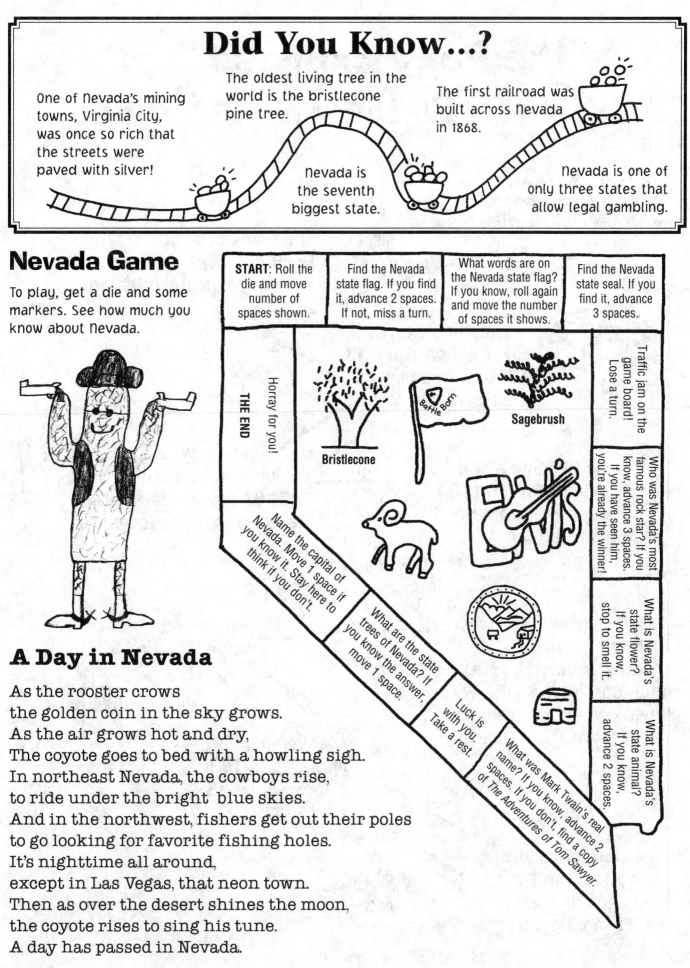

START: Roll the die and move number of spaces shown.

Find the Nevada state flag. If you find it, advance 2 spaces. If not, miss a turn.

What words are on the Nevada state flag? If you know, roll again and move the number of spaces it shows.

Find the Nevada state seal. If you find it, advance 3 spaces.

Traffic jam on the game board! Lose a turn.

Who was Nevada's most famous rock star? If you know, advance 3 spaces. If you have seen him, you're already the winner!

What is Nevada's state flower? If you know, stop to smell it.

What is Nevada's state animal? If you know, advance 2 spaces.

What was Mark Twain's real name? If you know, advance 2 spaces. If you don't, find a copy of *The Adventures of Tom Sawyer.*

Luck is with you. Take a rest.

What are the state trees of Nevada? If you know the answer, move 1 space.

Name the capital of Nevada. Move 1 space if you know it. Stay here to think if you don't.

Horray for you!

THE END

Bristlecone

Battle Born

Sagebrush

A Day in Nevada

As the rooster crows
the golden coin in the sky grows.
As the air grows hot and dry,
The coyote goes to bed with a howling sigh.
In northeast Nevada, the cowboys rise,
to ride under the bright blue skies.
And in the northwest, fishers get out their poles
to go looking for favorite fishing holes.
It's nighttime all around,
except in Las Vegas, that neon town.
Then as over the desert shines the moon,
the coyote rises to sing his tune.
A day has passed in Nevada.

Nevada

The Pony Express Trail Through Nevada's Past

It is **10,000 B.C.** Native Americans first come to Nevada.

The Comstock Lode starts in **1859**. It draws thousands of miners to western Nevada.

The Pony Express takes off on **April 13, 1860**. It delivers mail all over the state.

Yahoo! We're on our way to statehood. In **1861** Nevada territory is taken from Utah territory.

We become a state on **October 31, 1864**. President Lincoln needs us to help pay for the Civil War.

Gambling is first made legal in **1931**.

The last great Wild West bank robbery is on **September 19, 1900**. Butch Cassidy and the Wild Bunch creep into town and steal more than $32,000.

Hoover Dam is completed in **1936**. It took six years to finish.

In **August 1996**, the Top Gun Flight School moves to Fallon, Nevada.

COME TO SEE OUR NEVADA!

If you like **hunting** and **recreation**, come to Nevada.

Be sure to see the dolphins and tigers at Las Vegas's **family entertainment** casinos.

We suggest that while you are in Wells, take a hike to **Chimney Rock**.

Wells Elementary Fourth-Grade Class

Our state always has something to see!

Tourist Information:
Nevada Commission on Tourism
5151 South Carson Street
Carson City, NV 89710
(800) NEVADA8

http://www.state.nv.us

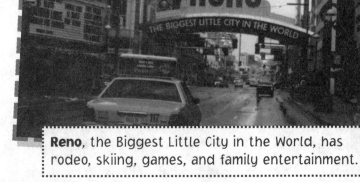

Reno, the Biggest Little City in the World, has rodeo, skiing, games, and family entertainment.

New Hampshire

The internationally known phenomenon carved by nature years ago, **the Old Man of the Mountain**, is a natural granite profile jutting out from a sheer cliff. It is 40 feet long from chin to forehead and located in Franconia Notch.

Some people refer to me as "the Great Stone Face."

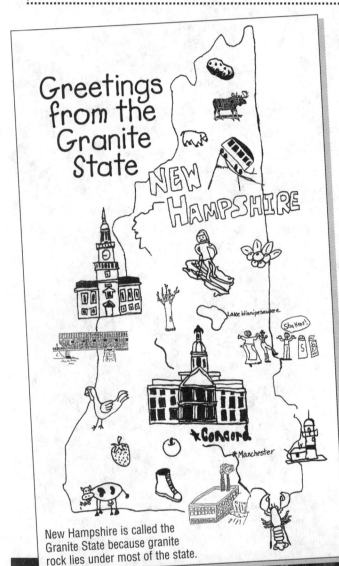

Greetings from the Granite State

NEW HAMPSHIRE

Lake Winnipesaukee

Sha Kers!

★ Concord

★ Manchester

New Hampshire is called the Granite State because granite rock lies under most of the state.

State Capital

★ Concord

SEAL OF THE STATE OF NEW HAMPSHIRE 1776

Dear Friends,

Greetings from the top of Mt. Washington, where the wind speed once reached 231 m.p.h.—the highest recorded wind speed on Earth. On a clear day you might be able to see Boston, Massachusetts, which is 90 miles away. We often take the Cog Railway down. Operating since 1869, it is the second steepest railway track in the world! Then we might go and have some pancakes with rich maple syrup from New Hampshire.

When you visit you must stop to see these sites: the Old Man of the Mountain, which is near Cannon Mountain. Cannon Mountain is one of the many ski areas in New Hampshire. Also be sure to visit the Flume, which is a natural 90-foot gorge in Franconia Notch. It is two miles long; you walk through it. The Lakes Region, which includes Lake Winnipesaukee, offers fun in the summer and ice fishing in the winter. (It is said there is one island for every day of the year in Lake Winnipesaukee. Do you know how many that would be?)

Hope to see you soon,

Mrs. Campbell's Sixth-Grade Class, Hooksett Memorial School, Hooksett, New Hampshire

P.S. Shopping is great! We have no state sales tax!

Sara Josepha Hale (1778–1879) was born in Newport. She had five children and her husband died when she was only 34 years old. To support her children, she became a magazine editor and writer. She wrote the song "Mary Had a Little Lamb." Mrs. Hale also worked toward making Thanksgiving a national holiday. In 1863 she succeeded in having it observed across the country.

Laura Bridgman (1829–1889) was born in Hanover. When she was two years old, she developed rheumatic fever. It left her deaf and blind. People then believed that a person who is deaf and blind could not be educated. Laura proved them wrong. She became America's first highly educated deaf and blind child. Helen Keller, who was also deaf and blind and lectured around the world, said that Laura Bridgman was her idol.

Robert Frost was not born in New Hampshire, but he spent most of his adult life on his farms in Derry and Franconia. His poems generally reflect life in New Hampshire. He won the Pulitzer Prize for his poetry four times (1924, 1931, 1937, and 1943). Do you know his poem "Stopping by Woods on a Snowy Evening"? It makes you want to run right out "to watch woods fill up with snow."

In the 1950s, just about every kid in America knew Archie and Veronica and their friends, the characters in *Archie*.
Bob Montana (1920–1975) was the cartoonist who created Archie. He based the characters on people he had known at his own high school, Central High, which is in Manchester.

Space is the last great frontier. So when NASA announced that it would choose an ordinary citizen to join the astronauts of the space shuttle *Challenger* on a journey, thousands of people applied. NASA gave the honor to **Christa McAuliffe** (1948–1986), a social studies teacher in Concord. On January 27, 1986, she and six other astronauts were aboard *Challenger* when it exploded on liftoff. Christa McAuliffe and the astronauts were all killed.

Alan B. Shepard, Jr. (1923–) was born in Derry. He was the first American in space and the fifth man to walk on the moon.

Check out these famous people who called NH home. Then check out my spots to learn some interesting things about the Granite State!

DID YOU KNOW...?

If you turn NH upside down it looks like VT.

Earl Tupper (inventor of Tupperware) is from Berlin, NH.

My state has the shortest coastline in the U.S. It is 18 miles long.

Rye and Sandwich are towns in NH.

Mount Monadnock is the most climbed mountain in North America.

Tourism is NH's biggest industry.

NH is divided into six regions so close to one another that you could visit them all in one day.

On Golden Pond was filmed on Squam Lake and *Jumanji* was filmed in Keene.

In 1842, NH made Christmas a legal bank holiday.

In the early 1900s, the Amoskeag Manufacturing Company was the largest textile factory in the world.

NH is the first state to hold Presidential primaries. All the candidates come here early to campaign.

Betty and Barney Hill claimed they were abducted by aliens near the Old Man of the Mountain.

the ladybug is NH's state insect.

AND . . . did you know that Shaker Village is located in Canterbury? The Shakers are a religious group that was founded in England in 1772 by Ann Lee. They were called Shakers because they shook while they were dancing during worship. Shaker Village was founded in 1792 and is now a museum.

Hey—check this out!

New Hampshire

Promenade Through the Granite State

1629 An Englishman, John Mason, sails up the Pisacataqua River and gives new Hampshire the name it has today.

1631 Strawbery Banke (now Portsmouth) is founded. It was named for the wild strawberries that blanketed it.

1679 New Hampshire becomes a separate royal province.

1700 About 5,000 settlers live here.

1728 General John Stark, new Hampshire's Revolutionary War hero and creator of the motto, "Live Free or Die," is born in Londonderry.

1741 Benning Wentworth is the first governor.

1769 Rah, Rah! Dartmouth College is founded in Hanover.

1776 State of independence. New Hampshire adopts its own constitution and becomes the first colony to declare independence from Great Britain.

1788 On June 21, New Hampshire becomes the ninth state to ratify the U.S. Constitution—the deciding factor.

1800 Anchors aweigh! Portsmouth navy Shipyard builds ships for the U.S. navy.

1808 Concord becomes the permanent capital.

1853 Franklin Pierce from Hillsborough is elected fourteenth U.S. President.

1866 The University of New Hampshire is started in Durham.

1929 Shuss! First ski school in the United States opens in Franconia.

1961 Alan Shepard, Jr., of Derry, becomes the first American in space.

1986 The space shuttle *Challenger* explodes on liftoff, killing all seven astronauts, including Christa McAuliff, a Concord High teacher.

1990 Protests don't stop the Seabrook Nuclear Power Plant from starting operations.

1997 Jeanne Shaheen becomes our first female governor.

NEW HAMPSHIRE
3 97
I LUV NH
LIVE FREE OR DIE

29

Moo-Hampshire

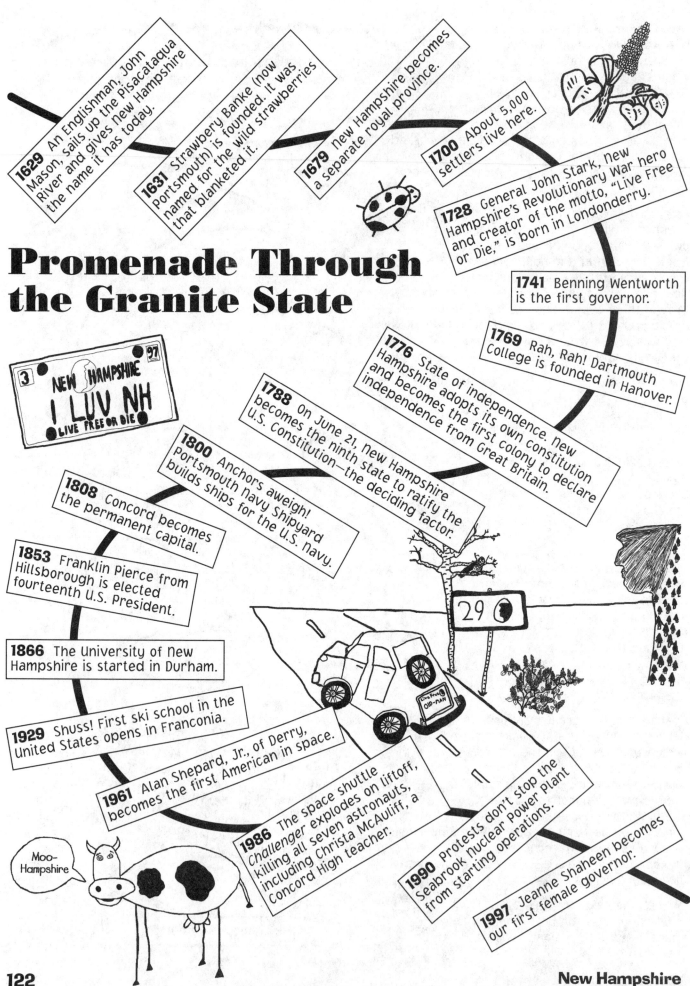

The Old Man says: Check out some facts about New Hampshire while you sing these word to the tune of "Mary Had a Little Lamb."

For more info about New Hampshire:
New Hampshire Office of Travel and Tourism Development
P.O. Box 1856, Dept. 125
Concord, NH 03302-1856
800-386-4664, ext. 125
http://www.visitnh.gov

 **Do It in New Hampshire!**

New Hampshire is definitely a four season state that has plenty of things to do!

WINTER
maple sugaring, cross-country skiing, downhill skiing, snowmobiling

SPRING
fishing, hiking, car racing (at Loudon International Speedway)

FALL
fishing, hunting, hiking, fall foliage viewing

SUMMER
swimming, camping, boating, fishing, hiking, car racing, biking

New Hampshire Song

Sarah Hale lived in New Hampshire
in New Hampshire
in New Hampshire
Sarah Hale lived in New Hampshire
and was the writer of this tune.

New Hampshire has a capital called Concord
capital called Concord
capital called Concord
New Hampshire has a capital called Concord
that was formed in 1659.

New Hampshire has a state flower
state flower
state flower
New Hampshire has a state flower
and it is the purple lilac.

New Hampshire has a state bird
state bird
state bird
New Hampshire has a state bird
and it is the purple finch.

New Hampshire has a state insect
state insect
state insect
New Hampshire has a state insect
and it is the ladybug.

New Hampshire has a state animal
state animal
state animal
New Hampshire has a state animal
and it is the white-tailed deer.

New Hampshire has an old man
old man
old man
New Hampshire has an old man
and it is made of granite rock.

We Had a Talk with Governor Jeanne Shaheen

Our class interviewed the governor, Jeanne Shaheen, and asked her a few questions. She is our state's first woman governor. She feels that it is exciting just to be governor, not a woman governor. She says that being elected and having a chance to lead our state is thrilling. Among her goals to improve the state are to have public kindergarten in every school district, to lower New Hampshire's high electric rates, to create good jobs and a healthy economic climate, and to have accessible health care for families.

New Jersey

Hi, I'm Hadrosaurus, and my bones were found in Haddonfield in 1858. Here's what I've learned about New Jersey.

Though New Jersey is the **fifth smallest state** in area, it has the **greatest population density** of all the states. New Jerseyans live so close together that we have to get along!

In 1881 along the Passaic River, John Holland launched the **first submarine**.

The **symbols of the Republican and Democratic parties** were created in Morristown. Do you know what they are? (Hint: One never forgets and the other is stubborn.)

Buzz Aldrin and Alan Shepard are two **astronauts** from New Jersey.

Jack Ford, host of the weekend TV show *Today*, graduated from our Point Pleasant Beach school system in 1968.

Joseph Campbell started canning tomatoes in Camden in 1869, which led to a big soup company. Can you guess the company's name?

State Capital

Trenton

Hi U.S.A.,
New Jersey is a great state! We are small in size but large in variety. Our state offers sandy beaches along the Atlantic Coast, farmlands filled with yummy vegetables and fruit, busy industries, beautiful suburbs, and mountains for hiking and skiing. Our warm summer weather is perfect for swimming, and winters bring a bit of snow for winter sports. Just think, all this variety and we are the fifth smallest state.
Mrs. Wolfesberger's Fourth Grade at
Antrim Elementary School, Pt. Pleasant Beach

Why We Love New Jersey

New Jersey is like a jigsaw puzzle. The pieces of the puzzle are our four regions.

The biggest region is the Atlantic Coastal Plain. Here you can fish, swim, go boating, and maybe even visit the casinos in Atlantic City.

The Piedmont is the home of New Jersey's state capital, Trenton. Most of New Jersey's industry is located here.

The Highlands, the land of many lakes and mineral resources, has many growing suburbs.

The Ridge and Valley Region is the place to go skiing and hiking. Come visit High Point, the highest point in New Jersey at 1,803 feet.

New Jersey

High Point

Ridge and Valley

Highlands

Delaware Water Gap

Delaware River

N. J. Industry

Piedmont

Trenton

Atlantic Coastal Plain

Camden
Home of Campbell Soup

Pinelands

Barnegat Lighthouse

Eastern Goldfinch

Cape May Lighthouse

The Garden State

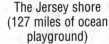

Jersey Devil

New Jersey Our Home

We live in New Jersey and we're proud to say
We've got the very best state in the U.S.A.

From the Kittatinny Mountains to the Jersey shore,
There is not another state that can offer you more.

We have skiing in the mountains and swimming at the shore
We grow strawberries, tomatoes, and cranberries galore.

Our nickname is the Garden State
Our bug, the honeybee
Our flower is the violet
We're very proud, you see.

The Jersey Devil roams our state
On that we say no more
Lenapes came long ago to our New Jersey shore.

Our capital is Trenton
It has the golden dome
We're all so very proud to claim New Jersey as our home!

The Jersey shore
(127 miles of ocean playground)

N.J. Lenape Indians build a longhouse.

Garden State Greats

The beat of musician **COUNT BASIE** (1904–1984) started in New Jersey.

He's way cool, he's totally famous. He's the Boss, born in New Jersey. He's **BRUCE SPRINGSTEEN** (1949–), from Freehold.

You may have heard the story of **MOLLY PITCHER** (1754–1830) who, it is said, carried pitchers of water to Revolutionary War soldiers during the Battle of Monmouth, 1778.

The lab where **THOMAS ALVA EDISON** (1847–1931) worked is in Menlo Park. Where would we be without his more than 1,000 inventions? Can you name one? (the incandescent electric lamp, the phonograph, the motion picture projector, for example)

Is *Superfudge* one of your favorite books? Then, like us, you're a fan of an author named **JUDY BLUME** (1938–) who was born in Elizabeth. Yes. *That* Judy Blume!

Do your parents think you're a real Einstein? Well, the actual **ALBERT EINSTEIN** (1879–1955), the one who discovered the secrets of atomic energy, was a professor at our Princeton University.

Take a Jersey Hike Through Time

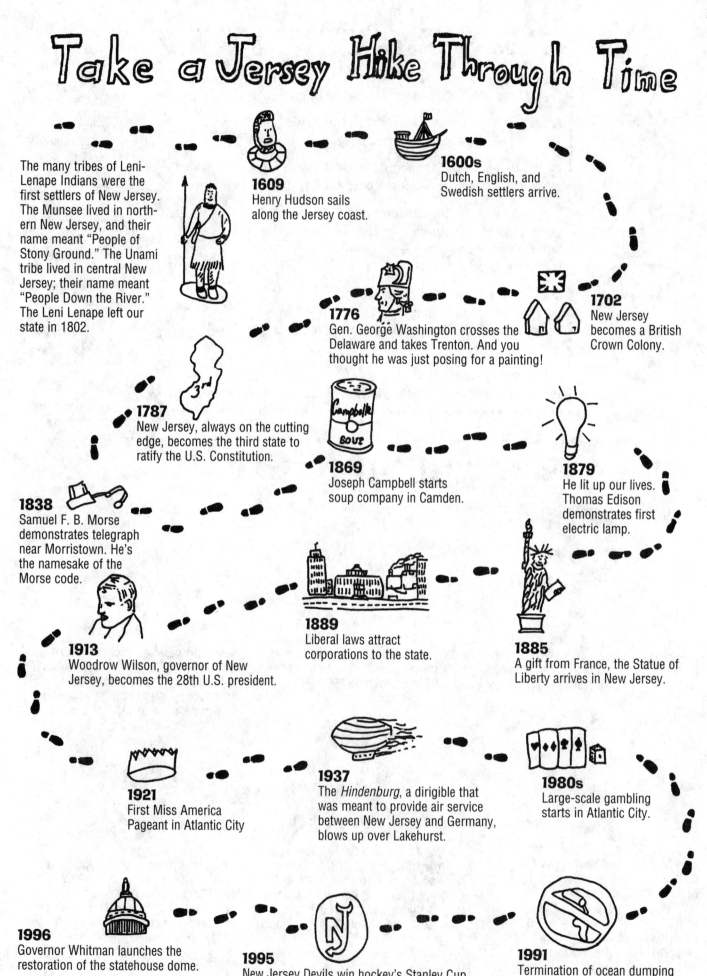

The many tribes of Leni-Lenape Indians were the first settlers of New Jersey. The Munsee lived in northern New Jersey, and their name meant "People of Stony Ground." The Unami tribe lived in central New Jersey; their name meant "People Down the River." The Leni Lenape left our state in 1802.

1609
Henry Hudson sails along the Jersey coast.

1600s
Dutch, English, and Swedish settlers arrive.

1776
Gen. George Washington crosses the Delaware and takes Trenton. And you thought he was just posing for a painting!

1702
New Jersey becomes a British Crown Colony.

1787
New Jersey, always on the cutting edge, becomes the third state to ratify the U.S. Constitution.

1869
Joseph Campbell starts soup company in Camden.

1879
He lit up our lives. Thomas Edison demonstrates first electric lamp.

1838
Samuel F. B. Morse demonstrates telegraph near Morristown. He's the namesake of the Morse code.

1889
Liberal laws attract corporations to the state.

1885
A gift from France, the Statue of Liberty arrives in New Jersey.

1913
Woodrow Wilson, governor of New Jersey, becomes the 28th U.S. president.

1921
First Miss America Pageant in Atlantic City

1937
The *Hindenburg*, a dirigible that was meant to provide air service between New Jersey and Germany, blows up over Lakehurst.

1980s
Large-scale gambling starts in Atlantic City.

1996
Governor Whitman launches the restoration of the statehouse dome.

1995
New Jersey Devils win hockey's Stanley Cup.

1991
Termination of ocean dumping

JOIN A JERSEY JOURNEY

Picnic in a state park.

Swim at the Jersey shore.

Party by Barnegat Bay.

Ski in northwest Jersey.

Farm in the Garden State.

Catch a big one in
New Jersey waters.

Tour the Pinelands,
a peaceful experience.

Escape an angry Atlantic
during a Jersey Nor'easter

Meet Mrs. Bonnie
Wolfesberger and
her fourth-grade class
from G. Harold Antrim
Elementary School

The New Jersey Division of Travel and Tourism
State House
CN 826 20 W. State Street
Trenton, New Jersey 08625   http://www.state.nj.us

New Mexico

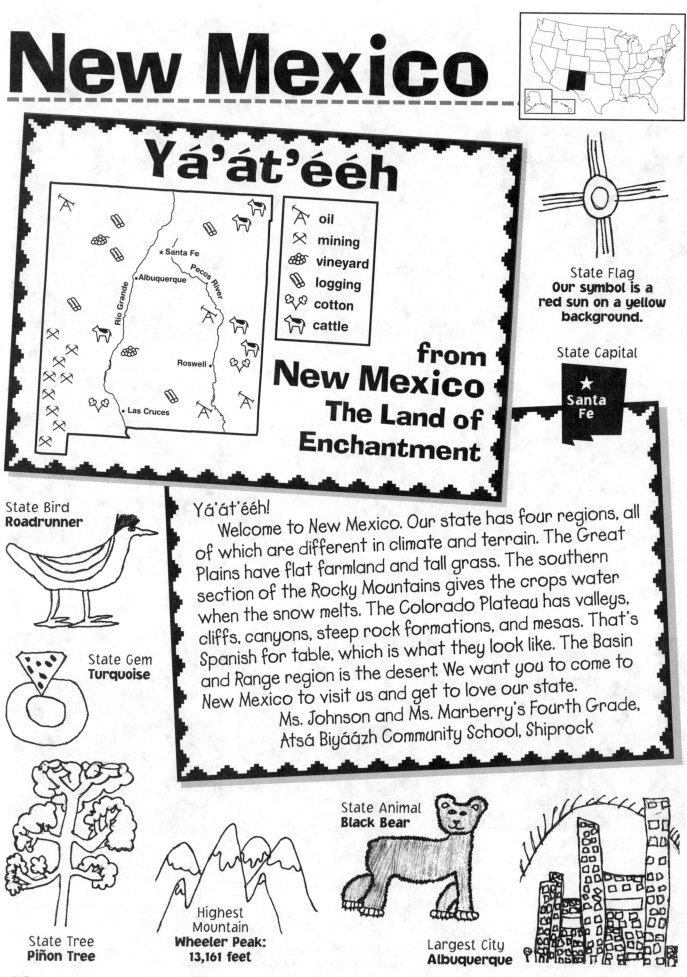

Yá'át'ééh

oil
mining
vineyard
logging
cotton
cattle

Santa Fe
Albuquerque
Rio Grande
Pecos River
Roswell
Las Cruces

from New Mexico
The Land of Enchantment

State Flag
Our symbol is a red sun on a yellow background.

State Capital
Santa Fe

State Bird
Roadrunner

State Gem
Turquoise

Yá'át'ééh!

Welcome to New Mexico. Our state has four regions, all of which are different in climate and terrain. The Great Plains have flat farmland and tall grass. The southern section of the Rocky Mountains gives the crops water when the snow melts. The Colorado Plateau has valleys, cliffs, canyons, steep rock formations, and mesas. That's Spanish for table, which is what they look like. The Basin and Range region is the desert. We want you to come to New Mexico to visit us and get to love our state.

Ms. Johnson and Ms. Marberry's Fourth Grade,
Atsá Biyáázh Community School, Shiprock

State Animal
Black Bear

State Tree
Piñon Tree

Highest Mountain
Wheeler Peak:
13,161 feet

Largest City
Albuquerque

Our State…It's Great… Here's Why

New Mexico is the place to see
high great white sands,
snowcapped mountains, dry prairies,
and tumbleweed land.

Horses and sheep,
roadrunners and bears,
ranches with begashi,
rattlesnakes, and hares.

In New Mexico we've got
many cultures you'll see
the Pueblo, the Navajo,
and the Apache.

Albuquerque is the place
to which all the Indian nations go
each spring to chill
for a giant pow wow show

Adios and
como estás:
In some places you'll see
that Spanish is boss.

Yá'át'ééh, Shima,
and Hagoónee'—
this language is part
of the Navajo way.

If you're a tourist here
and all your money is spent,
you'll still be happy to say
"I left it all in the Land of Enchantment."

Smokey Bear

A fire in New Mexico in 1950 orphaned a little bear. He became the mascot of the National Park Service fire prevention program. After he died in 1976 (at a good old age for a bear), he was buried in Smokey Bear Historical State Park.

We Have 25 Reservations

Indians first lived in New Mexico about 20,000 years ago. Today, more than eight million acres of New Mexico belong to the Pueblo, Apache, and Navajo Nations.

Navajo Code Talkers were used during World War II to send messages for the U.S. Navajo is such a difficult language that the enemy could not break the code.

Learn to speak Navajo!

Navajo Words

Word	Pronunciation	Translation
Ahéhee'	A•HYEH•hay	Thank you
Hágoonee'	Ha•go•NAY	Good-bye
Ma'ii	Ma•EEH	Coyote
Shil na aash	Sheelsh na ash	My cousin
Shi che	Shee chay	My grandfather
Yá'át'ééh	YAH•ah•t•eh	Greeting
Yee yah!	Yee yah	Ready for a fight
Ye'ii	Yeh•EEH	Navajo deity

The Mystery at Roswell

What really happened that day— July 8, 1947?

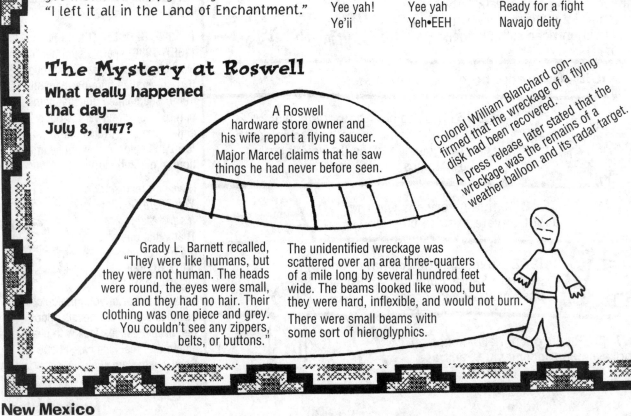

A Roswell hardware store owner and his wife report a flying saucer.

Major Marcel claims that he saw things he had never before seen.

Colonel William Blanchard confirmed that the wreckage of a flying disk had been recovered.

A press release later stated that the wreckage was the remains of a weather balloon and its radar target.

Grady L. Barnett recalled, "They were like humans, but they were not human. The heads were round, the eyes were small, and they had no hair. Their clothing was one piece and grey. You couldn't see any zippers, belts, or buttons."

The unidentified wreckage was scattered over an area three-quarters of a mile long by several hundred feet wide. The beams looked like wood, but they were hard, inflexible, and would not burn.

There were small beams with some sort of hieroglyphics.

STEPS TOWARD TODAY

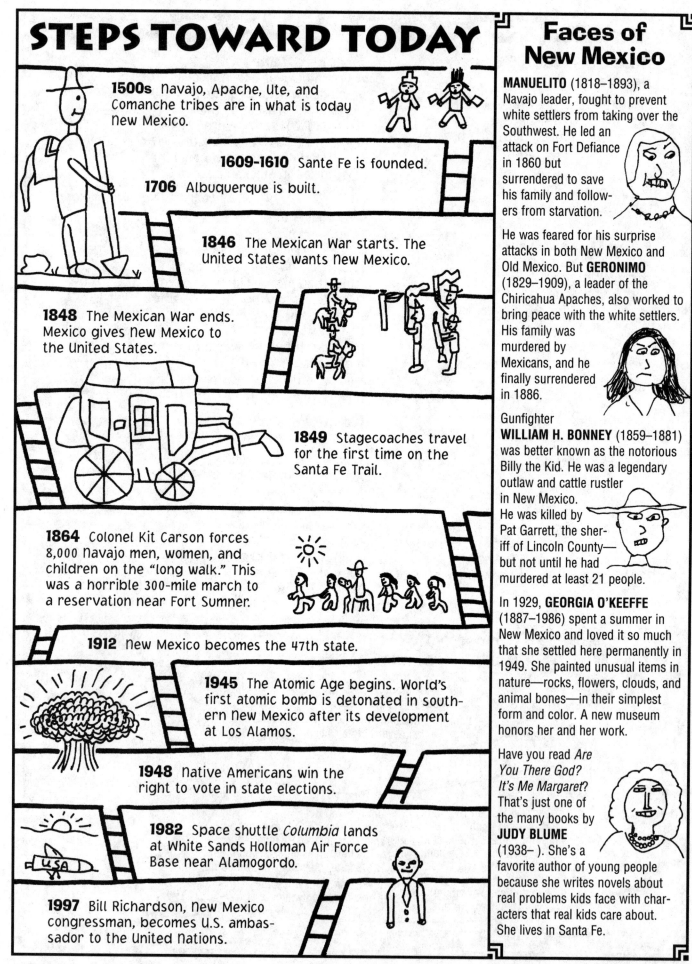

1500s Navajo, Apache, Ute, and Comanche tribes are in what is today New Mexico.

1609–1610 Sante Fe is founded.

1706 Albuquerque is built.

1846 The Mexican War starts. The United States wants New Mexico.

1848 The Mexican War ends. Mexico gives New Mexico to the United States.

1849 Stagecoaches travel for the first time on the Santa Fe Trail.

1864 Colonel Kit Carson forces 8,000 Navajo men, women, and children on the "long walk." This was a horrible 300-mile march to a reservation near Fort Sumner.

1912 New Mexico becomes the 47th state.

1945 The Atomic Age begins. World's first atomic bomb is detonated in southern New Mexico after its development at Los Alamos.

1948 Native Americans win the right to vote in state elections.

1982 Space shuttle *Columbia* lands at White Sands Holloman Air Force Base near Alamogordo.

1997 Bill Richardson, New Mexico congressman, becomes U.S. ambassador to the United Nations.

Faces of New Mexico

MANUELITO (1818–1893), a Navajo leader, fought to prevent white settlers from taking over the Southwest. He led an attack on Fort Defiance in 1860 but surrendered to save his family and followers from starvation.

He was feared for his surprise attacks in both New Mexico and Old Mexico. But **GERONIMO** (1829–1909), a leader of the Chiricahua Apaches, also worked to bring peace with the white settlers. His family was murdered by Mexicans, and he finally surrendered in 1886.

Gunfighter **WILLIAM H. BONNEY** (1859–1881) was better known as the notorious Billy the Kid. He was a legendary outlaw and cattle rustler in New Mexico. He was killed by Pat Garrett, the sheriff of Lincoln County—but not until he had murdered at least 21 people.

In 1929, **GEORGIA O'KEEFFE** (1887–1986) spent a summer in New Mexico and loved it so much that she settled here permanently in 1949. She painted unusual items in nature—rocks, flowers, clouds, and animal bones—in their simplest form and color. A new museum honors her and her work.

Have you read *Are You There God? It's Me Margaret*? That's just one of the many books by **JUDY BLUME** (1938–). She's a favorite author of young people because she writes novels about real problems kids face with characters that real kids care about. She lives in Santa Fe.

The Shiprock Giant

Enchanting Landscapes

Shiprock
• Chimayo
• Albuquerque
Alamogordo •   Carlsbad •

El Santuario de Chimayo
☐ Church

Legend says that if sick people dig a hole in the mud floor here and crawl into it, they'll have a quick recovery.

Shiprock
☐ Dead volcano
☐ 1,400–1,700 feet high

Navajo legend explains "that an enormous bird carried a group of Navajos from the north and, upon landing on the open plain, turned to stone."

Balloon Fiesta
☐ Albuquerque

Hundreds of differently shaped balloons fill the skies during this colorful event.

Carlsbad Caverns
☐ World's largest chamber
☐ Eerie and creepy

The caverns walking tour takes 3½ hours. The walls feel like dry ice. The caverns smell like salt. Visitors often feel as if spiders and bats are going to jump out at them any minute. The quiet is deafening.

White Sands
☐ National monument
☐ Sand white as snow

This range was first used to test rockets that were confiscated from the German armed forces after World War II.

For more information contact:
Sante Fe Chamber of Commerce
P.O. Box 1928
Sante Fe, NM 87504
phone (800) 777-2489
fax (505) 984-2205
http://www.nets.com/santafe

Mrs. Johnson and Ms. Marberry's fourth-grade New Mexico book project group.

New York

State Capital

State Tree
Sugar Maple

State Animal
Beaver

State Song
"I Love New York"

State Bird
Bluebird

New York Riddle: In New York Harbor it can be seen, what giant statue is pretty and green?

Answer: the Statue of Liberty

Hi! I'm Mr. Big Apple! See if you can find me throughout the New York pages!

New York Facts

State Motto: **Excelsior** (Ever upward)

State Shell: **Bay Scallop**

State Beverage: **Milk**

State Gem: **Garnet**

State Fruit: **Apple**

You Can Bite Into

New York became the 11th state in 1788. It is ranked 2nd in population and 30th in size.

The Empire State

A New York Song

Start telling your friends,
Here's where your search ends,
We've got so much for you to see,
New York, New York,

From super stores
to Long Island Shores
It's the best of every single thing,
New York, New York

I want to take you to the
mountains that are upstate,
To find some beautiful spots
on top of the peaks,

Our Empire State,
is very first rate,
We want to come and see the sights,
New York, New York,

If you have seen the rest,
Come to the state that's best,
It's up to you,
New York, New York

Sing this song to the tune of "New York, New York"
(Music and Original Lyrics by Kander and Ebb)

Dear Readers,
Welcome to the Empire State! We got our nickname from a remark made by George Washington. He thought New York might become the seat of the new empire. If you want to see tall buildings—really tall buildings!—then come to our state. If you want to walk on city streets with thousands of other people from all over the world, then come to our state. But maybe you're looking for peaceful country lanes, wide and wonderful beaches, incredible waterfalls, wide open spaces, mountains, and valleys...well, then, come to New York! We have it all. And we'd like to show it to you.
From the fifth-grade writers in Mrs. MacCarthy's class, Raymond J. Lockhart Elmentary School, Massapequa

State Flower
Rose

State Fish
Trout

State Flag

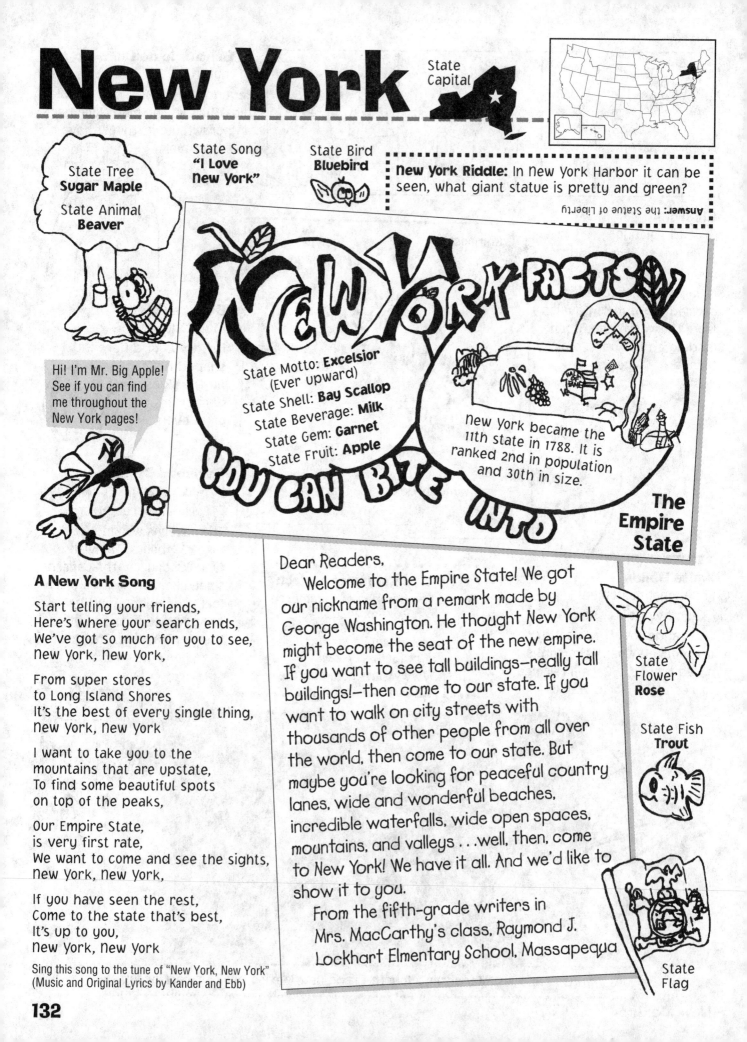

They've Made Our State Great

Theodore Roosevelt

A New Yorker through and through, **Theodore Roosevelt** was born in New York City in 1858 and died in Oyster Bay in 1919. From 1905 to 1909, he was the 26th President of the United States. In 1906, in recognition for helping to end a war between Russia and Japan, he became the first American to receive the Nobel Peace Prize.

Eleanor Roosevelt was born in New York City in 1884 and died there in 1962. She was born into a wealthy political family. As the wife of Franklin D. Roosevelt, president of the U.S. from 1933 to 1945, she was a great and good influence on him. But, more important, she made a name for herself as a writer, diplomat, and supporter of the rights of all people.

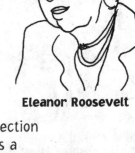

Eleanor Roosevelt

Joe DiMaggio

Joseph Paul DiMaggio was born in 1914. He played for the N.Y. Yankees for many years. A talented baseball player and great favorite with the fans, DiMaggio set many long-standing records. He was named Most Valuable Player in 1931, 1941, and 1947. He was elected to the National Baseball Hall of Fame in 1955.

The Schomburg Center for Research in Black Culture in Harlem, a section of New York City, was started thanks to **Arthur Schomburg**. He was a Puerto Rican of African descent who collected books, photographs, and paintings to do with black history. He lived from 1874 to 1938.

Do you know where the wild things are? **Maurice Sendak** does. He was born in New York City—in Brooklyn, actually—in 1928. In 1964, his book *Where the Wild Things Are* won the Caldecott Medal. He has illustrated more than 70 books and has written close to 20. Which have you read?

Alec Baldwin grew up in Massapequa, Long Island. His first acting experience was in a play, *Cheaper by the Dozen*, at Berner High School. He was 15 years old. As an adult, the movie he most enjoyed appearing in was *The Getaway*, because he got to work with his wife, Kim Bassinger. His goal in life is to be happily married and to have a family. He did achieve both. The toughest part of his job is the public exposure and getting up early.

Alec Baldwin

A Puzzle of New York State Places

The letters in the state nickname will give you a hint for each clue.

1. Site of the National Baseball Hall of Fame _ _ _ _ _ **E** _ _ _ _ _ _
2. Theodore Roosevelt's Oyster Bay Home _ _ _ _ _ **M** _ _ _ _
3. U.S. Military Academy on the Hudson River _ _ _ _ **P** _ _ _ _ _
4. Statue in New York Harbor _ _ **I** _ _ _ _ _
5. Mountains in northern New York State _ _ _ _ _ **R** _ _ _ _ _ _
6. Buffalo is on this Great Lake. _ _ _ **E**
7. A rockin' music festival was held here _ _ _ _ _ **S** _ _ _ _
8. Great Lake north of Rochester _ _ **T** _ _ _ _
9. 1980 Winter Olympics held here _ _ _ _ **A** _ _ _ _ _
10. Famous for springs and horse racing _ _ _ _ **T** _ _ _
11. Site of Franklin Roosevelt's home _ _ _ _ **E** _ _ _

Answers: 1. Cooperstown **2.** Sagamore Hill **3.** West Point **4.** Liberty **5.** Adirondacks **6.** Erie **7.** Woodstock **8.** Ontario **9.** Lake Placid **10.** Saratoga

New York Times

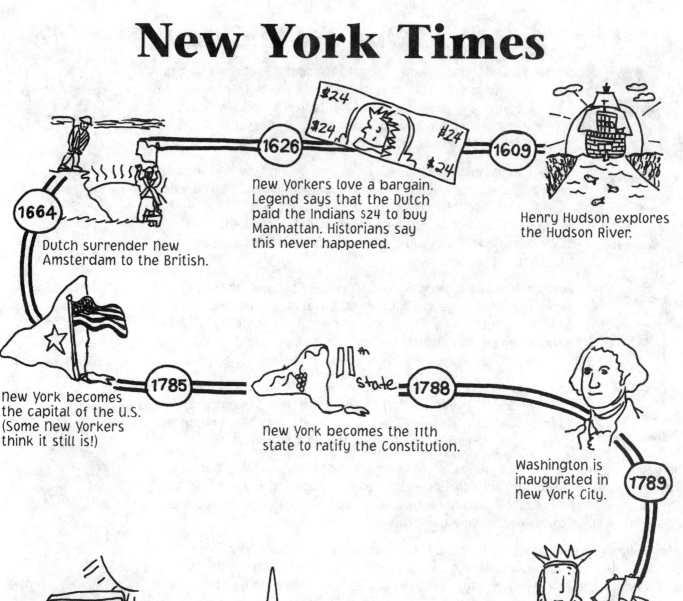

1626

New Yorkers love a bargain. Legend says that the Dutch paid the Indians $24 to buy Manhattan. Historians say this never happened.

1609

Henry Hudson explores the Hudson River.

1664

Dutch surrender New Amsterdam to the British.

1785

New York becomes the capital of the U.S. (Some New Yorkers think it still is!)

1788

New York becomes the 11th state to ratify the Constitution.

1789

Washington is inaugurated in New York City.

1939

New York hosts its first World's Fair.

1886

Statue of Liberty arrives from France.

1952

United Nations buildings are completed.

1969

The Woodstock festival celebrates the sixties with music and unexpected crowds.

1993

Terrorists bomb the World Trade Center.

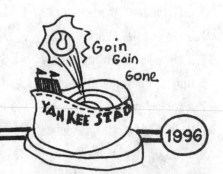

Goin
Goin
Gone

1996

New York Yankees win the baseball World Series.

THE NEW YORK SCENE

© Photodisc

Since 1886, the first sight many people have had of the United States has been the Lady in the Harbor, the magnificent **Statue of Liberty**. She was given to us by France as a symbol of friendship and freedom. She stands 305 feet from base to torch. But what she stands for is beyond measure.

Yours till **Niagara Falls**! This fabulous sight on our border with Canada is a favorite of honeymooners and all kinds of tourists. You can ride a boat in it. Just remember to wear a slicker or you'll get very wet.

Long Island has some of the most popular beaches in the U.S.

Between 1892 and 1924, **Ellis Island** in upper New York Bay was the place through which 16 million immigrants passed before they were allowed to enter the United States. It is now a popular museum.

All sorts of sports are popular in New York—including hiking the beautiful **Hudson River Valley**.

New York State Department of Economic Development
One Commerce Plaza
Albany, New York 12245
Or call: 800-Call-NYS
http://www.state.ny.us

Courtesy Howard Israel

We're in a New York state of mind! We're Mrs. MacCarthy's class.

North Carolina

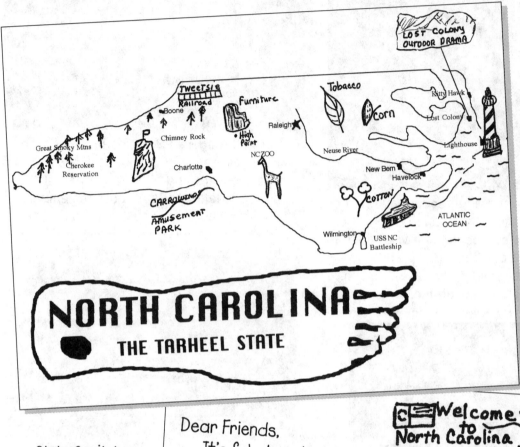

Map labels: Lost Colony Outdoor Drama, Tweetsie Railroad, Boone, Furniture, Tobacco, Corn, Kitty Hawk, Lost Colony, Great Smoky Mtns, Chimney Rock, Raleigh, High Point, NC ZOO, Neuse River, Lighthouse, Cherokee Reservation, Charlotte, New Bern, Havelock, Carrowinds Amusement Park, Cotton, ATLANTIC OCEAN, Wilmington, USS NC Battleship

NORTH CAROLINA
THE TARHEEL STATE

Tarheel Story

In colonial days, turpentine from pine trees was made into tar and pitch for sale to England. Workers often got tar stuck to their heels and were called tarheels. Another story comes from the Civil War. Troops fought so hard that the general said, "That N.C. regiment must have tar on their heels to make them stick as they do." Whatever the true story, we are all proud to be called "tarheels."

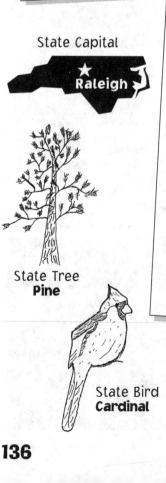

State Capital
Raleigh

State Tree
Pine

State Bird
Cardinal

State Flower
Flowering Dogwood

Welcome to North Carolina

Havelock

Dear Friends,
It's fabulous here in North Carolina. We always have something interesting to do. At island beaches we play in the sun and sand or ride ferries to visit the Outer Bank sights. We take walks in the forests across the state, seeing wildlife. It is fun to visit the state zoo in the spring and see all the baby animals. The mountains have beautiful waterfalls or it is a lot of fun to go skiing or snowboarding in the winter when it is cold. But it doesn't snow much in North Carolina except in the mountains. In fact, except for hurricanes, our weather is really great! As the song says, "It's great to be in Carolina."
Mrs. Thomas's Fifth-Grade Class,
Havelock Elementary, Havelock

Amazing Tarheel Facts

Bald-Headed Men of America meet yearly in Morehead City!

Carolina was named for King Charles I of England.

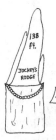

Jockey's Ridge, a 138-foot-high sand dune in Nag's Head, is the highest in the U.S.

A piece of the **Wright Brothers' airplane** was put on the moon by Neil Armstrong in 1969.

Pirating was an equal-opportunity profession in North Carolina. Two famous pirates were women, Anne Bonney and Mary Read.

Cape Hatteras is known as "the Graveyard of the Atlantic" because of the ships that have been wrecked and sunk in the area.

---

3 U.S. PRESIDENTS
They all came from NC
Andrew Jackson (7th)
James K. Polk (11th)
Andrew Johnson (17th)

4 MILITARY BASES
Air Force: Seymour Johnson
Navy/Marine: Cherry Point
Marine: Camp Lejeune
Army: Fort Bragg

4 UNIVERSITIES
UNC Tarheels
NCSU Wolfpack
DUKE Blue Devils
WAKE FOREST Deacons

We've Made History
North Carolina is the site of the first...
- English settlement in the New World.
- colony to ask for independence from England.
- home run hit by Babe Ruth as a professional. It was in 1914.
- town named for George Washington.

Daniel Boone's first home in North Carolina was in a cave named Devil's Den.

The **world's most famous chair**, made of metal and cement, is in Thomasville, the Chair City. The chair is 18 feet tall and sits on a 12-foot-high limestone stand.

Cherokees called the mountains **the Land of 1000 Smokes** because of the heavy haze.

The **Venus's-flytrap** grows in the wild in only North Carolina and South Carolina.

The **N.C. Mutual Life Insurance Company** of Durham is the largest business in the world owned and operated by black people.

There are MANY FAMOUS TARHEELS. Here are just a few.

Michael Jordan
He was born 1963 in Wilmington. An all-around athlete, he played basketball for the University of North Carolina, was on the "dream team" at the U.S. Olympic Games, and plays pro ball for the Chicago Bulls.

Maya Angelou

This poet, author, playwright, and actress recited one of her poems at President Clinton's first inauguration. She is now a professor at Wake Forest University in Winston-Salem.

Dolley Madison
Born in Guilford County; wife of James Madison, 4th president of the U.S. As first lady, she saved many White House art treasures when the British burned the president's house during the War of 1812.

Blackbeard
Born Edward Teach, he became the most famous North Carolina pirate. In his case, crime paid—he had homes in Bath, Beaufort, and Ocracoke—but not for long. Blackbeard was killed during a battle in 1718 on Ocracoke Island. In 1997, divers found his ship off the coast of Beaufort.

Andy Griffith

Name a role. He can play it. Born in Mt. Airy, Griffith was an up-and-coming actor when he played Sir Walter Raleigh in the N.C. outdoor drama *The Lost Colony*. On TV, he was Sheriff Andy Taylor on *The Andy Griffith Show* and then played a lawyer in the drama series *Matlock*.

Billy Graham
He was born on a farm near Charlotte, and now his name is known the world over. He became an inspiring television preacher and religious leader; millions have heard his sermons.

North Carolina

Tarheel Prints in Time

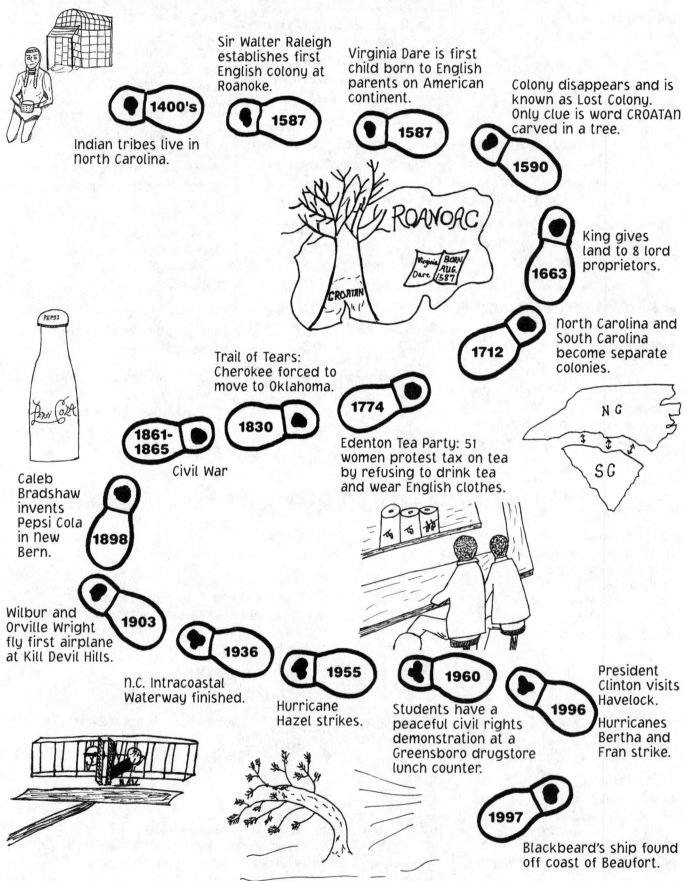

Indian tribes live in North Carolina.

1400's

Sir Walter Raleigh establishes first English colony at Roanoke.

1587

Virginia Dare is first child born to English parents on American continent.

1587

Colony disappears and is known as Lost Colony. Only clue is word CROATAN carved in a tree.

1590

King gives land to 8 lord proprietors.

1663

North Carolina and South Carolina become separate colonies.

1712

Trail of Tears: Cherokee forced to move to Oklahoma.

1830

Edenton Tea Party: 51 women protest tax on tea by refusing to drink tea and wear English clothes.

1774

Civil War

1861-1865

Caleb Bradshaw invents Pepsi Cola in New Bern.

1898

Wilbur and Orville Wright fly first airplane at Kill Devil Hills.

1903

N.C. Intracoastal Waterway finished.

1936

Hurricane Hazel strikes.

1955

Students have a peaceful civil rights demonstration at a Greensboro drugstore lunch counter.

1960

President Clinton visits Havelock.

Hurricanes Bertha and Fran strike.

1996

Blackbeard's ship found off coast of Beaufort.

1997

Tarheel Tourism

Cape Hatteras National Seashore
The famous Cape Hatteras Lighthouse was built in 1870. It is the tallest and oldest brick lighthouse in the U.S.

Wright Brothers National Memorial
Near Kitty Hawk and Kill Devil Hills is a museum built for the Wright Brothers' historic flight of the first power-driven airplane.

North Carolina Zoological Park
A total natural habitat zoo, with 42-acre African region and 200-acre North American region. Other regions are planned for completion over the next 10 years. An education center provides classrooms, library, and other facilities for the thousands of schoolchildren who visit the zoo each year.

USS North Carolina
This restored battleship is docked on the Cape Fear River in Wilmington. In 1961, when the U.S. government was going to junk the World War II battleship, schoolchildren helped purchase the USS *North Carolina* by donating their pennies, raising $345,000. Visitors are now able to tour the restored battleship seven days a week.

Fort Macon State Park
A restored pre–Civil War fort guarding the channel to Beaufort and Morehead City was used during the Civil War, W.W. I, and W.W. II. On-site museum and guided tours daily.

Cherokee Reservation
After the Trail of Tears, when many American Indians were forcibly moved to reservations in the 1830s, survivors hid in the mountains. In 1878 the U.S. government gave the Cherokees land that is now the town of Cherokee.

The Lost Colony
This outdoor drama in Manteo was written by Paul Green of Chapel Hill. It tells what life was like in Roanoke Island when Virginia Dare was a baby. The disappearance of this colony remains a mystery.

Hello from Mrs. Thomas and her fifth-grade class from Havelock Elementary School.

Tryon Palace
Located on the Trent River in New Bern, this was the home of the colonial governor, William Tryon. New Bern was the state capital until Raleigh, a more central location, became the capital. Tryon Palace is famous for its beautiful gardens. Visitors can enjoy tours led by costumed guides year-round.

n.C. Department of Commerce
Travel & Tourism Division
301 N. Wilmington Street
Raleigh, NC 27601
http://www.visitnc.com

North Carolina

North Carolina Travel and Tourism

North Dakota

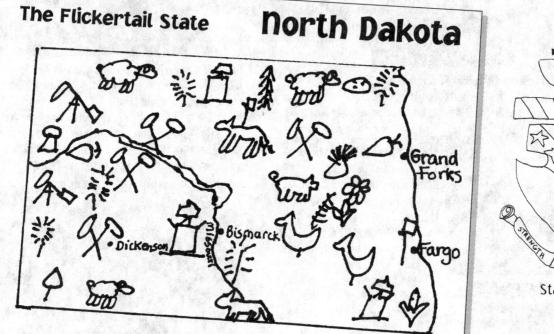

The Flickertail State

North Dakota

Grand Forks

Dickenson

Bismarck

Missouri

Fargo

State Shield

STRENGTH FROM THE SOIL

State Capital

Bismarck
★

State Flower
Wild Prairie Rose

State Bird
Western Meadowlark

Dear Readers,

Many of us come from ranching or farming families. That's because our state is mostly agricultural. It's not unusual to be on farms here that are larger than 1,000 acres. We've seen beautiful sunflower fields and waves of wheat in the summer. In fact, we grow more spring wheat than any other state. (Can you guess how the wheat got its name? Right! It's grown in the spring.) During our winter travels we've seen snow drifts so high they reach the roofs of some homes. In fact, we have some of the coldest temperatures in the country. Only Alaska is colder. And, because North Dakota has the least forest land of any state and because it is almost flat, we get some frosty winds. People here like to say, "There's nothing between us and the North Pole except some barbed-wire fences." So bundle up (or, if it's the summer, wear something light and cool) and visit us.

Mrs. Eppler's Fourth-Grade Class, Nativity School, Fargo

State Fish
Northern Pike

All About North Dakota

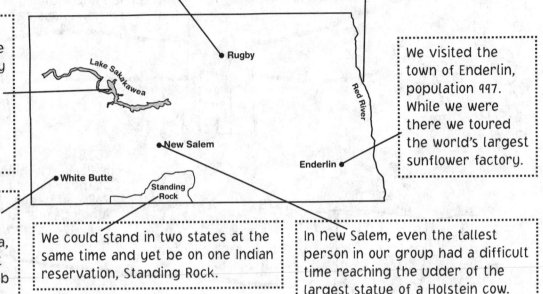

We sure felt like the center of attention while we were in Rugby. That's no surprise. Rugby is the center of the North American continent.

Had a great time canoeing on the Red River. This river flows north. Only two others in the world that do that, the Nile and the Rhine.

There's nothing like taking a dip in a lake on a hot summer day in North Dakota. This is Lake Sakakawea, the largest artificial lake within a single state.

We visited the town of Enderlin, population 997. While we were there we toured the world's largest sunflower factory.

While out west, we climbed the highest point in North Dakota, White Butte. It didn't take too long to climb 3,506 feet.

We could stand in two states at the same time and yet be on one Indian reservation, Standing Rock.

In New Salem, even the tallest person in our group had a difficult time reaching the udder of the largest statue of a Holstein cow.

Noted North Dakotans

She was born in 1920 in Jamestown with the name Norma Deloris Egstrom. But the world knows her as Miss **PEGGY LEE**. "Is That All There Is?" she asked in a famous song.

If you want to shake the powerful hands of **VIRGIL HILL**, just head for his hometown of Grand Forks. He was the WBA light heavyweight champ in 1987.

ROGER MARIS was born in Fargo. But his claim to fame happened all across the country. As a New York Yankee, he hit 61 home runs in 1961, beating a record set by the great Babe Ruth way back in 1927.

A one and a two... For many years, one of America's favorite ways to spend Saturday night was to watch **LAWRENCE WELK** play his accordion and lead his orchestra on TV. He was born in Strasburg, a German-speaking village, in 1903 and died in 1992.

North Dakota in Many Ways
by Thomas Seim

Listen, you may hear the wind speak.
If you look carefully,
You may see the stars of peace.

Wait! There are Red Hawks looking over you.
Watch the golden fields of wheat,
Wave in the wind.

Spring, summer, winter, fall,
Ice and grass.
Peaceful and calm are ways in North Dakota.

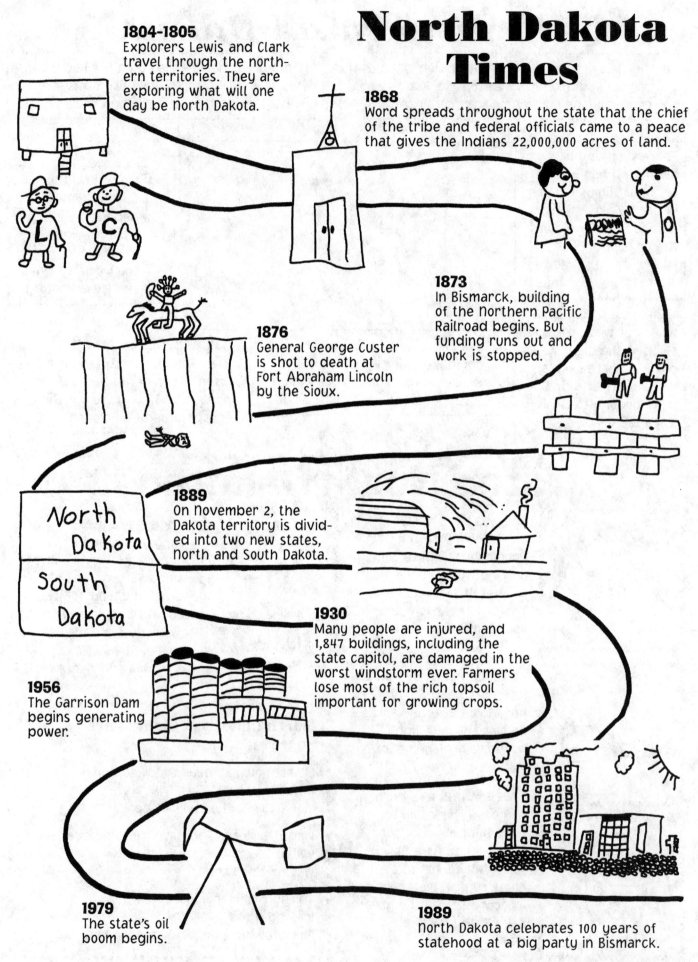

North Dakota Times

1804-1805
Explorers Lewis and Clark travel through the northern territories. They are exploring what will one day be North Dakota.

1868
Word spreads throughout the state that the chief of the tribe and federal officials came to a peace that gives the Indians 22,000,000 acres of land.

1873
In Bismarck, building of the Northern Pacific Railroad begins. But funding runs out and work is stopped.

1876
General George Custer is shot to death at Fort Abraham Lincoln by the Sioux.

1889
On November 2, the Dakota territory is divided into two new states, North and South Dakota.

1930
Many people are injured, and 1,847 buildings, including the state capitol, are damaged in the worst windstorm ever. Farmers lose most of the rich topsoil important for growing crops.

1956
The Garrison Dam begins generating power.

1979
The state's oil boom begins.

1989
North Dakota celebrates 100 years of statehood at a big party in Bismarck.

Through the Peace Garden State

Alycia, Shannon, Tyler, Tyler, Thomas, Heather, Giuliana, Courtney, Katherine, Nicole, Ross,

The **International Peace Garden** was dedicated to international peace. This monument is in two countries, the United States and Canada.

The **Red River Valley** is good for growing corn, sugar beets, sunflowers, wheat, and barley. This is a sunflower field near Valley City.

This is **Lake Sakakawea**, the largest artificial lake within a single state, near Dick City.

North Dakota is well known for its **cold winters** and large snowfalls.

Howdy from Mrs. Eppler's fourth-grade class in Fargo

Fargo Convention and Visitors Bureau
2001 44 Street S.W., Fargo, ND 58104
(800) 235-7684
http://www.state.nd.us

In New Salem, visit the largest statue of a Holstein cow, **Salem Sue**.

Nick, Alison, Aaron, Ashley, Rachel, Andrew, Samantha, Nick, Jeff, Laura, Aaron, Matthew

North Dakota

Ohio

State Capital

columbus ★

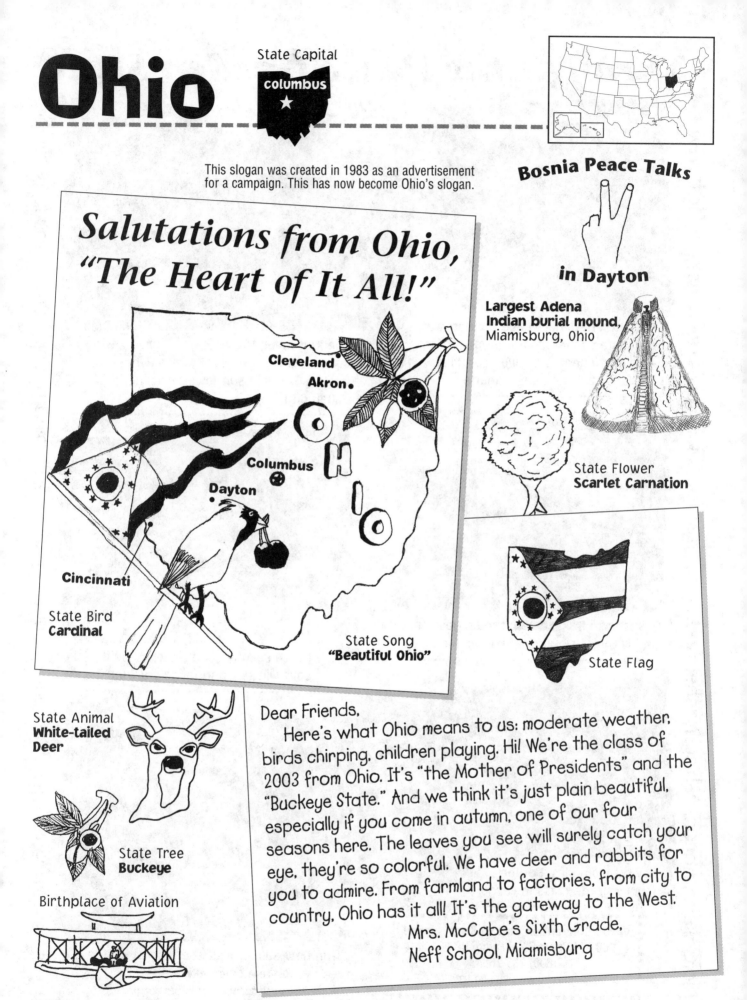

This slogan was created in 1983 as an advertisement for a campaign. This has now become Ohio's slogan.

Salutations from Ohio, "The Heart of It All!"

Cleveland
Akron
Columbus
Dayton
OHIO
Cincinnati

State Bird
Cardinal

State Song
"Beautiful Ohio"

Bosnia Peace Talks

in Dayton

Largest Adena Indian burial mound, Miamisburg, Ohio

State Flower
Scarlet Carnation

State Flag

State Animal
White-tailed Deer

State Tree
Buckeye

Birthplace of Aviation

Dear Friends,
Here's what Ohio means to us: moderate weather, birds chirping, children playing. Hi! We're the class of 2003 from Ohio. It's "the Mother of Presidents" and the "Buckeye State." And we think it's just plain beautiful, especially if you come in autumn, one of our four seasons here. The leaves you see will surely catch your eye, they're so colorful. We have deer and rabbits for you to admire. From farmland to factories, from city to country, Ohio has it all! It's the gateway to the West.
Mrs. McCabe's Sixth Grade,
Neff School, Miamisburg

144

Bursting with Buckeye Facts

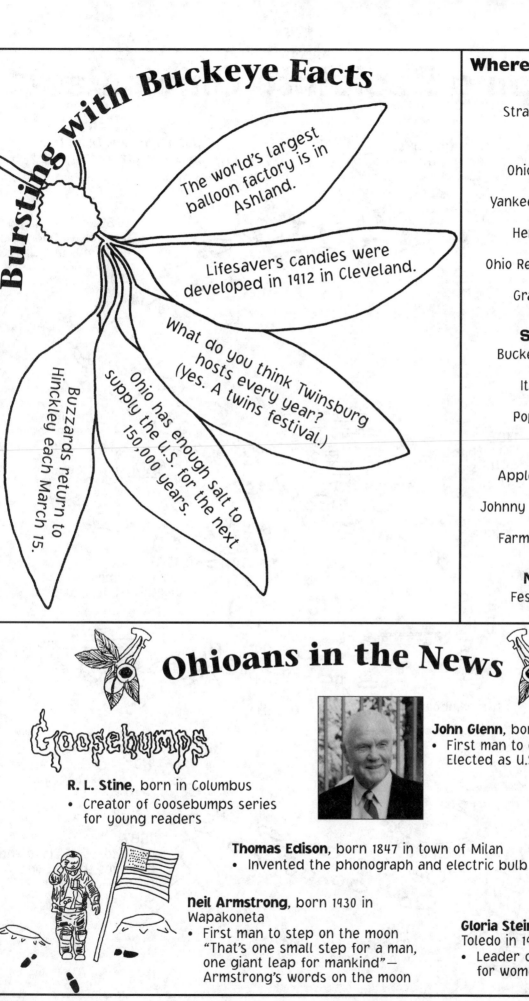

The world's largest balloon factory is in Ashland.

Lifesavers candies were developed in 1912 in Cleveland.

What do you think Twinsburg hosts every year? (yes. A twins festival.)

Ohio has enough salt to supply the U.S. for the next 150,000 years.

Buzzards return to Hinckley each March 15.

Where the Action Is

MAY
Strawberry Festival
Jefferson

AUGUST
Ohio Swiss Festival
Sugarcreek
Yankee Peddlar Festival
Fulton
Heritage Festival
Piqua
Ohio Renaissance Festival
Waynesville
Grape Jamboree
Geneva

SEPTEMBER
Buckeye Tree Festival
Utica
Italian Festival
Sandusky
Popcorn Festival
Marion

OCTOBER
Apple Butter Festival
Grand Rapids
Johnny Appleseed Festival
Defiance
Farmer's Fall Festival
Chillicothe

NOVEMBER
Festival of Lights
Cincinnati

Ohioans in the News

Goosebumps

R. L. Stine, born in Columbus
• Creator of Goosebumps series for young readers

John Glenn, born 1921 in Cambridge
• First man to orbit Earth in 1962
Elected as U.S. senator in 1974

Thomas Edison, born 1847 in town of Milan
• Invented the phonograph and electric bulb

Neil Armstrong, born 1930 in Wapakoneta
• First man to step on the moon
"That's one small step for a man, one giant leap for mankind"—
Armstrong's words on the moon

Gloria Steinem, born in Toledo in 1934
• Leader of campaign for women's rigths

Stepping Back into Ohio's Past

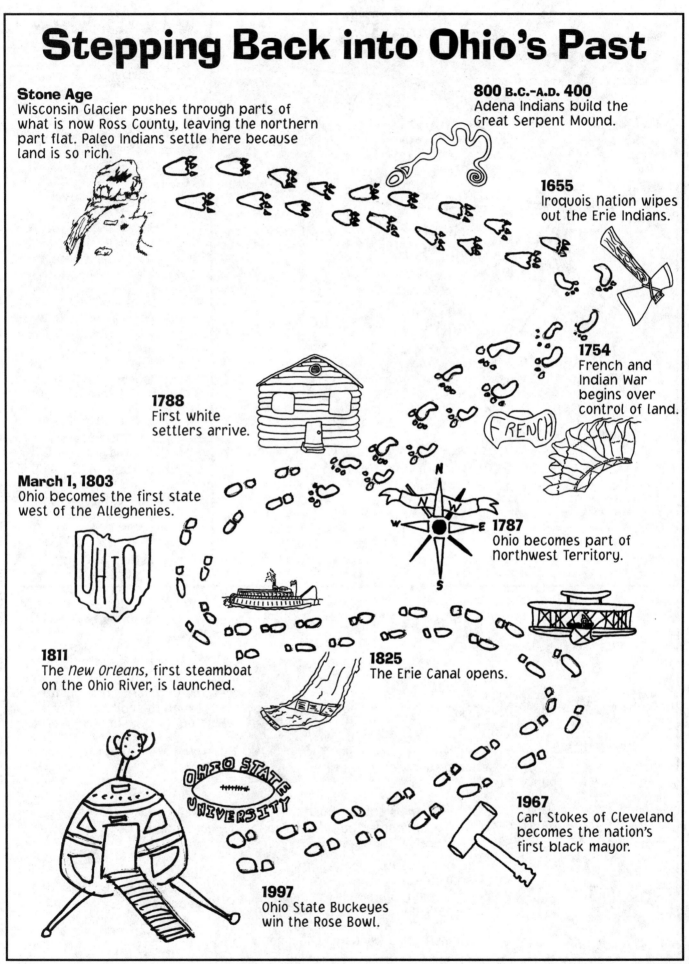

Stone Age
Wisconsin Glacier pushes through parts of what is now Ross County, leaving the northern part flat. Paleo Indians settle here because land is so rich.

800 B.C.–A.D. 400
Adena Indians build the Great Serpent Mound.

1655
Iroquois Nation wipes out the Erie Indians.

1754
French and Indian War begins over control of land.

1788
First white settlers arrive.

March 1, 1803
Ohio becomes the first state west of the Alleghenies.

1787
Ohio becomes part of Northwest Territory.

1811
The *New Orleans*, first steamboat on the Ohio River, is launched.

1825
The Erie Canal opens.

1967
Carl Stokes of Cleveland becomes the nation's first black mayor.

1997
Ohio State Buckeyes win the Rose Bowl.

Picture This...OHIO

Want to be turned upside down six times at 55 miles per hour? Then the **roller coaster** at Kings Island is for you! (Go before lunch.)

Serpent Mound

Adena Indian Mound is shaped like a serpent.

To find out more about Ohio, visit us online at: http://www.state.oh.us

Columbus, the capital of Ohio, is located in the center of the state where the Scioto and Olentangy rivers meet.

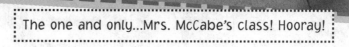

The one and only...Mrs. McCabe's class! Hooray!

Oklahoma OK!

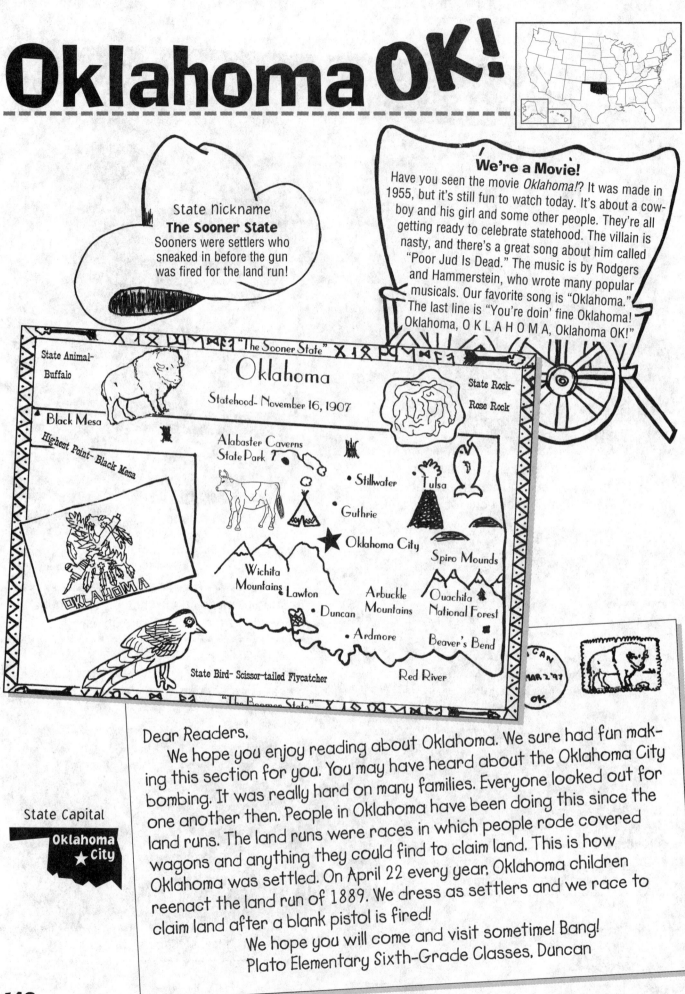

State nickname
The Sooner State
Sooners were settlers who sneaked in before the gun was fired for the land run!

We're a Movie!
Have you seen the movie *Oklahoma!*? It was made in 1955, but it's still fun to watch today. It's about a cowboy and his girl and some other people. They're all getting ready to celebrate statehood. The villain is nasty, and there's a great song about him called "Poor Jud Is Dead." The music is by Rodgers and Hammerstein, who wrote many popular musicals. Our favorite song is "Oklahoma." The last line is "You're doin' fine Oklahoma! Oklahoma, O K L A H O M A, Oklahoma OK!"

"The Sooner State"

State Animal- Buffalo

Oklahoma
Statehood- November 16, 1907

State Rock- Rose Rock

Black Mesa

Highest Point- Black Mesa

OKLAHOMA

Alabaster Caverns State Park

• Stillwater

• Tulsa

• Guthrie

★ Oklahoma City

Spiro Mounds

Wichita Mountains • Lawton

Arbuckle Mountains

Ouachita National Forest

• Duncan

• Ardmore

Beaver's Bend

State Bird- Scissor-tailed Flycatcher

Red River

"The Boomer State"

DUNCAN MAR 2 '97 OK

State Capital
Oklahoma ★ City

Dear Readers,
    We hope you enjoy reading about Oklahoma. We sure had fun making this section for you. You may have heard about the Oklahoma City bombing. It was really hard on many families. Everyone looked out for one another then. People in Oklahoma have been doing this since the land runs. The land runs were races in which people rode covered wagons and anything they could find to claim land. This is how Oklahoma was settled. On April 22 every year, Oklahoma children reenact the land run of 1889. We dress as settlers and we race to claim land after a blank pistol is fired!
    We hope you will come and visit sometime! Bang!
    Plato Elementary Sixth-Grade Classes, Duncan

Oklahoma Pride

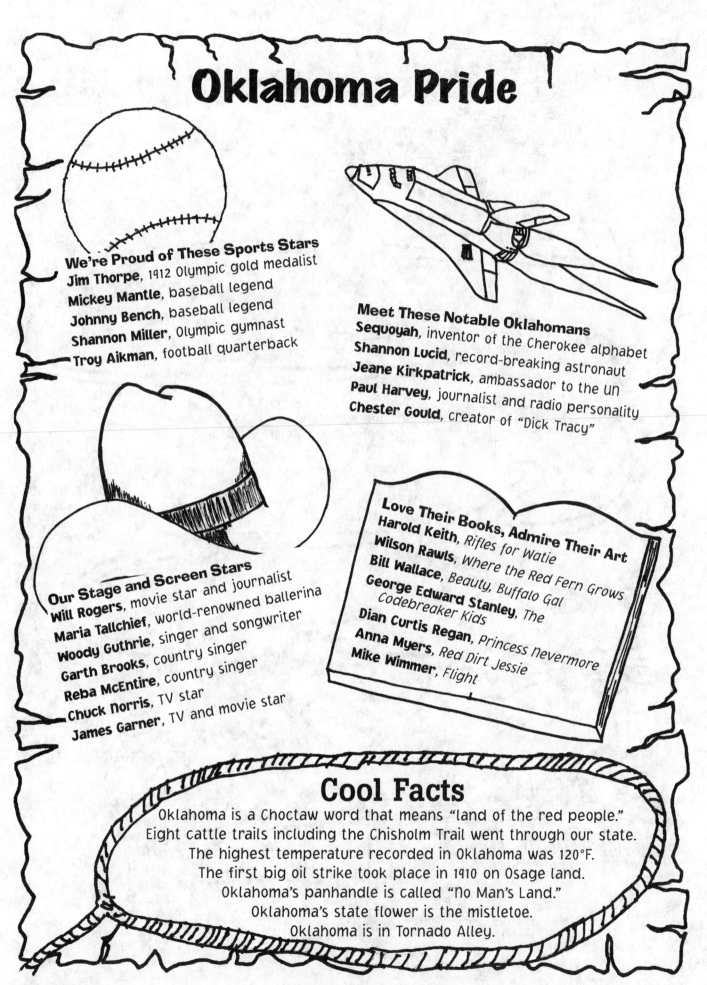

We're Proud of These Sports Stars
Jim Thorpe, 1912 Olympic gold medalist
Mickey Mantle, baseball legend
Johnny Bench, baseball legend
Shannon Miller, Olympic gymnast
Troy Aikman, football quarterback

Meet These Notable Oklahomans
Sequoyah, inventor of the Cherokee alphabet
Shannon Lucid, record-breaking astronaut
Jeane Kirkpatrick, ambassador to the un
Paul Harvey, journalist and radio personality
Chester Gould, creator of "Dick Tracy"

Our Stage and Screen Stars
Will Rogers, movie star and journalist
Maria Tallchief, world-renowned ballerina
Woody Guthrie, singer and songwriter
Garth Brooks, country singer
Reba McEntire, country singer
Chuck Norris, TV star
James Garner, TV and movie star

Love Their Books, Admire Their Art
Harold Keith, Rifles for Watie
Wilson Rawls, Where the Red Fern Grows
Bill Wallace, Beauty, Buffalo Gal
George Edward Stanley, The Codebreaker Kids
Dian Curtis Regan, Princess Nevermore
Anna Myers, Red Dirt Jessie
Mike Wimmer, Flight

Cool Facts
Oklahoma is a Choctaw word that means "land of the red people."
Eight cattle trails including the Chisholm Trail went through our state.
The highest temperature recorded in Oklahoma was 120°F.
The first big oil strike took place in 1910 on Osage land.
Oklahoma's panhandle is called "No Man's Land."
Oklahoma's state flower is the mistletoe.
Oklahoma is in Tornado Alley.

Blown Through Time

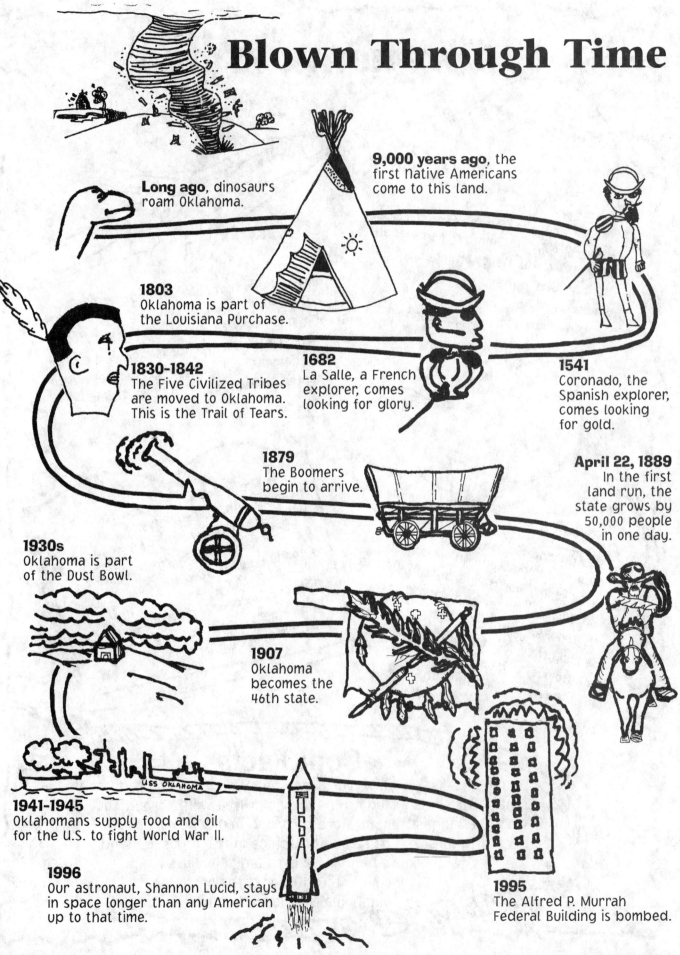

Long ago, dinosaurs roam Oklahoma.

9,000 years ago, the first Native Americans come to this land.

1803
Oklahoma is part of the Louisiana Purchase.

1830-1842
The Five Civilized Tribes are moved to Oklahoma. This is the Trail of Tears.

1682
La Salle, a French explorer, comes looking for glory.

1541
Coronado, the Spanish explorer, comes looking for gold.

1879
The Boomers begin to arrive.

April 22, 1889
In the first land run, the state grows by 50,000 people in one day.

1930s
Oklahoma is part of the Dust Bowl.

1907
Oklahoma becomes the 46th state.

USS OKLAHOMA

1941-1945
Oklahomans supply food and oil for the U.S. to fight World War II.

1996
Our astronaut, Shannon Lucid, stays in space longer than any American up to that time.

1995
The Alfred P. Murrah Federal Building is bombed.

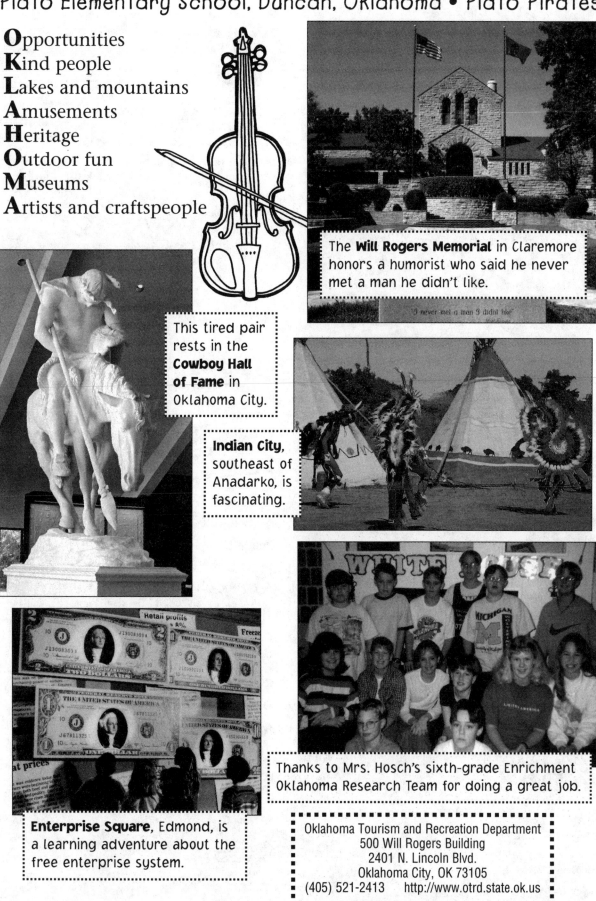

Opportunities
Kind people
Lakes and mountains
Amusements
Heritage
Outdoor fun
Museums
Artists and craftspeople

Lindsay Green • Scott Bryant • Kasey Moody • Crissy Spencer • Brandon Lowry • Josh Scott

Jeremy Graham • Mary Garis • Matt Kendall • Brandon Wright • Melinda Roop • 6th Grade

The **Will Rogers Memorial** in Claremore honors a humorist who said he never met a man he didn't like.

This tired pair rests in the **Cowboy Hall of Fame** in Oklahoma City.

Indian City, southeast of Anadarko, is fascinating.

Thanks to Mrs. Hosch's sixth-grade Enrichment Oklahoma Research Team for doing a great job.

Enterprise Square, Edmond, is a learning adventure about the free enterprise system.

Oklahoma Tourism and Recreation Department
500 Will Rogers Building
2401 N. Lincoln Blvd.
Oklahoma City, OK 73105
(405) 521-2413   http://www.otrd.state.ok.us

• Garrett Haviland • Abby Murphree • Jamie Wooten • Mrs. Hosch •

Oregon

State Capital
★ **Salem**

State Bird
Western Meadowlark

State Flower
Oregon Grape

Population: 3,181,000

Highest Point: Mt. Hood, 11,237 feet

Lowest Point: Sea Level

State motto
She flies with her own wings

State Drink
Milk

State Seal

State Fish
Chinook Salmon

State Tree
Douglas Fir

Dear Friends,
    Want to build a house? Come to Oregon, one of the world's leading suppliers of wood and wood products. We supply our nation with plywood. Ready for something scrumptious to eat? Have an Oregon feast. We produce cheese, cranberries, salmon, shrimp, sea oysters, vegetables, nuts, wine grapes, cattle, sheep, potatoes, corn, sugar beets, and melons, not to mention hay, grain, Christmas trees, flower bulbs, and lilies. Wow! We're proud. No wonder tourism is a big deal in Oregon. People also like to come here for rockhounding, waterskiing, snow skiing, hunting, and wind surfing. These are just a few of the fun things to do in Oregon.

                    Mrs. Alexander's Fourth Grade,
                    Vern Patrick Elementary School, Redmond

People We Want You to Meet

BEVERLY CLEARY, an Oregon author, is one of our favorites. She wrote the Ramona books and books about Ralph S. Mouse. "I like *The Mouse and the Motorcycle* because it's about a mouse who talks. He runs away on a motorcycle." That's what one student says. Another says, "*Ramona the Brave* is my favorite book because first grade was fun and I was naughty just like Ramona."

CHIEF JOSEPH was the chief of the Nez Percé Indians. His tribal name was Modoc. In 1872 he led his tribe in a war against the U.S. Army over the Indians' refusal to settle on Klamath Reservation in Oregon. Chief Joseph is said to have died of a broken heart, away from his beloved homeland.

TOM MCCALL was the governor of Oregon between 1967 and 1975. He cared about Oregon's natural beauty. He even won an award for a film he made about cleaning the Willamette River. He also helped ban throwaway bottles and cans.

See her run—but don't try to catch up! **MARY DECKER** broke Olympic running records in 1984. In spite of her asthma, she continues to run and break records today. Her running career has spanned 25 years—and hardly anyone's kept up with her pace.

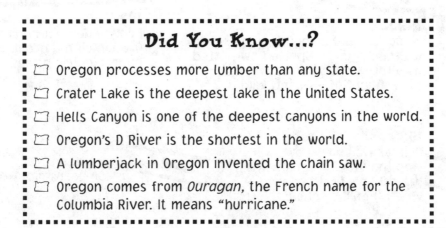

Did You Know...?

- ▱ Oregon processes more lumber than any state.
- ▱ Crater Lake is the deepest lake in the United States.
- ▱ Hells Canyon is one of the deepest canyons in the world.
- ▱ Oregon's D River is the shortest in the world.
- ▱ A lumberjack in Oregon invented the chain saw.
- ▱ Oregon comes from *Ouragan,* the French name for the Columbia River. It means "hurricane."

Oregon's History Trail

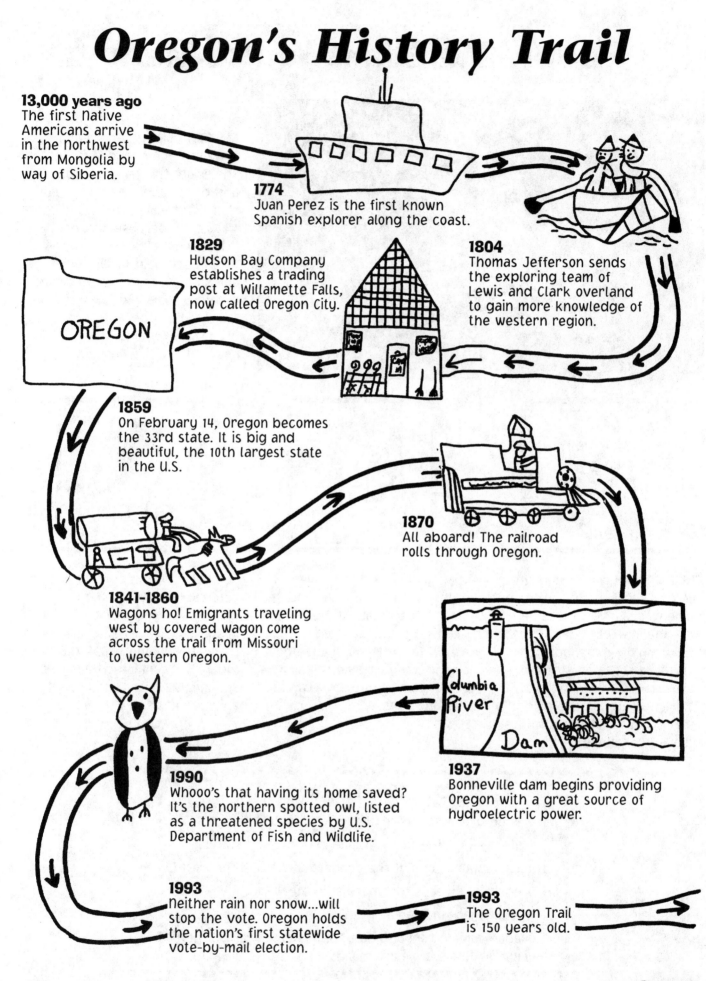

13,000 years ago
The first Native Americans arrive in the Northwest from Mongolia by way of Siberia.

1774
Juan Perez is the first known Spanish explorer along the coast.

1829
Hudson Bay Company establishes a trading post at Willamette Falls, now called Oregon City.

1804
Thomas Jefferson sends the exploring team of Lewis and Clark overland to gain more knowledge of the western region.

OREGON

1859
On February 14, Oregon becomes the 33rd state. It is big and beautiful, the 10th largest state in the U.S.

1870
All aboard! The railroad rolls through Oregon.

1841-1860
Wagons ho! Emigrants traveling west by covered wagon come across the trail from Missouri to western Oregon.

Columbia River

Dam

1990
Whooo's that having its home saved? It's the northern spotted owl, listed as a threatened species by U.S. Department of Fish and Wildlife.

1937
Bonneville dam begins providing Oregon with a great source of hydroelectric power.

1993
Neither rain nor snow...will stop the vote. Oregon holds the nation's first statewide vote-by-mail election.

1993
The Oregon Trail is 150 years old.

Places to Go, People to See

© Photodisc

Crater Lake is in the gorgeous Cascade Mountains. It lies in a sunken volcano.

For great skiing and timberline lodge, head for **Mt. Hood**.

A Whale of a Tale

Our very own movie star. That's Keiko, the orca whale that starred in *Free Willy*. Commonly called a killer whale, Keiko was freed—just as Willy was. Our whale lived in Mexico in a small tank. There, he became ill. His fans campaigned to get him a better home. And in 1996 he came to Oregon, where he got a nice roomy tank in which he could recover. His new home is in New Port on the Oregon coast.

WE LOVE HAPPY ENDINGS.

For further information to visitors:
Oregon Economic Development Department
Tourism Department
775 Summer St. NE
Salem, Oregon 97310
Oregon Tourist Commission Web site:
http://www.traveloregon.com

Mrs. Alexander's fourth-grade class at Vern Patrick Elementary school, Redmond, sends a huge hello! (And Mrs. Burton, our principal, does too!)

Pennsylvania

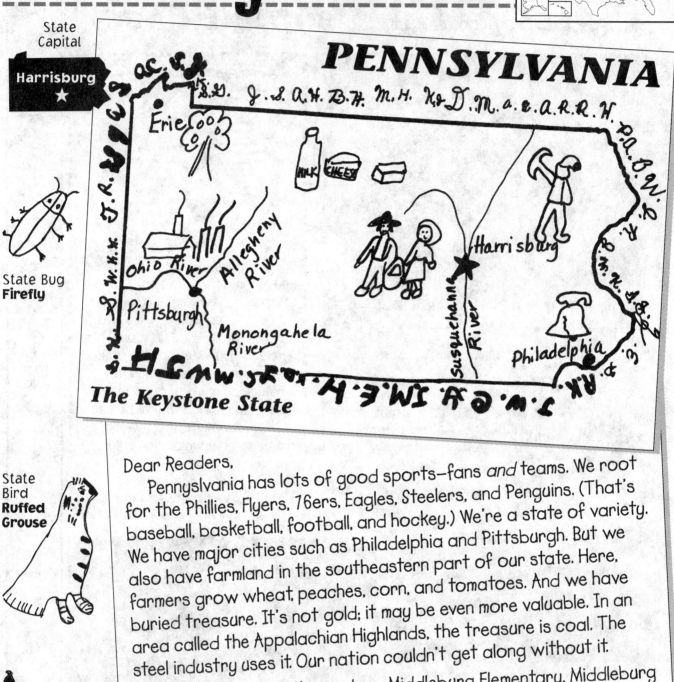

PENNSYLVANIA

Erie

Ohio River
Allegheny River
Pittsburgh
Monongahela River
Harrisburg
Susquehanna River
Philadelphia

The Keystone State

State Bug
Firefly

State Bird
Ruffed Grouse

Dear Readers,

Pennysylvania has lots of good sports–fans *and* teams. We root for the Phillies, Flyers, 76ers, Eagles, Steelers, and Penguins. (That's baseball, basketball, football, and hockey.) We're a state of variety. We have major cities such as Philadelphia and Pittsburgh. But we also have farmland in the southeastern part of our state. Here, farmers grow wheat, peaches, corn, and tomatoes. And we have buried treasure. It's not gold; it may be even more valuable. In an area called the Appalachian Highlands, the treasure is coal. The steel industry uses it. Our nation couldn't get along without it.

Mrs. Fincke's Fourth-graders, Middleburg Elementary, Middleburg

State Flag

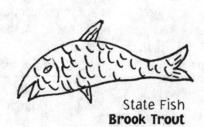

State Fish
Brook Trout

State Deer
White-tail Deer

Pennsylvania's Proud of...

The Great Man

Thomas Jefferson, who wrote the Declaration of Independence, said **William Penn** was "the greatest lawgiver the world has produced." Penn (1644–1718) came from a wealthy family in England. He believed that all people should be treated fairly. He said there should be freedom of religion. Because of his unusual beliefs, he was sent to prison several times.

In 1655, Penn saw a group called the Quakers remain in London to care for the sick during a terrible epidemic. He was very impressed. Like him, the Quakers bowed to no man and were against violence and war. Penn became a Quaker.

When the king of England repaid a debt to Penn with land in America, Penn decided to leave England. America seemed a place he and other Quakers could follow their beliefs freely and in peace. They called land on which they settled *Pennsylvania*, which means "Penn's Woods." There, as the first governor of Pennsylvania, Penn wrote a set of laws. He made treaties with Native Americans of the area that he never broke, saying, "I consider us all the same flesh and blood joined by one heart."

The Flag Lady

You can visit the house in which **Betsy Ross** lived in Philadelphia. It's said that, in 1776, she was asked to make the first flag for the brand-new United States. The flag had 13 red and white stripes, a field of blue, and a circle of 13 white stars. Ross completed the flag on June 14, 1777. That's why we celebrate Flag Day on June 14.

A Restless Pioneer

In one movie about his life, he was called the "King of the Wild Frontier." **Daniel Boone** was born on a farm near Reading in 1734. He had 10 brothers and sisters. As a child, he learned to hunt and to survive in the wild. In 1755, at the start of the French and Indian War, he served with the British Army. That's when he first saw western lands. A restless man, unhappy among groups of people, Boone spent his adult life on the move, clearing, settling, and farming. He had many adventures and died peacfully at the age of 86.

There Wasn't Anything He Couldn't Do

Benjamin Franklin came to Philadelphia from Boston when he was 17 years old. He found many ways to make his new home a better place. He planned the first library, hospital, and university. He organized firefighters, police, and street sweepers. He made discoveries about electricity, invented many useful things, and wrote books. Most of all, he helped write the first laws for the United States. We still follow them today.

Our Very Own Superstar

Everyone knows **Bill Cosby** from TV. This popular comedian grew up in Philadelphia and tells funny stories of his boyhood there. But he is more than an entertainer. Dr. William Cosby has a doctoral degree in education from Temple University in Philadelphia. He believes in the importance of education and spends a lot of time spreading the word about it.

The Doctor of Dunk

Julius Erving was a popular basketball player. His nickname was Dr. J. Traded to the Philadelphia 76ers in 1976, he was a skillful player known for his dazzling moves and soaring slam dunks. His electrifying play helped the 76ers reach the NBA finals four times, including the championship in 1983. When he retired in 1987, he had scored more than 30,000 career points.

10 Really Neat Things to Know About the Keystone State

1. Pennsylvania had the first radio station in the world, KDKA.
2. Little League baseball started in 1939 in Williamsport.
3. The Philadelphia Zoo was America's first zoo. It also had the country's first white lions.
4. Pennsylvania has 350 covered bridges, more than any other state.
5. Caves dot our state. It's said that the first colonial child was born in a cave.
6. On February 2, you can see if the groundhog will see his shadow at Punxsutawney.
7. The groudhog is known as Punxsutawney Phil.
8. The hills, valleys, and plains here were formed by glaciers more than one million years ago.
9. Pennsylvania products include glass, steel, cement, farming, and dairy products. Tourism also helps our economy.
10. We lead the country in mushrooms and in Christmas tree farming.

Pennsylvania's Early Days

Native Amercans live in Pennsylvania for more than 5,000 years before Europeans arrive.

1777-1778
George Washington's army spends the winter at Valley Forge.

1682
William Penn founds the colony of Pennsylvania.

1812
Harrisburg becomes the capital of Pennsylvania.

1850s
Henry Bessemer and William Kelly discover a new way to make steel.

1859
The first oil well is drilled by Edwin Drake in Titusville.

1852
The first Pennsylvania railroad is completed.

1872
The first tin cans are designed in Pittsburgh.

1905
America's first movie theater opens in Pittsburgh.

The Great Train Robbery

1863
The Battle of Gettysburg, biggest of the Civil War, takes place in Pennsylvania. Our state plays an important part in the war.

1879
Frank W. Woolworth opens the first five and dime in Lancaster.

158

Pennsylvania

Popular Pennsylvania Places

Chocolate World is located near a theme park called Hershey Park. There, a factory tour shows how Hershey makes its candy.

When you visit Clyde Peeling's **Reptiland**, you will see snakes, crocodiles, and turtles. It's fun to have a birthday party there.

You can learn all about the Civil War at **Gettysburg National Park**. This is where President Lincoln made the Gettysburg Address.

Hiking is great in the **Pennsylvania Grand Canyon**.

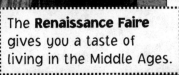

The **Renaissance Faire** gives you a taste of living in the Middle Ages.

For more information
Hershey-Carlisle Tourism & Convention Bureau
114 Walnut Street, P.O. Box 969
Harrisburg, PA 17108-0969
(717) 232-1377 or (800) 995-0969
http://www.state.pa.us

One of the world's finest collections of plants is at **Longwood Gardens**—more than 11,000 types of plants. Be sure to roam through the topiary garden.

Mrs. Fincke's and Mrs. Hackenberg's fourth-grade team at Middleburg Elementary.

The **Liberty Bell** rang from 1776 to 1835 when it cracked at the funeral of Chief Justice John Marshall. You can see it in a park near Independence Hall.

Rhode Island

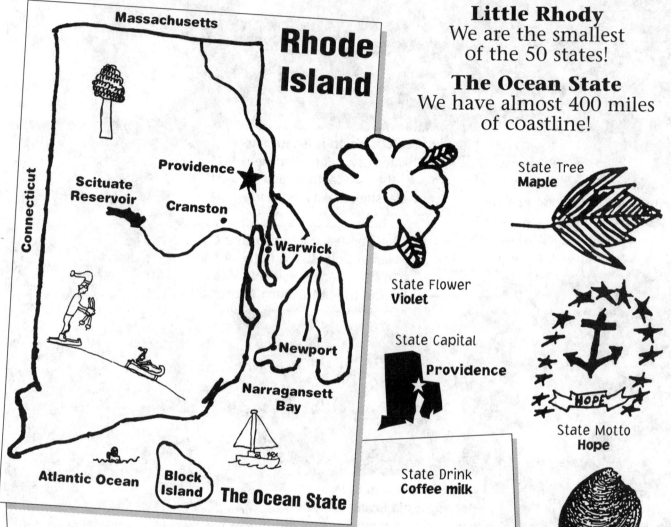

Massachusetts

Rhode Island

Connecticut

Scituate Reservoir

Providence ★

Cranston

Warwick

Newport

Narragansett Bay

Atlantic Ocean

Block Island

The Ocean State

Little Rhody
We are the smallest of the 50 states!

The Ocean State
We have almost 400 miles of coastline!

State Flower
Violet

State Tree
Maple

State Capital
★ **Providence**

State Motto
Hope

HOPE

State Drink
Coffee milk

State shell
Quahog

Dear Friends,
   We may be a small state, but we're big in sights, nature, and history. We have interesting cities. Our capital, Providence, has many neighborhoods to explore—each with a character all its own. We have many important schools, including the University of Rhode Island, Brown University, and the Rhode Island School of Design. We have farms and factories. But, best of all, we have the most beautiful wide, sandy beaches. Some have dunes. And, if you go to a little beach town called Watch Hill, you can ride on a real old carousel. Maybe you'll grab the brass ring. We feel as if we already have—'cause we live in Rhode Island!
   Mrs. Treichler's Fourth-Grade Class,
   B. F. Norton School, Cumberland

State Bird
Rhode Island Red Hen

They're Big in Little Rhody

If it weren't for **SAMUEL SLATER**, what would we wear? He founded the cotton industry in the U.S. and opened the first spinning mill in the U.S. It's called Slater Mill.

JULIA WARD HOWE, who lived from 1819 to 1910, spent her long life trying to make the world better. She worked for women's rights. And she supported the end of slavery. She wrote the words for "The Battle Hymn of the Republic." She also wrote poetry and articles about issues that were important to her.

AMBROSE BURNSIDE was a general in the Civil War. Do you know anyone with sideburns? His thick whiskers gave them the name!

When **ROGER WILLIAMS** founded Providence in 1636, he declared that all people who lived there could worship as they pleased.

GILBERT STUART was a portrait painter who is probably best known for his paintings of our first president, George Washington.

NICHOLAS COLASANTO was a much-loved and special TV and film actor. Just before his death in 1985, he played the role of Coach Ernie Pantusso on the TV show *Cheers*.

Born in 1933, **WILLIAM ANDERS**, a pilot and astronaut, was on the crew of *Apollo 8*. He was on the first piloted spacecraft to circle the moon. He set several world flight records. He was also the president of the conglomerate Texton Inc.

HOW TO SPEAK RHODE ISLAND

In R.I.	In U.S.
johnnycake	doughboy
hamburgs	hamburgers
ng	no good
blinkers	turning signals
pahster	pasta
summa	summer
grinder	sandwich
cabinet	milkshake
bubbler	fountain

TWO SPECIAL REASONS TO LIKE LIVING IN LITTLE RHODY

1 Del's Lemonade is what people in other places might call frozen lemonade. It is crushed ice with lemon flavoring and is very refreshing. You can get it only in the warm months. It began in Cranston.

2 Rhode Island's official state drink is coffee milk. It was first introduced in the early 1920s. It is made by mixing coffee syrup (just like chocolate) into milk. It really became popular in the 1940s. If you ask for it in your state, you may get a blank stare!

Meeting Natalie Babbitt

NATALIE BABBITT, a well-known children's book author who lives in Rhode Island, came to visit our class. Mrs. Babbitt originally wanted to be an illustrator. Instead, at the age of 33, she wrote her first book, *Dick Foot and the Shark*. Other popular books she wrote are *Bub, Tuck Everlasting, Knee Knock Rise,* and *The Search for Delicious*. It was a great book. Natalie Babbitt likes Rhode Island's lakes and ocean areas and its small size.

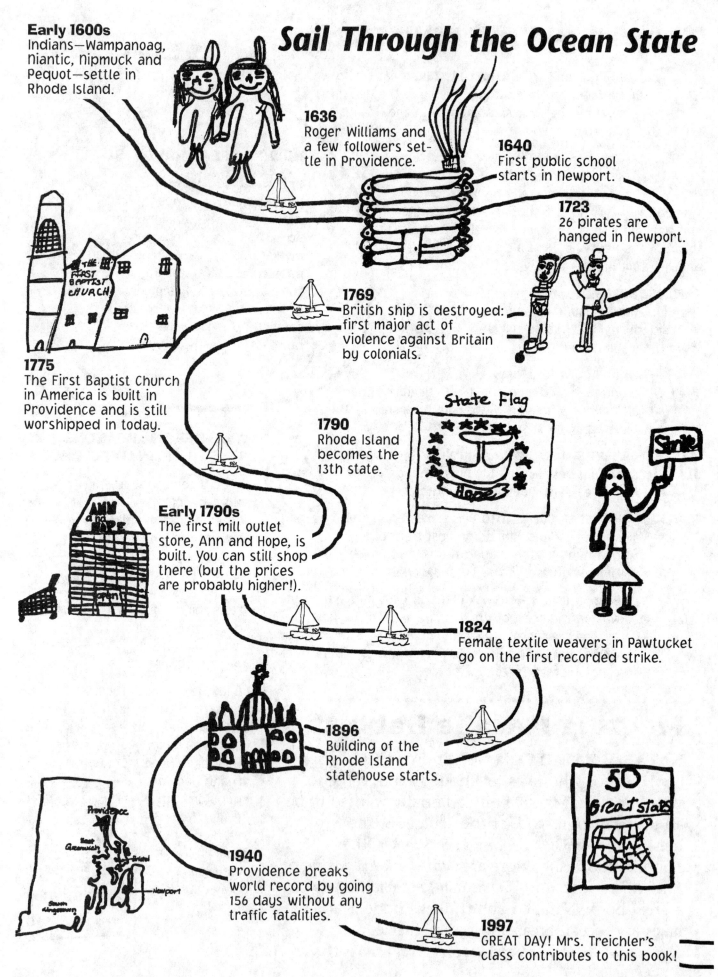

Sail Through the Ocean State

Early 1600s
Indians—Wampanoag, Niantic, Nipmuck and Pequot—settle in Rhode Island.

1636
Roger Williams and a few followers settle in Providence.

1640
First public school starts in Newport.

1723
26 pirates are hanged in Newport.

1769
British ship is destroyed: first major act of violence against Britain by colonials.

1775
The First Baptist Church in America is built in Providence and is still worshipped in today.

1790
Rhode Island becomes the 13th state.

State Flag

Hope

Strike

Early 1790s
The first mill outlet store, Ann and Hope, is built. You can still shop there (but the prices are probably higher!).

1824
Female textile weavers in Pawtucket go on the first recorded strike.

1896
Building of the Rhode Island statehouse starts.

50 Great state

1940
Providence breaks world record by going 156 days without any traffic fatalities.

1997
GREAT DAY! Mrs. Treichler's class contributes to this book!

Rocking Through Rhode Island

The **Pawtucket Red Sox** are the Boston Red Sox's farm team. They play at McCoy Stadium in Pawtucket. Come see a game.

We interviewed **Don Bousquet**, who drew this cartoon for us. He has an unlimited number of characters he uses that represent family members, friends, and himself. His favorite character is the Qua Hog, which is our state shell. Don Bousquet lives in Narragansett. He says he chose Rhode Island to live in because he was born here, his family lives here, people in R.I. love his books, and he loves it!

Rhode Island's **statehouse** is 235 feet high. It has the 4th largest unsupported dome in the world.

Newport mansions were the summer houses of the rich and famous. They are definitely a sight to see.

Slater Mill was built in 1793 by Samuel Slater. It was our nation's first operational mill. Today it is a museum.

For further information contact:
Tourism Division of Rhode Island
1 West Exchange Street
Providence, RI 02903
http://www.RIEDC.com

RI Tourism Division

Block Island is 1 of 36 islands in Rhode Island. People go there to relax or for sand, sun, and fun. Rhode Island has more than 400 miles of coastline.

Hello from Mrs. Treichler and her fourth-grade class at Bernard F. Norton School in Cumberland.

South Carolina

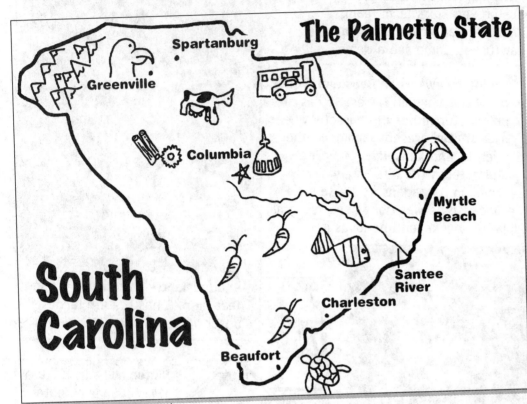

The Palmetto State

Spartanburg

Greenville

Columbia

Myrtle Beach

Santee River

Charleston

Beaufort

South Carolina

State Capital
Columbia

State Reptile
Loggerhead Sea Turtle

State Flower
Yellow Jasmine

Dear Friends,

We're having a ball in South Carolina! The weather is great. The beaches are just waiting for someone to take a swim. You can get a nice tan and be on your way to the Midlands, to visit the capital. You can go for a hike in the mountains of the Uplands and take your rope to rappel back down. We have beautiful wildlife, such as loggerhead turtles. Did we forget the bald eagle? It soars over us. So come on down to South Carolina. From the mountains to the sea, it's the place you want to be!

Y'all come down now,

Mr. Embrey's Class, James J. Davis Elementary School, Dale

State Bird
Wren

State Flag

Did you know...?

The tree on the state flag is the Palmetto tree. Not only is it the state tree but it has also earned a place in history. During the Revolutionary War, a fort was made of Palmetto trees to fight a British fleet. When the British fired their cannons, the cannon balls just bounced off the walls. The trees and sand made the walls like rubber. The Americans won the battle and the British left. Because the tree helped win the battle it was placed on the state flag.

South Carolina R-R-R-Rap

South Carolina is the place to be.
It feels just right for you and me.
With the wren, jasmine, and palmetto tree,
South Carolina has lots of hist'ry

Only gold producer east of the Mississippi River

First shots of the War Between the States fired at Ft. Sumter

First state to secede from the Union before the War Between the States

Although there are mountains, there is no skiing due to lack of snow.

One of the original 13 colonies

First state to use the Adopt-A-Highway Program

Far Out S.C. Facts

Oldest Senator in history: Strom Thurmond age 94, in 1997

More Facts About the Palmetto State

Capital: Columbia

Population: 3,673,287 (1995)

Area: 32,008 square miles

Highest Point: Sassafras Mountain (3,560 ft.)

Lowest Point: many beaches (sea level)

Main Rivers: Pee Dee, Savannah, Santee

Climate: humid subtropical and humid continental (in the mountains)

South Carolina

Cool South Carolinians

Mary McLeod Bethune (1875-1955)

Ms. Bethune was an African American who led the fight for equal rights through example. She was an educator who started Bethune-Cookman College and held important positions.

Ron and Natalie Daise

Ron and Natalie Daise are from the Beaufort area. They are the stars of the children's show *Gullah Gullah Island* on Nickelodeon.

Representative James E. Clyburn

Mr. Clyburn is a United States representative. His district includes parts of Low Country region.

(Smokin') Joe Frazier

Joe Frazier was one of the greatest heavyweight boxers of the 20th century. He made his way from poor beginnings to world stardom in the boxing ring.

Edward Rutledge (1749-1800)

Mr. Rutledge was one of the two South Carolinians to sign the Declaration of Independence. He was a statesman who helped lead South Carolina in the early years of the United States.

Jonathan Green

He is a nationally known painter. His paintings can be seen all over the country.

Katie Coleman

Ms. Coleman is one of many astronauts who have called South Carolina home. She, like the others, is always in training to be ready to go into space.

Hootie and the Blowfish

This band that plays Top 40 music has several albums out. "Time" is one of their most famous songs. They formed in Columbia and are very popular throughout South Carolina and the country.

River of Time

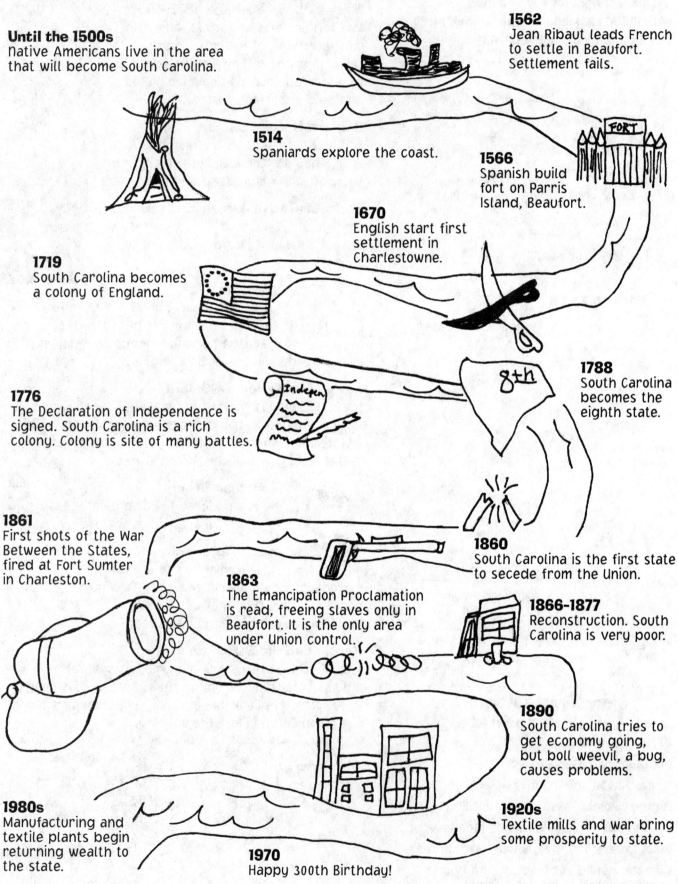

Until the 1500s
Native Americans live in the area that will become South Carolina.

1562
Jean Ribaut leads French to settle in Beaufort. Settlement fails.

1514
Spaniards explore the coast.

1566
Spanish build fort on Parris Island, Beaufort.

1670
English start first settlement in Charlestowne.

1719
South Carolina becomes a colony of England.

1788
South Carolina becomes the eighth state.

1776
The Declaration of Independence is signed. South Carolina is a rich colony. Colony is site of many battles.

1861
First shots of the War Between the States, fired at Fort Sumter in Charleston.

1860
South Carolina is the first state to secede from the Union.

1863
The Emancipation Proclamation is read, freeing slaves only in Beaufort. It is the only area under Union control.

1866-1877
Reconstruction. South Carolina is very poor.

1890
South Carolina tries to get economy going, but boll weevil, a bug, causes problems.

1980s
Manufacturing and textile plants begin returning wealth to the state.

1920s
Textile mills and war bring some prosperity to state.

1970
Happy 300th Birthday!

From the Mountains to the Sea...

Ranger Mike Walker from Hunting Island State Park works with *Gullah Gullah Island*. His first job is to be a ranger for his park. The television show is his second job. He says he likes doing it, but he is not a show-off. Ranger Mike doesn't watch the shows very much. He told us that the house on the show is actually in Florida, but the beach is in Beaufort.

The **State House** in Columbia is great to visit, but not when it is under construction.

Storms and **hurricanes** are not rare on the coast.

The **Yorktown** is a museum that used to be an aircraft carrier. There are other ships in Charleston to see too.

The park ranger gives talks about the history of **Fort Sumter**.

During the War Between the States, some raised grave sites at **churches in Beaufort** were used as operating tables.

Riding a carriage is a fun way to see **historical places** in Charleston and Beaufort.

Mr. Embrey and his intermediate multiage class from James J. Davis Elementary

Tourist Information
S.C. Dept. of Parks, Recreation & Tourism
1205 Pendleton St., Columbia, SC 29201
http://www.travelsc.com/home.html

South Carolina

South Dakota

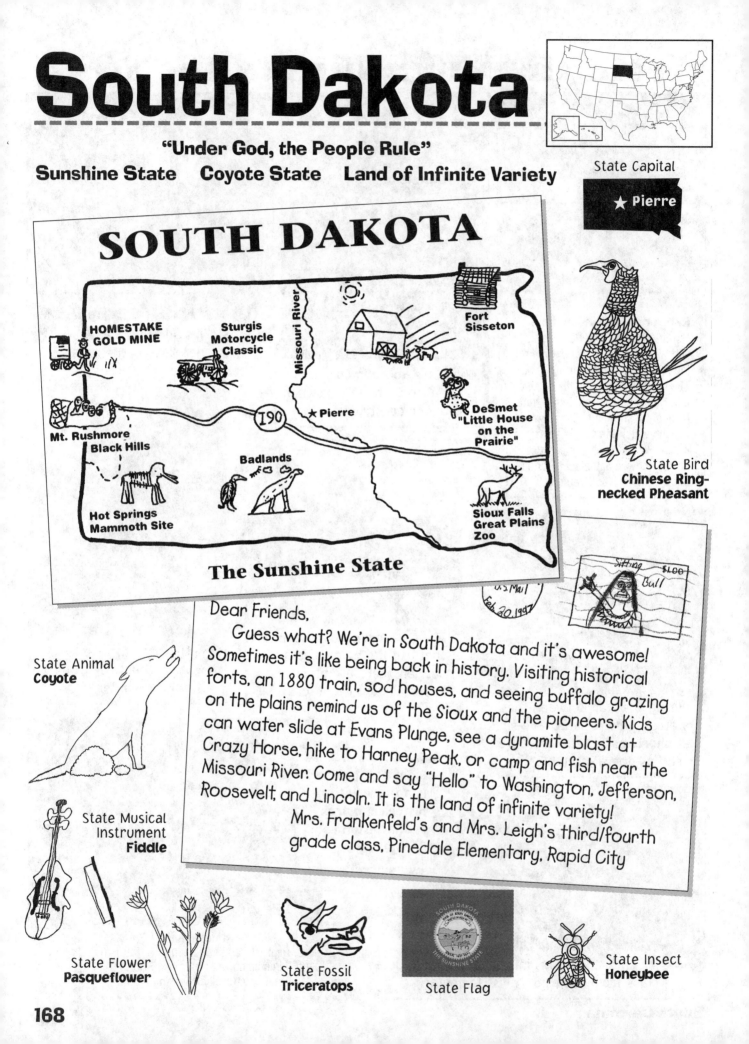

"Under God, the People Rule"

Sunshine State   **Coyote State**   **Land of Infinite Variety**

State Capital
★ Pierre

SOUTH DAKOTA

HOMESTAKE GOLD MINE

Sturgis Motorcycle Classic

Missouri River

Fort Sisseton

★ Pierre

I90

DeSmet "Little House on the Prairie"

Mt. Rushmore Black Hills

Badlands

Hot Springs Mammoth Site

Sioux Falls Great Plains Zoo

The Sunshine State

State Bird
Chinese Ring-necked Pheasant

Sitting Bull $1.00
U.S. Mail Feb. 20, 1997

State Animal
Coyote

Dear Friends,
　　Guess what? We're in South Dakota and it's awesome! Sometimes it's like being back in history. Visiting historical forts, an 1880 train, sod houses, and seeing buffalo grazing on the plains remind us of the Sioux and the pioneers. Kids can water slide at Evans Plunge, see a dynamite blast at Crazy Horse, hike to Harney Peak, or camp and fish near the Missouri River. Come and say "Hello" to Washington, Jefferson, Roosevelt, and Lincoln. It is the land of infinite variety!
　　Mrs. Frankenfeld's and Mrs. Leigh's third/fourth grade class, Pinedale Elementary, Rapid City

State Musical Instrument
Fiddle

State Flower
Pasqueflower

State Fossil
Triceratops

State Flag

State Insect
Honeybee

MONUMENTAL FACTS

George Washington — One of my eyes is five feet higher than the other!

Thomas Jefferson — South Dakota has a palace made of corn!

Theodore Roosevelt — Ten school buses can fit inside Crazy Horse Monument's armpit!

Abraham Lincoln — My nose on Mt. Rushmore is bigger than Egypt's *Sphinx!*

State Facts

Statehood . . . . November 2, 1889
Population 729,034 (1995)
U.S. Congress . . . . . 2 senators, 1 representative
Land Area . . . . 77,116 sq. miles
(17th largest state)
Highest Point . . . . . Harney Peak (7,242 ft.)

Crops

Corn makes up almost 50% of the state's crops. The world's only corn palace is in Mitchell.

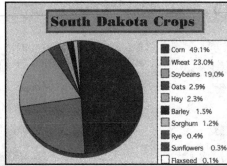

South Dakota Crops

- Corn 49.1%
- Wheat 23.0%
- Soybeans 19.0%
- Oats 2.9%
- Hay 2.3%
- Barley 1.5%
- Sorghum 1.2%
- Rye 0.4%
- Sunflowers 0.3%
- Flaxseed 0.1%

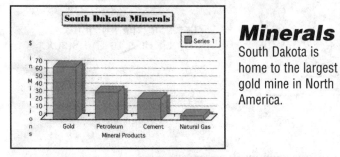

South Dakota Minerals

Series 1

$ in Millions — 0, 10, 20, 30, 40, 50, 60, 70

Gold, Petroleum, Cement, Natural Gas

Mineral Products

Minerals

South Dakota is home to the largest gold mine in North America.

Animals

Big Mammals	Small Mammals	Birds	Fish
Elk	Snowshoe Hare	Pheasant	Trout
Antelope	Squirrel	Partridge	Salmon
Bighorn Sheep	Prairie Dog	Grouse	Perch
Bison	Badger	Prairie	Sturgeon
Mountain Goat	Marten	Chicken	Smelt
Cougar	Fisher	Eagle	Pike
Wolf	Oppossum	Falcon	Bass
Black Bear		Woodchuck	Sunfish
Deer			Mooneye
			Sucker
			Catfish
			Drum
			Minnow

Famous South Dakotans

James Butler Hickok (1837–1876) was shot and killed while playing poker in a saloon in Deadwood. The hand he held was a pair of eights and a pair of aces and is known as the "dead man's hand."

Martha Jane Canary (1852–1903), better know as **Calamity Jane**, wasn't an ordinary woman. She dressed like a man and was a great shot with a gun. She served as a scout with the U.S. Cavalry and carried mail between Custer, South Dakota, Montana, and Deadwood, South Dakota.

Sitting Bull was one of the leaders who crushed General Custer's forces at the Battle of Little Big Horn. Sitting Bull was born near what is now Bullhead, South Dakota. He was a great medicine man and religious leader. He also planned the Battle of Little Big Horn. His real name is Tatanka Yotanka. Sitting Bull was arrested on December 15, 1890. He was shot and killed during a rescue attempt.

Gutzon Borglum (1867–1941) carved the faces of Mt. Rushmore. He was a painter, sculptor, engineer, inventor, statesman, and author. He started work on Mt. Rushmore but died in 1941 before it was completed. His son, Lincoln, continued the work.

Tom Brokaw (1940–), the anchor of NBC's *Nightly News*, was born in Webster. He was educated at the University of South Dakota in Vermillion.

Korczak Ziolkowski (1909–1982) was sculptor of Chief Crazy Horse out of Thunderhead Mountain. Although he was born in Boston, Ziolkowski spent the last half of his life in South Dakota. The Sioux people invited Ziolkowski to carve a memorial for them. Korczak referred to himself as a "storyteller in stone."

Thomas A. Daschle (1947–) is our senator and is the leader of the senate minority. He was born in Aberdeen. He was the first South Dakotan to hold a Senate leadership position.

South Dakota Time Tracks

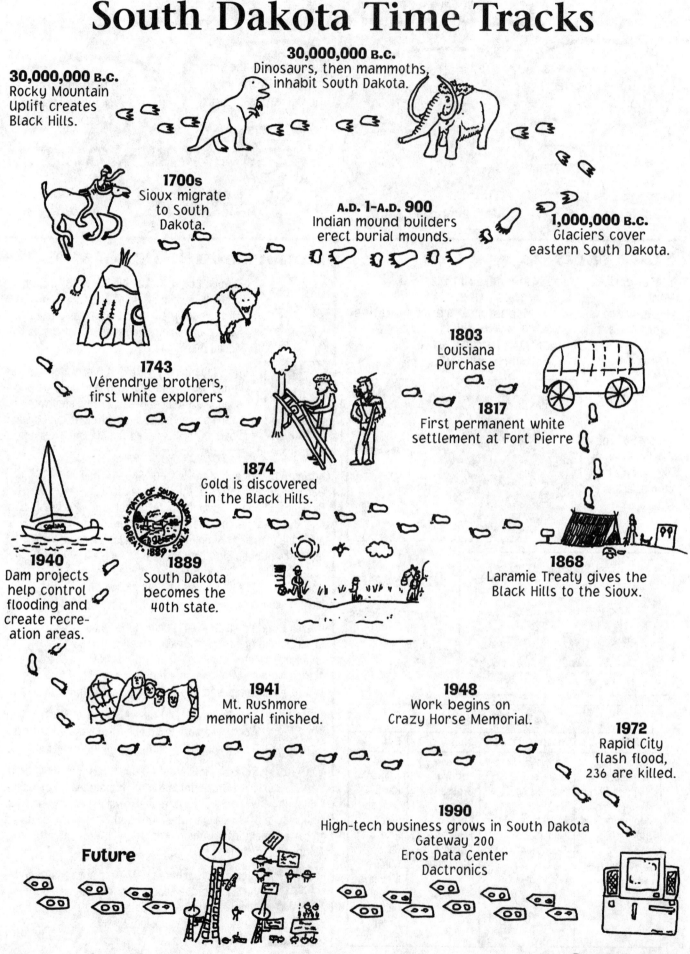

30,000,000 B.C.
Rocky Mountain Uplift creates Black Hills.

30,000,000 B.C.
Dinosaurs, then mammoths, inhabit South Dakota.

1,000,000 B.C.
Glaciers cover eastern South Dakota.

A.D. 1–A.D. 900
Indian mound builders erect burial mounds.

1700s
Sioux migrate to South Dakota.

1743
Vérendrye brothers, first white explorers

1803
Louisiana Purchase

1817
First permanent white settlement at Fort Pierre

1874
Gold is discovered in the Black Hills.

1868
Laramie Treaty gives the Black Hills to the Sioux.

1940
Dam projects help control flooding and create recreation areas.

1889
South Dakota becomes the 40th state.

1941
Mt. Rushmore memorial finished.

1948
Work begins on Crazy Horse Memorial.

1972
Rapid City flash flood, 236 are killed.

1990
High-tech business grows in South Dakota
Gateway 200
Eros Data Center
Dactronics

Future

South Dakota Photo Album

Mt. Rushmore, the largest sculpture in the world, was started by sculptor Gutzon Borglum in 1927. It contains the faces of four great presidents: George Washington, Thomas Jefferson, Theodore Roosevelt, and Abraham Lincoln. You can learn more about this in the new visitor center building.

Our state capital is **Pierre**. Pierre has great fishing areas, one of which is the Missouri River. If you like engineering feats like the Oahe Dam or following the trail of Lewis and Clark, Pierre is the place for you! Come to our Cultural Heritage Center.

Harney Peak is a 7,242-foot-high mountain. It is the highest point between the Rocky Mountains and Europe. If you hike it, you can see an extraordinary view. Harney Peak is located in Custer State Park. The hike to the top is an old jeep trail. It leads to an old fire lookout tower.

Crazy Horse was a brave warrior and chief of the Oglala Sioux Indians. You can see Crazy Horse being sculpted out of a mountain in the Black Hills of South Dakota today. The Crazy Horse mountain carving now in progress will be the world's largest sculpture when completed. Almost 8 million tons of rock have been blasted away already.

South Dakota Department of Tourism
711 E. Wells Avenue
Pierre, SD 57501-3369
(605) 773-3301
http://www.state.sd.us/state/tourism

South Dakota

171

Tennessee

Come See Tennessee!

Reelfoot Lake

Mississippi River

World's Largest Fish

Paris

Memphis

Tennessee River

Shiloh National Battlefield

Clarksville Home of Wilma Rudolph

Nashville

Chattanooga

Lookout Mountain

Big South Fork National Recreation Area

Tennessee River

Knoxville

Smoky Mountains

Dear Friends,

We're having fun in Tennessee! There's so much to do here. There's great action on the field at University of Tennessee football games. You can see sharks in tanks three stories tall at the Tennessee Aquarium in Chattanooga. For exciting rides and great music we have Opryland and Dollywood theme parks. We have three zoos with exotic animals from all over the world and a few children's museums. More music is recorded in Nashville than anywhere else in the world. Tennessee even hosts the World's Biggest Fish Fry in Paris every year. THERE'S A LOT TO SEE IN TENNESSEE!

From Mary Lou Reed's Sixth Graders, Oakmont Elementary, Dickson

Tennessee Trivia

Capital: Nashville, Music City, U.S.A.

Nickname: Volunteer State (because Tennessee has played such important roles in all the wars since the War of 1812).

Tennessee's name probably came from "Tanasi," a large Overhill Cherokee town in East Tennessee.

Three presidents called Tennessee home even though none were born here: Andrew Jackson, James K. Polk, and Andrew Johnson. All three are buried in Tennessee.

Happy Birthday Tennessee! The state celebrated it's 200th year of statehood in 1996 with parades, block parties, concerts, art exhibits, and quilt shows. We opened the Tennessee Bicentennial Mall State Park where each county has a time capsule to be opened in 2096!

Top Student Picks for Fun Places to See in Tennessee

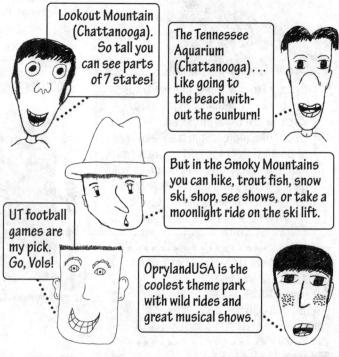

Lookout Mountain (Chattanooga). So tall you can see parts of 7 states!

The Tennessee Aquarium (Chattanooga)... Like going to the beach without the sunburn!

But in the Smoky Mountains you can hike, trout fish, snow ski, shop, see shows, or take a moonlight ride on the ski lift.

UT football games are my pick. Go, Vols!

OprylandUSA is the coolest theme park with wild rides and great musical shows.

Can You Name These Famous Leaders of Tennessee?
(Match the clue to the face in the picture.)

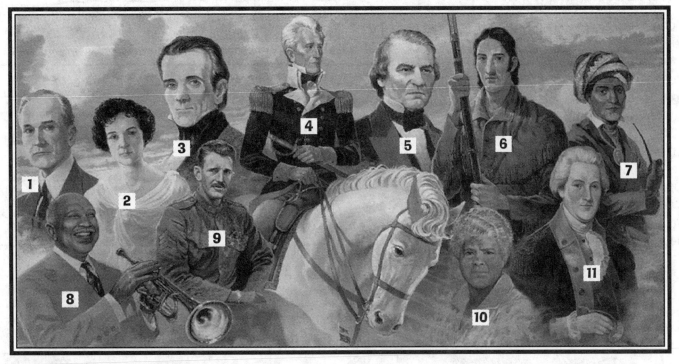

a. Alvin C. York, World War I hero

b. John Sevier, first Tennessee governor

c. James K. Polk, U.S. President who annexed Texas, California, Oregon, and New Mexico Territory

d. Sequoyah, developed the Cherokee alphabet

e. Andrew Jackson, U.S. president nicknamed "Old Hickory"

f. David Crockett, hero killed at the Alamo

g. Ida B. Wells Barnett, famous speaker and publisher of an antilynching newspaper in England

h. Cordell Hull, longest-serving U.S. secretary of state

i. Anne Dallas Dudley, president of National Woman Suffrage Association that helped ratify the 19th Amendment

j. Andrew Johnson, only U.S. president to be impeached

k. W. C. Handy, Father of the Blues

Tennessee Treasures

T is for the **Tennessee River** that runs through our state.

E is for the **eagles** that winter at Reelfoot Lake.

N is for **Nashville**, Music City, U.S.A.

N is for the **Natchez Trace**, a travelers' route for centuries.

E is for the **essential** pioneer Spirit that settled our state.

S is for the **Smoky Mountains** that border us on the east.

S is for the Tennessee **State Museum** full of important artifacts.

E is for **events** like the Old-time Fiddlers' Contest and Roly Hole Tournament and the National Walking Horse Celebration.

E is for **everything** that's special about Tennessee!

State Insect
Ladybug

State Bird
Mockingbird

State Capital

Davy Crockett's 'coon skin cap

1982 World's Fair Sunsphere

Wilma Rudolph's Olympic Gold

Key to Famous Leaders: a=9, b=11, c=3, d=7, e=4, f=6, g=10, h=1, i=2, j=5, k=8

DIGGING INTO TENNESSEE'S PAST

Archaeologists in Tennessee have found many fossils and artifacts at sites throughout the state. These help archaeologists piece together the history of Tennessee. Many of these artifacts can be seen in exhibits at museums like the Tennessee State Museum (Nashville), the McClung Museum (Knoxville), and Mud Island (Memphis). They all help tell the story of the great state of Tennessee.

Dig with this archaeologist into the layers of Tennessee's past to see the animals and people that lived here.

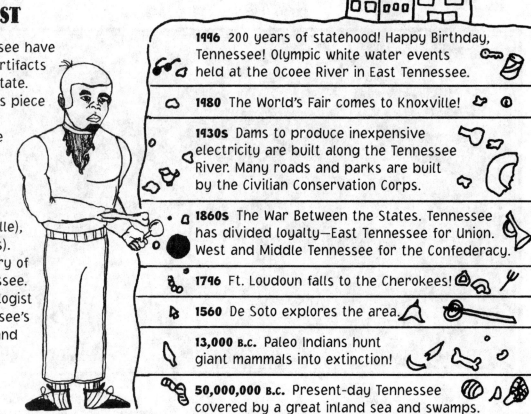

1996 200 years of statehood! Happy Birthday, Tennessee! Olympic white water events held at the Ocoee River in East Tennessee.

1980 The World's Fair comes to Knoxville!

1930s Dams to produce inexpensive electricity are built along the Tennessee River. Many roads and parks are built by the Civilian Conservation Corps.

1860s The War Between the States. Tennessee has divided loyalty—East Tennessee for Union. West and Middle Tennessee for the Confederacy.

1796 Ft. Loudoun falls to the Cherokees!

1560 De Soto explores the area.

13,000 B.C. Paleo Indians hunt giant mammals into extinction!

50,000,000 B.C. Present-day Tennessee covered by a great inland sea and swamps.

Other Famous Tennesseans: Texas freedom fighter Sam Houston, Civil War Admiral David Farragut; Vice President Al Gore; Senator Howard Baker; Singers Uncle Dave Macon, Minnie Pearl, Bessie Smith, Dolly Parton, Tina Turner; Talk show hostess Oprah Winfrey; Author Alex Haley; Olympic Winner Wilma Rudolph; Actress Cybill Shepard; Actor Alan Jackson

TENNESSEE HEROES FOR TODAY

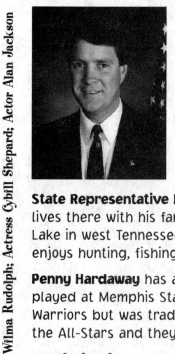

Dr. Bill Frist is a U.S. senator and a heart surgeon from Nashville. Senator Frist has three children. His favorite place to visit as a boy was Cumberland Mountain State Park in Crossville. Now his favorite Tennessee site is Jonesboro, home of the national storytelling festival. Frist thinks the most important thing for today's youth is to get the BEST education so they will have the opportunity to have the American dream and be what they want to be in life.

State Representative Doug Jackson was born and raised in Dickson and still lives there with his family. As a kid his favorite place to visit was Kentucky Lake in west Tennessee. Now his favorite place to visit is at home where he enjoys hunting, fishing, and playing different sports with his own kids.

Penny Hardaway has a great NBA career. He is from Memphis and played at Memphis State. Penny was drafted to the Golden State Warriors but was traded to the Orlando Magics. He was voted onto the All-Stars and they won. Hardaway played on the 1996 Olympic U.S. Dream Team.

Did you know...? Krystal (that hamburger place with the tiny square burgers on tiny square buns) started in Chattanooga in 1932. There's a country music star with hair down to her feet (Crystal Gayle). Elvis Presley is buried in the backyard of his Memphis mansion, Graceland. You could be a movie star (or at least an extra) in Tennessee where lots of movies like **Ernest Goes to Camp**, **Jungle Book**, and **Pure Country** have been filmed.

Traveling Through Tennessee

Celebrating Tennessee's 200th Birthday
Tennessee 1796–1996

1996 was our state's bicentennial. Here are a few things you might have seen if you'd decided to visit us.

This bridge on the **Natchez Trace Parkway** is the only bridge like this in the world. It is 155 feet tall.

Tennessee still has many **small farms** in scenic rural areas.

History come alive at sites like **Fort Loudoun** in East Tennessee.

Andrew visited **Pilot's Knob**, the site of a Confederate victory. This tall bluff was used by riverboat pilots as a navigation landmark because it is the highest spot on the Tennessee River in West Tennessee.

Nathan inspects a monument at **Stones River National Park**, which commemorates one of the many Civil War battles fought in Tennessee.

Mrs. Reed's family enjoys fishing in one of the many lakes found in Tennessee's **56 state parks**.

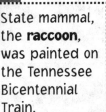

State mammal, the **raccoon**, was painted on the Tennessee Bicentennial Train.

Here are some of us doing a little research for the book. Kristen, Joey, Arlington, and Rebecca were camera shy and are not pictured.

For more information:
Tennessee Tourism
320 6th Avenue North
Nashville, TN 37202
(615)741-2159
Tennessee State Parks
401 Church Street
Nashville, TN 37243-0440
(800)421-6683
http://www.state.tn.us

Texas

State Capital
Austin

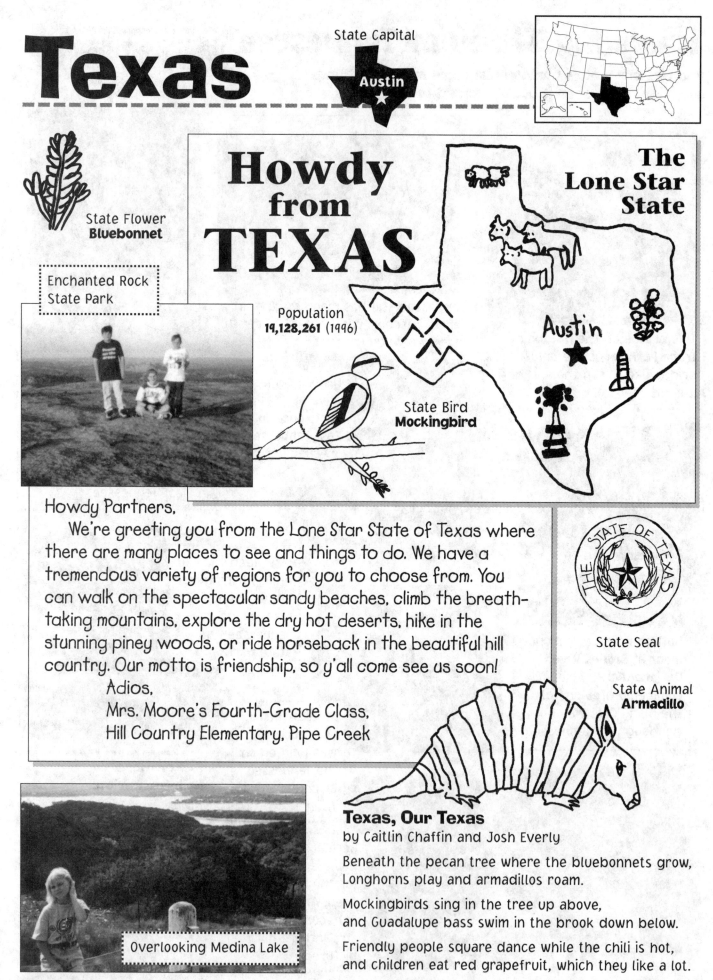

State Flower
Bluebonnet

Enchanted Rock
State Park

Howdy from TEXAS

The Lone Star State

Population
19,128,261 (1996)

Austin

State Bird
Mockingbird

Howdy Partners,

We're greeting you from the Lone Star State of Texas where there are many places to see and things to do. We have a tremendous variety of regions for you to choose from. You can walk on the spectacular sandy beaches, climb the breathtaking mountains, explore the dry hot deserts, hike in the stunning piney woods, or ride horseback in the beautiful hill country. Our motto is friendship, so y'all come see us soon!

Adios,
Mrs. Moore's Fourth-Grade Class,
Hill Country Elementary, Pipe Creek

State Seal

State Animal
Armadillo

Texas, Our Texas
by Caitlin Chaffin and Josh Everly

Beneath the pecan tree where the bluebonnets grow,
Longhorns play and armadillos roam.

Mockingbirds sing in the tree up above,
and Guadalupe bass swim in the brook down below.

Friendly people square dance while the chili is hot,
and children eat red grapefruit, which they like a lot.

Overlooking Medina Lake

TALL TEXANS

Davy Crockett was best known in history as one of the brave Texas patriots who lost their lives in the battle of the Alamo.

Sam Houston's army freed Texas from Mexico, and he became the first president of Texas.

Two U.S. presidents were born in Texas: **Dwight D. Eisenhower**, who served from 1953 to 1961, and **Lyndon B. Johnson**, who served from 1963 to 1969.

Country music star **George Strait** is from Texas.

Barbara Jordan grew up in Houston. She became a U.S. representative, lawyer, and teacher.

Baseball legend **Nolan Ryan** holds the major league record for the most strikeouts in a lifetime—5,668!

Ty Murray, who has been the World Champion All Around Cowboy for six years, lives in Texas.

Davy Crockett

Sam Houston

Dwight D. Eisenhower

Lyndon B. Johnson

Nolan Ryan

Ty Murray

STRANGE BUT TRUE

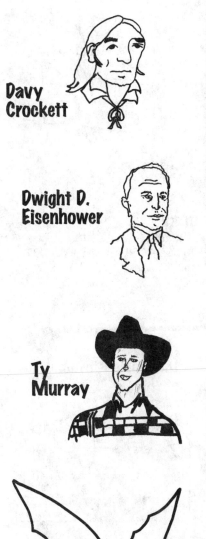

One of the **world's largest bat colonies** (20,000,000) lives in Bracken Cave near Austin.

Govenor James Hogg named his daughter Ima in 1882. That's **Ima Hogg**, as in "I'm a hog!"

Have you ever seen a **jackelope**? We have! It looks like a jackrabbit with deer antlers.

Texas has seven professional **sports teams**.

The name Texas came from the Spanish word *tejas*, which means "friends."

Four **poisonous snakes** live in Texas: copperhead, coral, cottonmouth, and rattlesnake.

Texas has more than 4,000 species of **wildflowers**; some grow along our state's more than 70,000 miles of highway.

New England, New York, Pennsylvania, and Ohio could fit inside Texas.

In 1984, a Beaumont girl set the record for the **longest name** on a birth certificate: Rhoshandiatellyneshiaunneveshenk Koyaanisquatsiuty Williams.

Dinosaur Valley State Park in Glen Rose is famous for the enormous dinosaur prints along the Paluxy River.

Texas Through Time

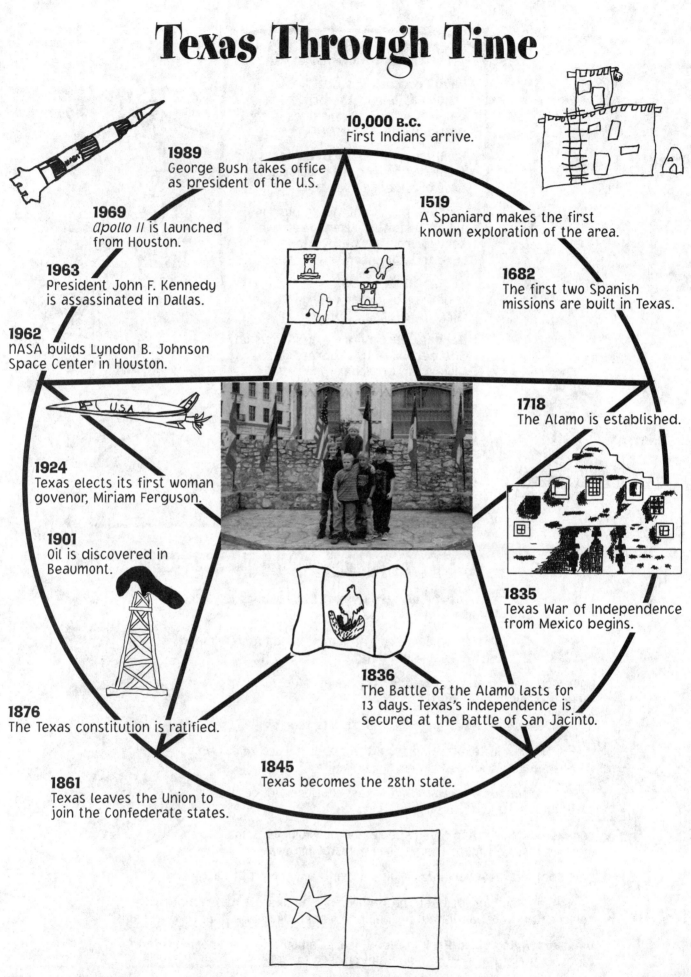

10,000 B.C.
First Indians arrive.

1989
George Bush takes office as president of the U.S.

1519
A Spaniard makes the first known exploration of the area.

1969
Apollo 11 is launched from Houston.

1682
The first two Spanish missions are built in Texas.

1963
President John F. Kennedy is assassinated in Dallas.

1962
NASA builds Lyndon B. Johnson Space Center in Houston.

1718
The Alamo is established.

1924
Texas elects its first woman govenor, Miriam Ferguson.

1901
Oil is discovered in Beaumont.

1835
Texas War of Independence from Mexico begins.

1876
The Texas constitution is ratified.

1836
The Battle of the Alamo lasts for 13 days. Texas's independence is secured at the Battle of San Jacinto.

1845
Texas becomes the 28th state.

1861
Texas leaves the Union to join the Confederate states.

TAKE A TRIP TO TEXAS

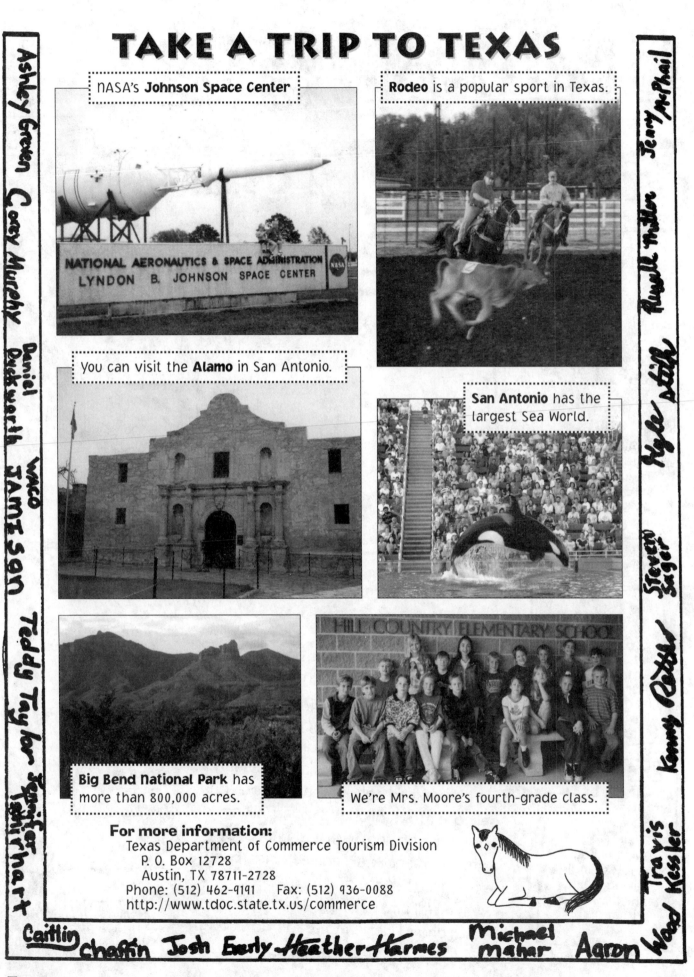

NASA's **Johnson Space Center**

Rodeo is a popular sport in Texas.

You can visit the **Alamo** in San Antonio.

NATIONAL AERONAUTICS & SPACE ADMINISTRATION
LYNDON B. JOHNSON SPACE CENTER

San Antonio has the largest Sea World.

Big Bend National Park has more than 800,000 acres.

We're Mrs. Moore's fourth-grade class.

For more information:
Texas Department of Commerce Tourism Division
P. O. Box 12728
Austin, TX 78711-2728
Phone: (512) 462-9191   Fax: (512) 936-0088
http://www.tdoc.state.tx.us/commerce

Ashley Green Corey Murphy Daniel Duckworth WACO JAMIESON Teddy Taylor Jennifer Reinhart

Jenny McPhail Russell Miller Kyle Stith Steven Sager Kenny Rother Travis Kessler Wood

Caitlin Chaffin Josh Everly Heather Harmes Michael Mahar Aaron

Utah A Pretty Great State

State Capital
★ Salt Lake City

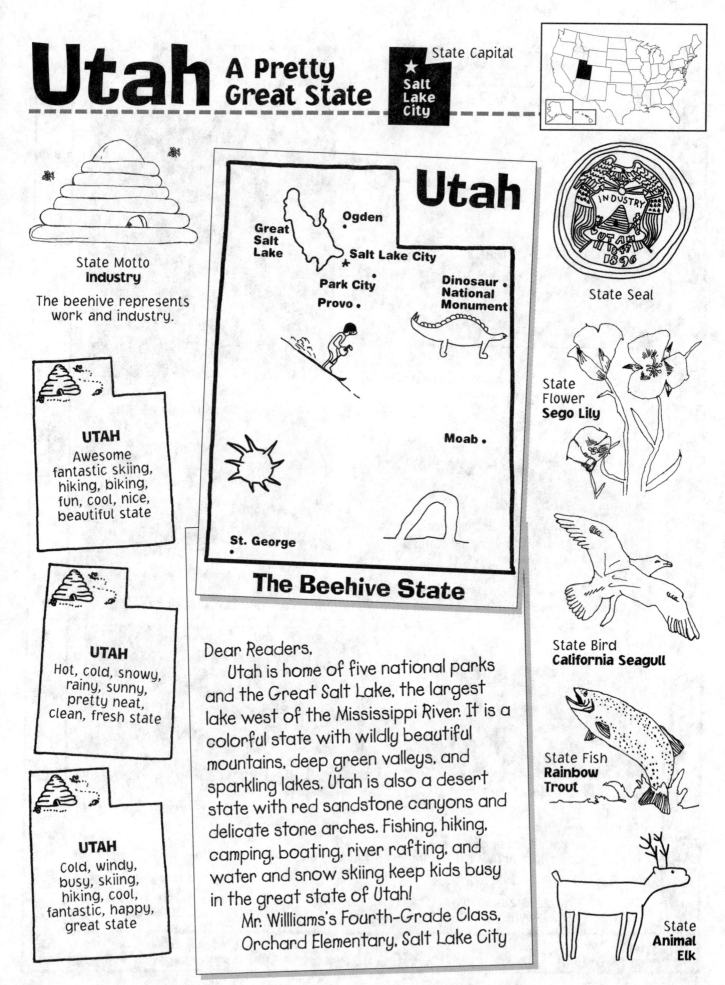

State Motto
Industry

The beehive represents work and industry.

UTAH
Awesome fantastic skiing, hiking, biking, fun, cool, nice, beautiful state

UTAH
Hot, cold, snowy, rainy, sunny, pretty neat, clean, fresh state

UTAH
Cold, windy, busy, skiing, hiking, cool, fantastic, happy, great state

Utah

Ogden
Great Salt Lake
Salt Lake City
Park City
Provo
Dinosaur National Monument
Moab
St. George

The Beehive State

Dear Readers,
Utah is home of five national parks and the Great Salt Lake, the largest lake west of the Mississippi River. It is a colorful state with wildly beautiful mountains, deep green valleys, and sparkling lakes. Utah is also a desert state with red sandstone canyons and delicate stone arches. Fishing, hiking, camping, boating, river rafting, and water and snow skiing keep kids busy in the great state of Utah!
Mr. Williams's Fourth-Grade Class, Orchard Elementary, Salt Lake City

State Seal

State Flower
Sego Lily

State Bird
California Seagull

State Fish
Rainbow Trout

State
Animal Elk

180

QUICK FACTS

Population	2,000,494 (1996)
Area	84,904 square miles
Highest Point	King's Peak, 13,528 ft.
Gem	Topaz
Mineral	Copper
Rock	Coal
Folk Dance	Square dance

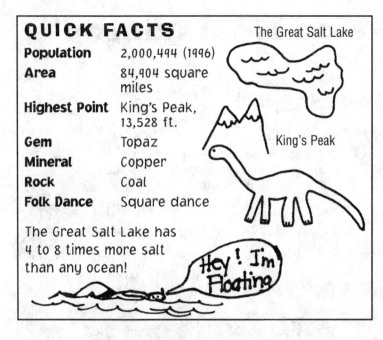

The Great Salt Lake

King's Peak

The Great Salt Lake has 4 to 8 times more salt than any ocean!

Hey! I'm Floating

People We'd Like You to Meet

Mary Jane Dilworth

Brigham Young

Philo Farnsworth

Mary Jane Dilworth was the first schoolteacher in Utah.

Lester Wire invented the traffic light.

Robert Redford is a movie star and environmentalist who lives in Utah.

Brigham Young was the first governor of Utah and western states colonizer.

Robert Jarvik was the inventor of the artificial heart.

Philo T. Farnsworth developed the idea of the image dissector, which led to the invention of television.

Roseanne, television comedian, is a native of Utah, as is **Steve Young**, football quarterback.

Jack Dempsey was a champion boxer and thought Utah was a great place.

UTAH'S NATIVE AMERICANS

Utah has had five main tribes: the Utes, Paiutes, Gosiutes, Shoshones, and Navajos.

The Legend of Turquoise

Once, a very long time ago, a Navajo maiden was digging in front of her home. She wanted to make a beautiful earthenware bowl for her mother, a bowl with many bright colors and designs. Suddenly she dug up an exquisite blue stone, a piece of turquoise. She carried it to the highest mountain in the village where the sun brightly shone, so she might better see the kind of stone it was. The Navajo girl was never seen again.

The piece of turquoise had brought flashes of lightning down toward the cliff itself. The bright light caused the startled girl to fall off the cliff. To this day, Navajo tribes' most prized possessions are turquoise stones.

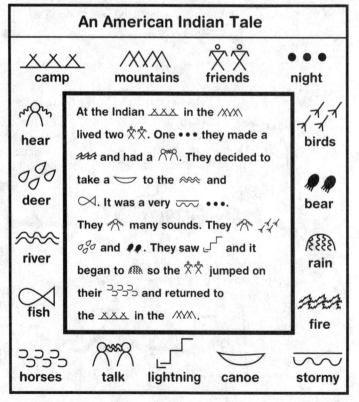

An American Indian Tale

camp   mountains   friends   night

hear   deer   river   fish

birds   bear   rain   fire

At the Indian ⚊ camp in the ⚊ mountains lived two ⚊ friends. One ⚊ night they made a ⚊ and had a ⚊. They decided to take a ⚊ canoe to the ⚊ river and ⚊ fish. It was a very ⚊ stormy ⚊ night. They ⚊ hear many sounds. They ⚊ ⚊ birds ⚊ deer and ⚊ bear. They saw ⚊ lightning and it began to ⚊ rain so the ⚊ friends jumped on their ⚊ horses and returned to the ⚊ camp in the ⚊ mountains.

horses   talk   lightning   canoe   stormy

Utah

Utah Means "Home on Mountaintop"

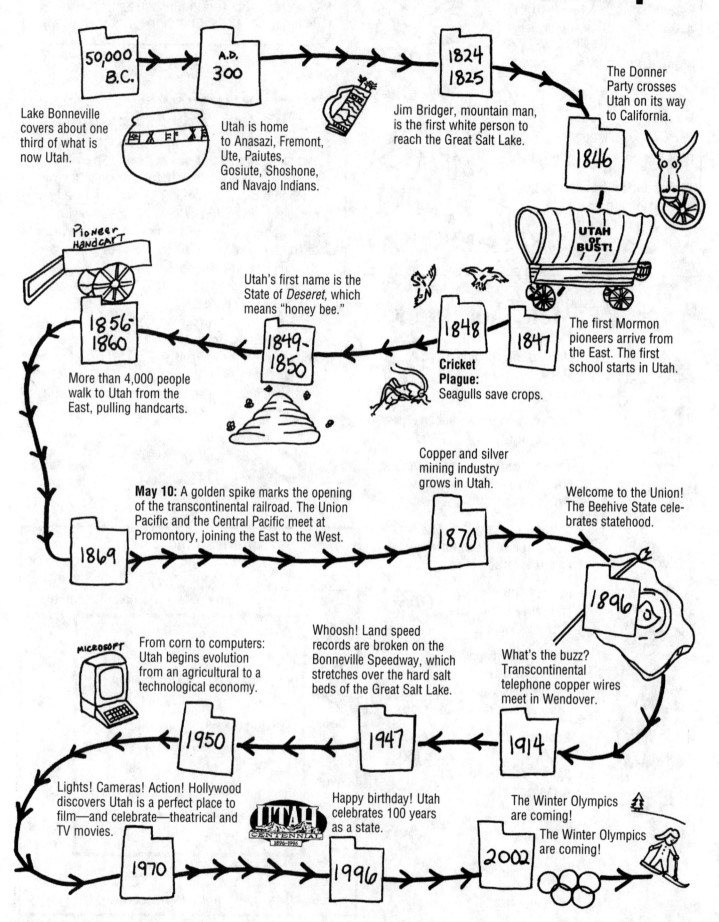

50,000 B.C.
Lake Bonneville covers about one third of what is now Utah.

A.D. 300
Utah is home to Anasazi, Fremont, Ute, Paiutes, Gosiute, Shoshone, and Navajo Indians.

1824 1825
Jim Bridger, mountain man, is the first white person to reach the Great Salt Lake.

The Donner Party crosses Utah on its way to California.

1846

UTAH or BUST!

The first Mormon pioneers arrive from the East. The first school starts in Utah.

1847

1848
Cricket Plague: Seagulls save crops.

Utah's first name is the State of *Deseret*, which means "honey bee."

1849-1850

Pioneer Handcart

1856-1860
More than 4,000 people walk to Utah from the East, pulling handcarts.

May 10: A golden spike marks the opening of the transcontinental railroad. The Union Pacific and the Central Pacific meet at Promontory, joining the East to the West.

1869

Copper and silver mining industry grows in Utah.

1870

Welcome to the Union! The Beehive State celebrates statehood.

1896

What's the buzz? Transcontinental telephone copper wires meet in Wendover.

MICROSOFT
From corn to computers: Utah begins evolution from an agricultural to a technological economy.

Whoosh! Land speed records are broken on the Bonneville Speedway, which stretches over the hard salt beds of the Great Salt Lake.

1950

1947

1914

Lights! Cameras! Action! Hollywood discovers Utah is a perfect place to film—and celebrate—theatrical and TV movies.

Happy birthday! Utah celebrates 100 years as a state.

The Winter Olympics are coming!
The Winter Olympics are coming!

UTAH CENTENNIAL 1896-1996

1970

1996

2002

UTAH Wonders

Utah has **more than 43 state parks** and **five national parks**: Arches, Bryce Canyon, Capitol Reef, Canyonlands, and Zion, and **national monuments** such as Dinosaurland and America's newest, the Escalante Staircase.

You can see American Indian **petroglyphs** and **pictographs** in most canyons of southeastern Utah.

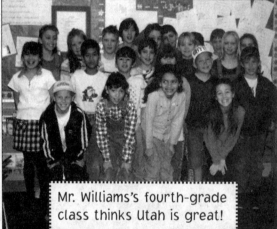

Mr. Williams's fourth-grade class thinks Utah is great!

UTAH
Mountainous, green, pretty, quiet, dreamy state

Information About Utah
Salt Lake Convention and Visitors Bureau
90 South West Temple
Salt Lake City, UT 84101
(801) 521-2822

http://www.state.ut.us

UTAH
Where dreams come true!

Vermont

State Capital
Montpelier ☆

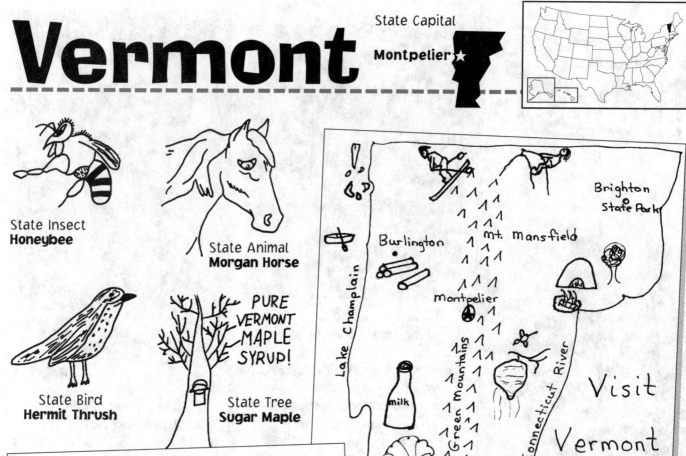

State Insect
Honeybee

State Animal
Morgan Horse

State Bird
Hermit Thrush

PURE VERMONT MAPLE SYRUP!

State Tree
Sugar Maple

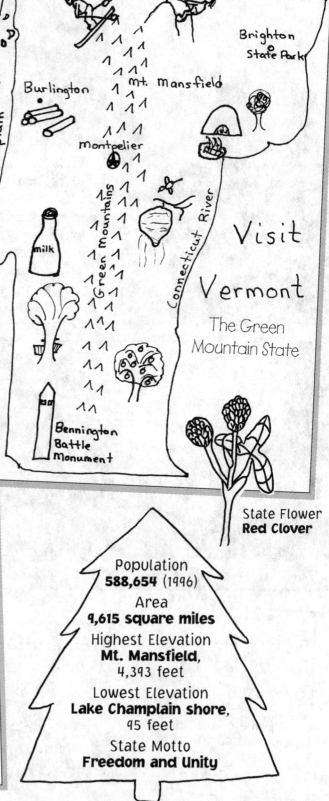

Brighton State Park

Burlington

Mt. Mansfield

Lake Champlain

Montpelier

milk

Green Mountains

Connecticut River

Visit Vermont
The Green Mountain State

Bennington Battle Monument

State Flower
Red Clover

Dear Reader,

Greetings from the Green Mountain State. Vermont is one of the smallest, prettiest, and sweetest states. We're the home of maple syrup. We call the late winter "sugaring time." Just before the snow (and we have lots of that, too) melts, is when the sap starts flowing from sugar maples. Did you know that sugaring time is over when spring nears and buds begin to show on trees? The sap tastes sour then.

We have to wait a whole year until the good stuff begins to drip from the trees again. In the meantime, we can look at fields of wildflowers. It rains a lot in spring and then we have a mud season. Still, farms, corn fields, and orchards cover the landscape, creating superb views. Hope you visit soon.

Ms. Freeman's Class, Brewster Pierce Memorial School, Huntington

Population
588,654 (1996)
Area
9,615 square miles
Highest Elevation
Mt. Mansfield,
4,393 feet
Lowest Elevation
Lake Champlain shore,
95 feet
State Motto
Freedom and Unity

SOME OF VERMONT'S BEST

Though **Ethan Allen** was born in Connecticut in 1737, he moved to Vermont as a young man and bought a huge amount of land. When the Revolutionary War began he fought hard for Vermont's freedom. He led the Green Mountain Boys in the capture of Fort Ticonderoga.

Two U.S. presidents came from Vermont. That's a lot for such a small state!

Chester A. Arthur, born in Fairfield in 1829, was the 21st president. He served from 1881 to 1885. He was a teacher in Vermont before becoming a lawyer and politician. He died in 1886.

Calvin Coolidge, the 30th president from 1923 to 1929, was born in Plymouth in 1872. He became famous when, as the governor of Massachusetts, he opposed a strike by police. He said, "There is no right to strike against the public safety by anyone, anywhere, anytime." He died in 1933.

Norman Rockwell painted America. He portrayed real Americans with dignity, humor, and sensitivity. Rockwell left New York State in 1937 to make Vermont his home. Some of his most famous works were on magazine covers.

WHY WE'RE PROUD OF OUR STATE

In 1791, when it entered the Union, Vermont was the **first state to give all adult white males the vote**.

The **first postage stamp** used in America was made in Brattleboro in 1846.

On July 8, 1777, Vermont became the **first state to outlaw slavery**.

Fanny Burnham Kilgore of Craftsbury was the **first female lawyer** in the United States.

In 1790, Samuel Hopkins received the **first U.S. patent**.

Bill Koch of Guilford was the **first American to win a medal** in Olympic Nordic skiing in 1976.

MEET A VERMONTER:
Bonnie Christensen, Illustrator and Author

Bonnie Christensen has written and/or illustrated six children's books. Among them are *The Edible Alphabet, Putting the World to Sleep,* and *Rebus Riot.* She also illustrates posters, magazines, catalogs, and book covers when she's not teaching art classes.

She uses many different styles in her illustrations. She does scratch board, ink blocks, watercolors, cutouts, oil pastels—and the most interesting medium of all, powder paint and egg.

She told us that she always wears black because of the ink she uses. She also told us that she hides her daughter's name in her book illustrations. She's a great illustrator.

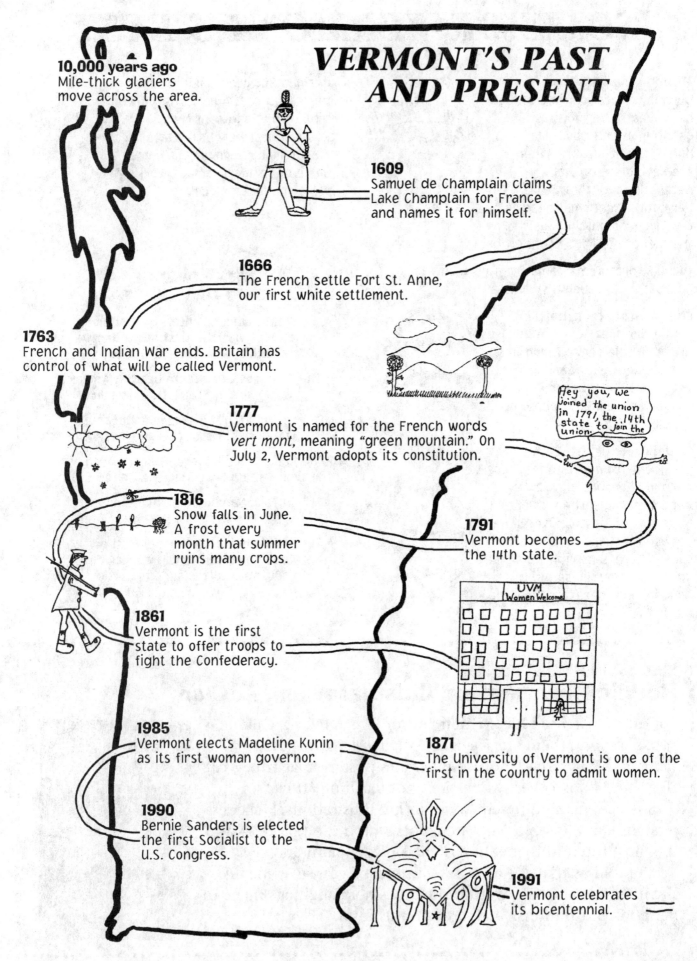

VERMONT'S PAST AND PRESENT

10,000 years ago
Mile-thick glaciers
move across the area.

1609
Samuel de Champlain claims
Lake Champlain for France
and names it for himself.

1666
The French settle Fort St. Anne,
our first white settlement.

1763
French and Indian War ends. Britain has
control of what will be called Vermont.

1777
Vermont is named for the French words
vert mont, meaning "green mountain." On
July 2, Vermont adopts its constitution.

Hey you, we
joined the union
in 1791, the 14th
state to join the
union.

1816
Snow falls in June.
A frost every
month that summer
ruins many crops.

1791
Vermont becomes
the 14th state.

UVM
Women Welcome

1861
Vermont is the first
state to offer troops to
fight the Confederacy.

1985
Vermont elects Madeline Kunin
as its first woman governor.

1871
The University of Vermont is one of the
first in the country to admit women.

1990
Bernie Sanders is elected
the first Socialist to the
U.S. Congress.

1991
Vermont celebrates
its bicentennial.

VISIT VERMONT'S VIEWS

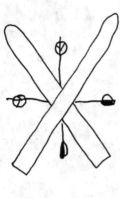

Skiing is a big deal in our state. In 1934, the **first ski tow** in the U.S. was set up on Clinton Gilbert's farm in Woodstock. The **first chair lift** was at Mt. Mansfield in Stowe in 1940.

The **oldest log cabin** in the U.S. is the Hyde log cabin. It was named for Jedediah Hyde and built in 1783.

The **Bennington Monument** marks the Battle of Bennington in 1777 during the Revolutionary War.

Take me to that gas station in Burlington—the one in which **Ben and Jerry's** ice cream was started.

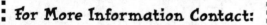

The first **Morgan horse** was developed in Vermont in 1795. It's a combination riding and work horse. You can visit the Morgan Horse Farm.

The **Richmond Round Church** isn't really round—but it's easy to spot. Sixteen men each built one of its sides. The money to build it was raised by selling pews. The total cost of the church was $2,305.42.

For More Information Contact:
Vermont Tourist Department
134 State Street
Montpelier, Vermont 05602
(802) 828-3237

Web sites
www.discover-vermont.com/vtlinks.ht
www.travel-vermont.com/tourism/vermont1.htm

We're Mrs. Freeman's class.

Virginia

State Capital
Richmond

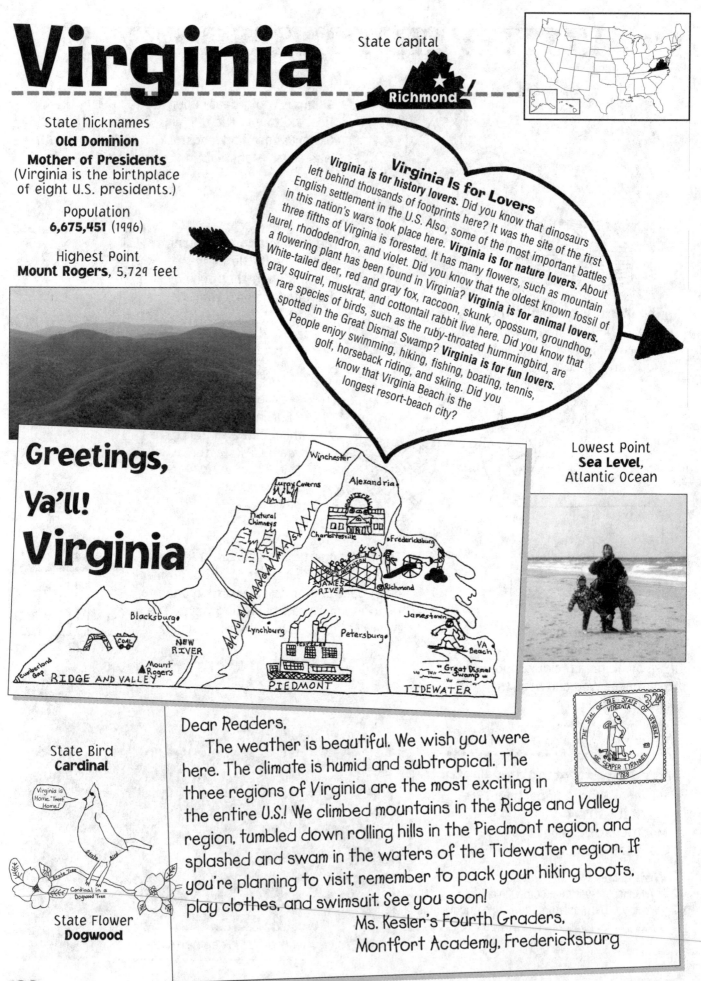

State Nicknames
Old Dominion

Mother of Presidents
(Virginia is the birthplace of eight U.S. presidents.)

Population
6,675,451 (1996)

Highest Point
Mount Rogers, 5,729 feet

Virginia Is for Lovers

Virginia is for history lovers. Did you know that dinosaurs left behind thousands of footprints here? It was the site of the first English settlement in the U.S. Also, some of the most important battles in this nation's wars took place here. **Virginia is for nature lovers.** About three fifths of Virginia is forested. It has many flowers, such as mountain laurel, rhododendron, and violet. Did you know that the oldest known fossil of a flowering plant has been found in Virginia? **Virginia is for animal lovers.** White-tailed deer, red and gray fox, raccoon, skunk, opossum, groundhog, gray squirrel, muskrat, and cottontail rabbit live here. Did you know that rare species of birds, such as the ruby-throated hummingbird, are spotted in the Great Dismal Swamp? **Virginia is for fun lovers.** People enjoy swimming, hiking, fishing, boating, tennis, golf, horseback riding, and skiing. Did you know that Virginia Beach is the longest resort-beach city?

Lowest Point
Sea Level,
Atlantic Ocean

Greetings, Ya'll! Virginia

State Bird
Cardinal

Virginia is Home,'Tweet' Home!

Cardinal in a Dogwood Tree

State Flower
Dogwood

Dear Readers,
   The weather is beautiful. We wish you were here. The climate is humid and subtropical. The three regions of Virginia are the most exciting in the entire U.S.! We climbed mountains in the Ridge and Valley region, tumbled down rolling hills in the Piedmont region, and splashed and swam in the waters of the Tidewater region. If you're planning to visit, remember to pack your hiking boots, play clothes, and swimsuit. See you soon!
                    Ms. Kesler's Fourth Graders,
                    Montfort Academy, Fredericksburg

☆ Hats Off to Virginians ☆

Fran Tarkenton (1940–) was a professional football player who made it into the Football Hall of Fame.

Booker T. Washington (1856–1915) was a leader in education. He worked hard to help African Americans advance in America.

Roy Clark (1933–) was named Entertainer of the Year in 1973 by the Country Music Association.

Virginius Dabney (1901–) won the Pulitzer Prize for editorial writing in 1947.

PRESS

Ella Fitzgerald (1918–1996) was a jazz singer who won eight Grammy awards. She has been called the First Lady of Song.

Arthur Ashe (1943–1993) was the first African American to win the tennis tournament at Wimbledon, England, in 1975.

Pocahontas (1595–1617) was a Powhatan Indian who brought about a good relationship between the Indians and the Jamestown colonists.

Thomas Jefferson (1743–1826) was the governor of Virginia and the third president of the U.S. He wrote most of the Declaration of Independence.

SPLASH!
Swimming Gold Medalist Jeff Rouse Returns to Virginia

FREDERICKSBURG, Virginia—Stafford County native and Olympic gold medal swimmer Jeff Rouse wowed his audience at a Montfort Academy school assembly. Jeff, who hopes to live in Virginia for the rest of his life, dived into swimming at age five. At 12, he broke the national record for backstroke, which has become his best and favorite stroke. In 1992, at the Olympics held in Barcelona, Spain, Jeff won a gold medal as part of the men's medley relay team and a silver medal in the 100-meter backstroke. During the 1996 Olympics in Atlanta, Georgia, he achieved his goal—gold medal in the 100-meter backstroke, as well as another gold for the men's medley relay team!

Believe it or not, he said that he was actually glad he did not reach his lifelong goal of winning a gold medal in the 100-meter backstroke in 1992. Why? Because he had four more years to strengthen his character and become a stronger athlete. According to Jeff, having earned Olympic gold medals "feels like the end of a journey and the start of another." Jeff worked hard for many years to earn his medals. If you work hard, someday you might get an Olympic medal, too!

Jeff and 4B students "go for the gold!"

KEEPING TRACK OF VA'S HISTORY

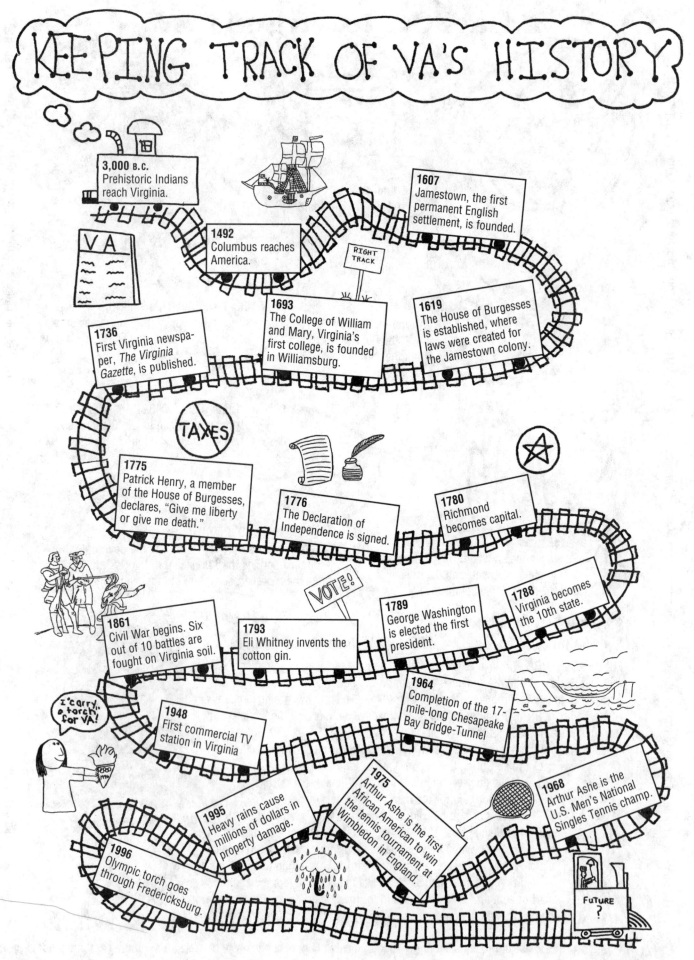

3,000 B.C. Prehistoric Indians reach Virginia.

1492 Columbus reaches America.

1607 Jamestown, the first permanent English settlement, is founded.

RIGHT TRACK

1693 The College of William and Mary, Virginia's first college, is founded in Williamsburg.

1619 The House of Burgesses is established, where laws were created for the Jamestown colony.

1736 First Virginia newspaper, *The Virginia Gazette*, is published.

TAXES

1775 Patrick Henry, a member of the House of Burgesses, declares, "Give me liberty or give me death."

1776 The Declaration of Independence is signed.

1780 Richmond becomes capital.

VOTE!

1861 Civil War begins. Six out of 10 battles are fought on Virginia soil.

1793 Eli Whitney invents the cotton gin.

1789 George Washington is elected the first president.

1788 Virginia becomes the 10th state.

I carry a torch for VA!

1948 First commercial TV station in Virginia

1964 Completion of the 17-mile-long Chesapeake Bay Bridge-Tunnel

1995 Heavy rains cause millions of dollars in property damage.

1975 Arthur Ashe is the first African American to win the tennis tournament at Wimbledon in England.

1968 Arthur Ashe is the U.S. Men's National Singles Tennis champ.

1996 Olympic torch goes through Fredericksburg.

FUTURE ?

Virginia's Picture-Perfect Highlights

Brrr! Exprerience the thrilling stalactites and stalagmites during an underground adventure at **Luray Caverns**.

Don't turn around! Legends are plentiful at the **Great Dismal Swamp**.

Wheee! White Water Rapids is just one of many exciting rides at **King's Dominion Park**.

Ms. Kesler and her history-loving fourth-grade class at Montfort Academy prepared these Virginia pages.

Jamestown's reenactments take you back many many years.

The Virginia Peanut

I visited a peanut farm in Surry, Virginia, where I sampled

_____ _____ peanuts. I was surprised to find a (an)
  large number   adjective

_____ in one of the shells! On my visit, I learned a lot about
  noun

peanuts. In Virginia the peanut is a (an) _____ crop. The
                                          large number

_____ grows the peanut, and the soil must be rich and
  animal

_____. The peanuts _____ underground. _____
  color   verb   Person's name

uses peanuts for _____ and _____. If you grow peanuts,
                  -ing verb   -ing verb

make sure to _____ them often! Peanuts are _____!
              verb   adjective

For further information for visitors
Virginia Chamber of Commerce
9 South 5th Street
Richmond, VA 23219
(804) 644-1607
http://www.state.va.us

A Bonus from Us
Find a partner and a sheet of paper. Without letting your partner see the story at left, ask for the needed words to fill in the blanks. Write the answers on the lines. Read the story with your partner's words in the blanks. Enjoy a good laugh!

Washington

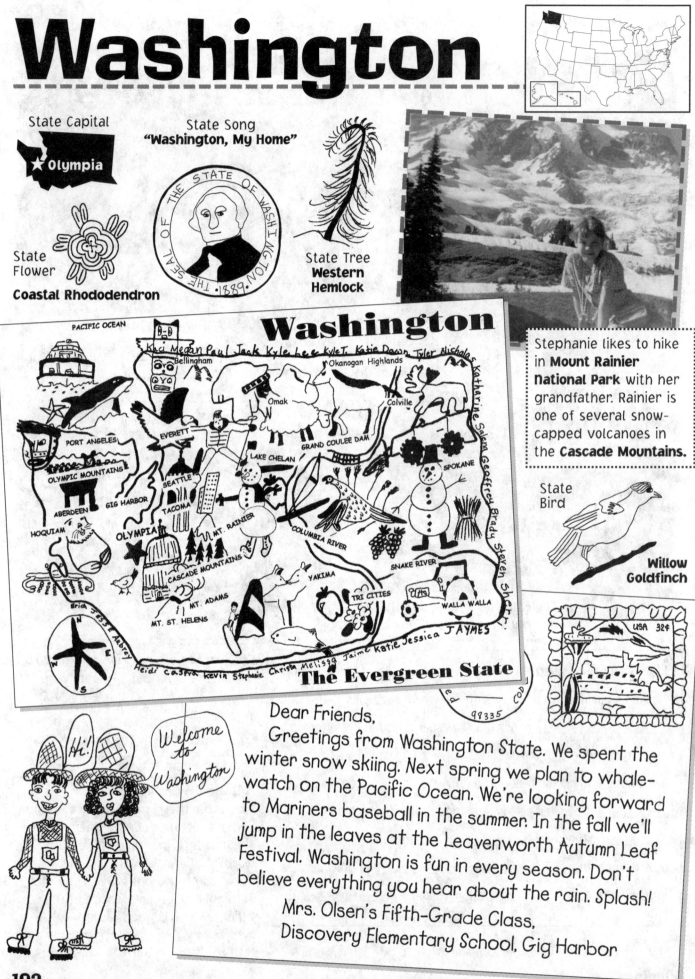

State Capital
★ Olympia

State Song
"Washington, My Home"

THE SEAL OF THE STATE OF WASHINGTON • 1889 •

State Tree
Western Hemlock

State Flower
Coastal Rhododendron

Stephanie likes to hike in **Mount Rainier National Park** with her grandfather. Rainier is one of several snow-capped volcanoes in the **Cascade Mountains.**

State Bird

Willow Goldfinch

USA 32¢

PACIFIC OCEAN

Bellingham
Okanogan Highlands
Omak
Colville
EVERETT
GRAND COULEE DAM
PORT ANGELES
LAKE CHELAN
SPOKANE
OLYMPIC MOUNTAINS
SEATTLE
GIG HARBOR
TACOMA
ABERDEEN
OLYMPIA
MT. RAINIER
COLUMBIA RIVER
HOQUIAM
CASCADE MOUNTAINS
SNAKE RIVER
MT. ADAMS
YAKIMA
TRI CITIES
WALLA WALLA
MT. ST. HELENS
N E S W

The Evergreen State

98335

Welcome to Washington

Hi!

Dear Friends,
Greetings from Washington State. We spent the winter snow skiing. Next spring we plan to whale-watch on the Pacific Ocean. We're looking forward to Mariners baseball in the summer. In the fall we'll jump in the leaves at the Leavenworth Autumn Leaf Festival. Washington is fun in every season. Don't believe everything you hear about the rain. Splash!
Mrs. Olsen's Fifth-Grade Class,
Discovery Elementary School, Gig Harbor

🏴 Washington State Rap 🏴

Come on out to the Evergreen State
We've got some stuff that's really great
Cascade Mountains through the middle run
Making two different regions become as one.

On the western side of the mountain chain
You get real wet 'cause there's lots o' rain
On the eastern side there's places to go
You can ski on the lakes or slide in the snow.

Visit our volcanoes: Baker, Adams, or Rainier
But it's Mt. St. Helens yuh really gotta fear.
In 1980 I hope you didn't stop
'Cause that's the year St. Helens blew her top.

Follow the Columbia from its head to its mouth
Watch the salmon go north while the river runs south.
With irrigation pumps, fresh water is drawn
To grow apples and wheat and sprinkle the lawn.

West of the mountains fruits and veggies grow fine
'Cause they get lots o' sun and it rains all the time
But on the east—feel the desert sun fry
Without irrigation, all the plants would die.

Everyone who comes to Washington State
Enjoys Seattle—Pike Place Market is great!
From the top of the space needle you can see
A panoramic view of King County

Watch the Sonics boom or the Seahawks punt
Hook a fish, take a hike, or even hunt
But to see Mariners baseball—hurry on down
The team's for sale—they might leave town.

Olympia is the capital of the state
Spokane, Long Beach, Port Angeles are great
Yakima is fine and Wenatchee is cool
Chelan has its own giant natural pool.

With the railroads gone and logging days past
Theme towns like Leavenworth can be a blast
If sailing's your game—or even if it's "knot"
Shop in Gig Harbor—You don't need a yacht.

So we hope you'll come and visit our state
Before too long—before it's too late
We'll flash a smile—we'll shake your hand.
Folks are friendly out here in latte land.

Washington State History Game

Sir Hemlock
(Washington State Tree)

So tall and proud you seem to stand
A fortress from a distant land
You spread your arms and
bow just so
In the crystal light
You breathe and grow
Needle armor—majestic scene
Cones of gold—fine gift for a queen.

Katie Dawn shows off her first catch—a sunfish. Commercial **fishing** is a major industry in Washington State.

Mount St. Helens erupted in 1980, covering the state in volcanic ash. Some parts of the state got a light dusting; other places were buried in 10 feet of ash.

Mountain goats walk nimbly along Olympic ridges.

Some of Washington's famous people:

- **Ken Griffey, Jr.**—center fielder for Mariners baseball team
- **Randy Johnson**—pitcher for Mariners baseball team
- **Dale Chihuly**—world-class glass artist
- **Bill Gates**—Founder and CEO of Microsoft—software giant
- **Glenn T. Kelly**—Music educator and composer of the *Columbia River Suite*

Other famous folks include: **Steve Largent**—Seattle Seahawks receiver; **Bing Crosby**—popular actor and singer; **Gary Larson**—*Far Side* creator; **Jimi Hendrix**—rock star; **Betty MacDonald**—author of *Mrs. Piggle Wiggle* series. **Matt Groening**, *Simpson* creator, graduated from Evergreen State College.

Richard Berry never lived in Washington, but his song "Louie Louie," made famous by Seattle Grunge bands of the '60s, lives in our hearts.

Our teacher, Carol Olsen, is the author of **funny books** for kids about Louie and his pet **banana slug,** Slime. You can visit them on the internet. http://www.web-pac.com/mall/slugs

A mini-wetland at **Discovery Elementary School** teaches kids about wetlands. Blackbird pond was named for a red-winged blackbird that nests in the willows. **Wetlands** control floods and clean our water. Animals find shelter. People enjoy wetlands.

White-capped **Mount Rainier** may be seen from Gig Harbor. Covered by twenty-six glaciers, this volcano rises 14,410 feet above sea level. Mount Rainier is a **dormant volcano.** It last erupted 150 years ago.

Jaime wades in the **Yakima River** with her dad.

PHOTO ALBUM

Twin **pileated wood-peckers** drill holes in a Douglas fir tree.

Douglas fir trees are popular for building, landscaping, and decorating as Christmas trees.

The first **Narrows Bridge,** built in 1940, was nicknamed **Galloping Gertie.** On windy days it galloped. Galloping Gertie soon fell apart and crashed into the water below.

Space Needle

Seattle's spectacular rotating restaurant
Perched at the top
A panoramic view as the restaurant turns
Enjoy the clam chowder in
Delightful, enchanting
Latte Land—otherwise known as the
Emerald City

Geoffrey and his friends dig for littleneck clams. **Geoducks** (gooey-ducks) have long necks and are too fast for the average clam digger. Commercial companies must use hydraulic pumps to harvest geoducks (*Panopea abrupta*).

Washington

West Virginia

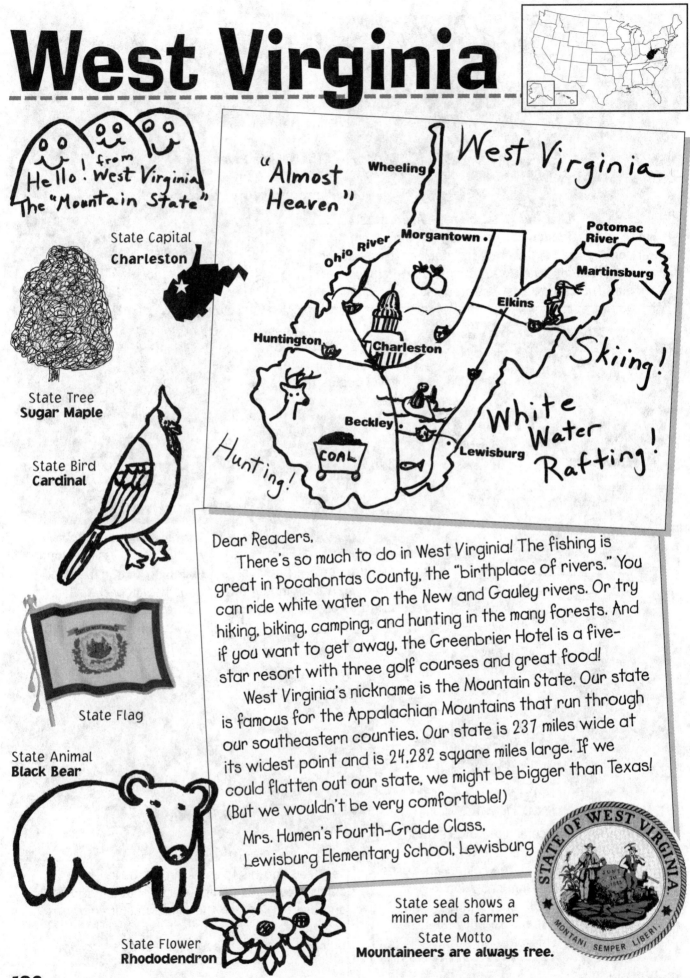

Hello! from West Virginia
The "Mountain State"

State Capital
Charleston

State Tree
Sugar Maple

State Bird
Cardinal

State Flag

State Animal
Black Bear

State Flower
Rhododendron

"Almost Heaven"

West Virginia

Wheeling
Ohio River
Morgantown
Potomac River
Martinsburg
Elkins
Huntington
Charleston
Skiing!
Beckley
COAL
Lewisburg
White Water Rafting!
Hunting!

Dear Readers,
    There's so much to do in West Virginia! The fishing is great in Pocahontas County, the "birthplace of rivers." You can ride white water on the New and Gauley rivers. Or try hiking, biking, camping, and hunting in the many forests. And if you want to get away, the Greenbrier Hotel is a five-star resort with three golf courses and great food!
    West Virginia's nickname is the Mountain State. Our state is famous for the Appalachian Mountains that run through our southeastern counties. Our state is 237 miles wide at its widest point and is 24,282 square miles large. If we could flatten out our state, we might be bigger than Texas! (But we wouldn't be very comfortable!)

Mrs. Humen's Fourth-Grade Class,
Lewisburg Elementary School, Lewisburg

State seal shows a miner and a farmer

State Motto
Mountaineers are always free.

STATE OF WEST VIRGINIA
MONTANI SEMPER LIBERI

Great Mountain State People

Variety is the word that describes the show business career of **Stan Sweet**, a native of White Sulphur Springs. He has done commercials, movies, radio and TV work, and appearances on talk shows. He is best known for his eight National Fast-Draw Championships!

Jerry West was born in Cabin Creek. He attended West Virginia University where he was named an All-American. Jerry helped the Los Angeles Lakers win the NBA title in 1972. His number was 44. After Jerry became manager of the Lakers in 1982, they won the title in 1982, 1985, 1987, and 1988.

Johnny Appleseed's real name was John Chapman. Johnny was a pioneer who became legendary in American history. He planted orchards in much of what later became West Virginia.

Mary Lou Retton was a newcomer to international competition in 1984, but she was America's best hope for an Olympic medal in gymnastics. After a very close contest, she scored a perfect 10 on the vault, her final event, and became the first American to win the overall title.

And then there's the legendary **John Henry**. Do you know the song about him? It's said that he helped build the Big Bend Tunnel at Talcott. John claimed that he could dig a tunnel faster than a steam drill. He won a race doing just that, but "laid down his hammer and died" when it was over. No one knows how true the story is, but there are twin tunnels through the mountain. And one looks as if it were carved with a hammer!

From the Pens of Local Authors

All the books we've reviewed are by West Virginia authors and take place in West Virginia.

Shiloh, by Phyllis Naylor, is about a hunting dog that is afraid of the sound of guns. Shiloh and the boy who befriends him will touch your heart. The story takes place near Friendly, West Virginia, a town on the Ohio River.

No Star Nights, by Anna Smucker, brings to life the steel-making way of life in Weirton, West Virginia. Life was hard and dangerous for the steel workers, but there was also fun to be had. In July, the workers got their vacation pay, and it was almost like Christmas! Once the school year began, children didn't often see their fathers because of the shift work. The air in Weirton was always full of soot and graphite. Most of the mills are closed now. But the grandchildren of those workers love to hear stories of the old days when the skies were red and you couldn't see the stars.

In *A Little Excitement*, by Marc Harshman, a farm boy longs for something exciting to happen. His grandmother warns him to be careful what he wishes for! The something exciting turned out to be a fire in the chimney of the farmhouse. Our class liked the book because it was full of action. If you ever get the chance, read *A Little Excitement*!

Rocks in My Pockets, by Marc Harshman, is about a very poor family that lives on a very windy hill. In order to live there, they have to put rocks in their pockets to keep form blowing away! This is a very funny book, and we liked reading it very much.

Believe us, you'll like **When I Was Young in the Mountains**, by Cynthia Rylant. The story relates how things were in West Virginia's past, when nearly everyone worked in the coal mines. It's interesting to read what happens in this book and compare it to the way our lives are today.

You're sure to enjoy *The Relatives Came*, by Cynthia Rylant. It has hilarious illustrations by Stephen Gammell. It has a lot of hugging and laughing. And when the relatives get home they think about next summer, because this summer was so wonderful!

Tracks Through Time

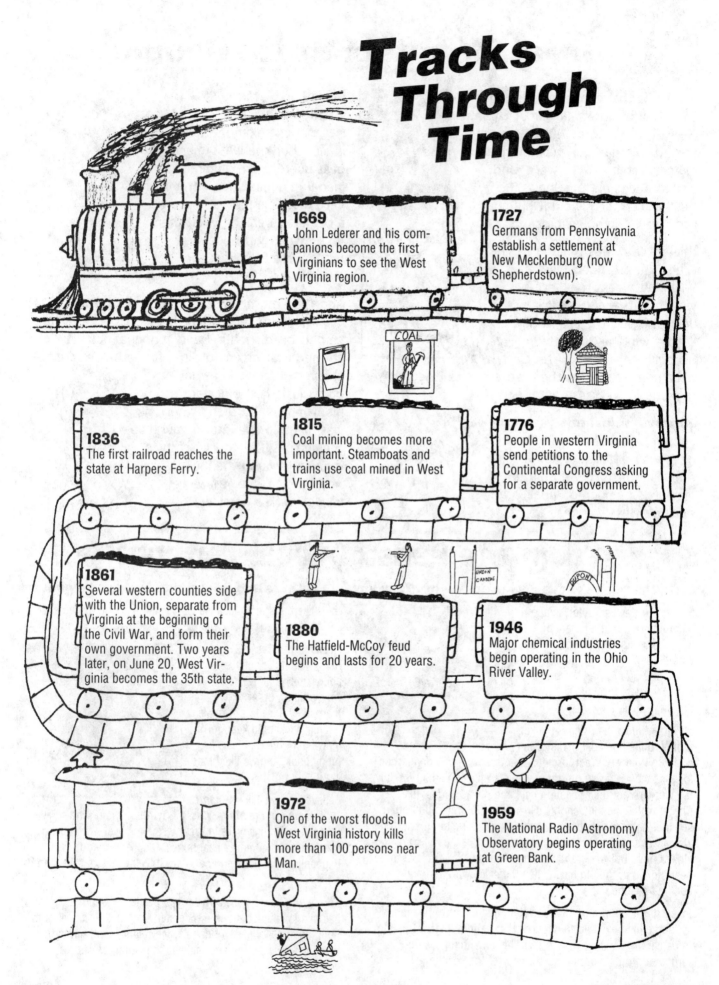

1669
John Lederer and his companions become the first Virginians to see the West Virginia region.

1727
Germans from Pennsylvania establish a settlement at New Mecklenburg (now Shepherdstown).

1836
The first railroad reaches the state at Harpers Ferry.

1815
Coal mining becomes more important. Steamboats and trains use coal mined in West Virginia.

1776
People in western Virginia send petitions to the Continental Congress asking for a separate government.

1861
Several western counties side with the Union, separate from Virginia at the beginning of the Civil War, and form their own government. Two years later, on June 20, West Virginia becomes the 35th state.

1880
The Hatfield-McCoy feud begins and lasts for 20 years.

1946
Major chemical industries begin operating in the Ohio River Valley.

1972
One of the worst floods in West Virginia history kills more than 100 persons near Man.

1959
The National Radio Astronomy Observatory begins operating at Green Bank.

Wild Wonderful West Virginia

Seneca Rocks, a great place for climbers!

West Virginia has wild, wonderful **skiing**!

The view from **Spruce Knob**, elevation 4,380 feet.

New River Gorge Bridge near Fayetteville on U.S. 19, the largest arched bridge in the world.

White water rafting on the New River.

Greetings from Mrs. Humen's fourth-grade class

Contact WV tourism at 800-225-5982

Web site: http://www.state.wv.us

Dustin, Keri, Kelly, Justin, Rachel J., Joey, Rachel I., Donald, Hali Jo, Zack,

Hayley, Shananah, Geoffrey, Mallory, Michael T., Mitchell, Brandon W., Kim

Michael H., Brandon F., Jacob, Tricia, Kevin, Brandon H.,

Wisconsin

State Capital

Madison

State Tree
Sugar Maple

State Flower
Wood Violet

State Insect
Honeybee

State Bird
Robin

Dear Friends,

Wisconsin is a great place to be a kid! In the fall, when the leaves turn many scrumptious colors, attend a farmer's market, enjoy Oktoberfest, have loads of fun at fall festivals. Come winter, our sparkling snow is super for skiing, sledding, snowmobiling, and ice fishing. Go biking in the spring on our many state bike trails and enjoy camping at public and private campgrounds. Summer brings us bright sun and warm weather for swimming, waterskiing, and boating! We have two Great Lakes, Superior and Michigan, and many state and national forests. We are rich in many recreational spots including the mighty Mississippi. Come visit soon.

Your friends, Mrs. Liska's Grade-Five Students,
Onalaska Middle School, Onalaska

Here's a Wisconsin riddle.

Q. What's black and white and black and white and black and white and . . . ?

A. A Holstein cow rolling down the hill.

Lake Onalaska, Onalaska, Wisconsin

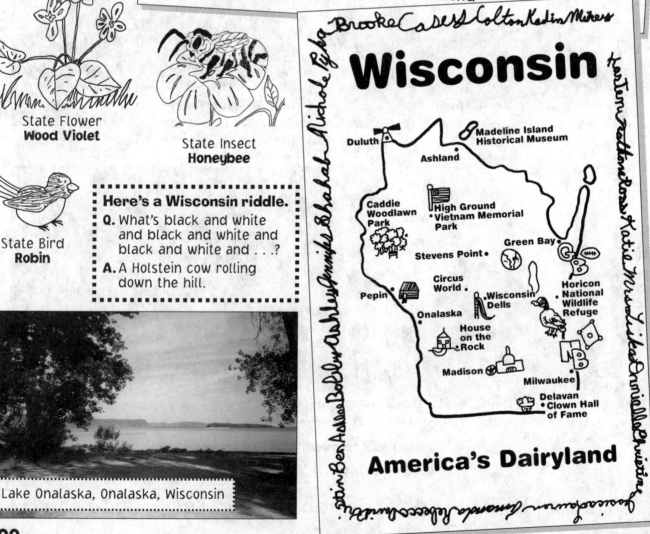

Wisconsin

- Duluth
- Madeline Island Historical Museum
- Ashland
- Caddie Woodlawn Park
- High Ground Vietnam Memorial Park
- Green Bay
- Stevens Point
- Pepin
- Circus World
- Wisconsin Dells
- Horicon National Wildlife Refuge
- Onalaska
- House on the Rock
- Madison
- Milwaukee
- Delavan Clown Hall of Fame

America's Dairyland

People We're Proud Of

Arnold Schwarzenegger was born in Austria on July 30, 1947. But we're proud of him because he was graduated from University of Wisconsin-Superior in 1979. He earned a degree in marketing and business. He also taught fitness for life classes on the UW-Superior staff in 1979. He received an honorary doctorate for community service.

Harry Houdini was one of the world's best and most famous magicians. He said that he had two birthdays, just like George Washington—April 6, 1864, and March 24, 1862. Either way, he was born in Appleton. Harry could escape from locked boxes that were thrown into a river or get out of handcuffs. He claimed he never got more than five hours of sleep at a time in his adult life. On May 16, 1908, he announced he was going to retire. He had a short retirement. He died on October 31, 1926. You may think that's Halloween. But, to the many people who revere Houdini's memory, October 31 is now National Magic Day.

Dr. Nicholas Senn was born in Switzerland and came to America as a child with his parents. When he grew up he became a doctor and practiced medicine in Wisconsin for 40 years. He improved operating room procedures in America by using sterilized tools and antiseptics to kill bacteria and prevent infection.

Weird, Wacky, and Wonderful Wisconsin

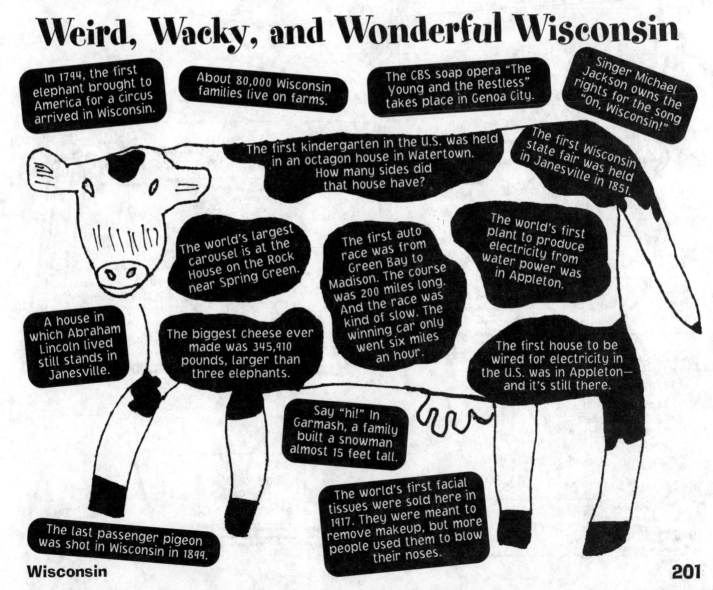

In 1794, the first elephant brought to America for a circus arrived in Wisconsin.

About 80,000 Wisconsin families live on farms.

The CBS soap opera "The Young and the Restless" takes place in Genoa City.

Singer Michael Jackson owns the rights for the song "On, Wisconsin!"

The first kindergarten in the U.S. was held in an octagon house in Watertown. How many sides did that house have?

The first Wisconsin state fair was held in Janesville in 1851.

The world's largest carousel is at the House on the Rock near Spring Green.

The first auto race was from Green Bay to Madison. The course was 200 miles long. And the race was kind of slow. The winning car only went six miles an hour.

The world's first plant to produce electricity from water power was in Appleton.

A house in which Abraham Lincoln lived still stands in Janesville.

The biggest cheese ever made was 345,910 pounds, larger than three elephants.

The first house to be wired for electricity in the U.S. was in Appleton—and it's still there.

Say "hi!" In Garmash, a family built a snowman almost 15 feet tall.

The world's first facial tissues were sold here in 1917. They were meant to remove makeup, but more people used them to blow their noses.

The last passenger pigeon was shot in Wisconsin in 1899.

Timber! Time Line

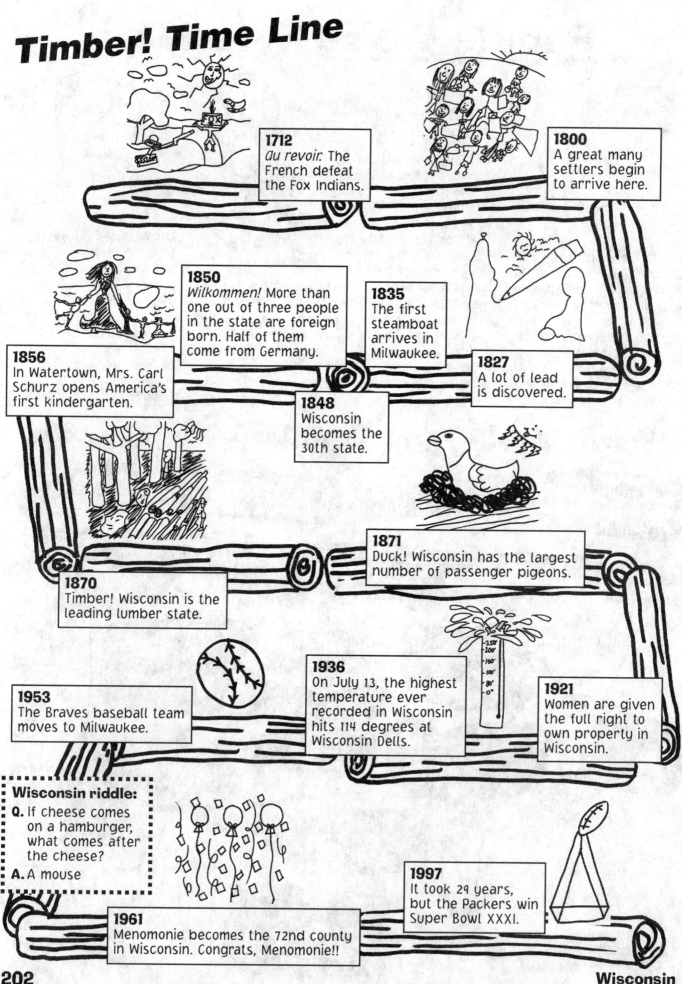

1712
au revoir: The French defeat the Fox Indians.

1800
A great many settlers begin to arrive here.

1850
Wilkommen! More than one out of three people in the state are foreign born. Half of them come from Germany.

1835
The first steamboat arrives in Milwaukee.

1856
In Watertown, Mrs. Carl Schurz opens America's first kindergarten.

1827
A lot of lead is discovered.

1848
Wisconsin becomes the 30th state.

1871
Duck! Wisconsin has the largest number of passenger pigeons.

1870
Timber! Wisconsin is the leading lumber state.

1953
The Braves baseball team moves to Milwaukee.

1936
On July 13, the highest temperature ever recorded in Wisconsin hits 114 degrees at Wisconsin Dells.

1921
Women are given the full right to own property in Wisconsin.

Wisconsin riddle:
Q. If cheese comes on a hamburger, what comes after the cheese?
A. A mouse

1997
It took 29 years, but the Packers win Super Bowl XXXI.

1961
Menomonie becomes the 72nd county in Wisconsin. Congrats, Menomonie!!

The Seasons of Wisconsin

What a sight! **Goose Island Park** in La Crosse is on the national bird migration flyway.

You can guess what's for dinner. **Northern pike** abound in our lakes and rivers.

The **Wisconsin Dells** are a beautiful sight.

Another Wisconsin riddle:
Q. Which vegetable grows on a farmer's foot?
A. (A) corn

A fresh snow softly falls on a house in Onalaska.

Wisconsin is beautiful in all seasons.

For information, call:

**1-800-432-8747
or
1-800-372-2737**

http://www.state.wi.us

Get some exercise while you're having fun. Canoe our creeks.

Hello from Mrs. Liska's Grade-Five students

Wyoming

The Equality State! Ours was the first state to let women vote.

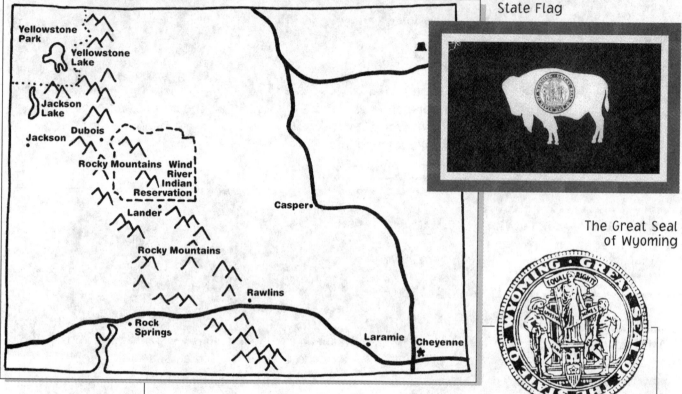

Yellowstone Park
Yellowstone Lake
Jackson Lake
Jackson
Dubois
Rocky Mountains
Wind River Indian Reservation
Lander
Rocky Mountains
Casper
Rawlins
Rock Springs
Laramie
Cheyenne

State Flag

The Great Seal of Wyoming

THIS IS WYOMING, PARTNER!

Dear Friends,

We are having a great time in wilderness-filled, mountain-studded Wyoming. The knolls of hills are a great sight. And, as the song says, we really can watch the antelope play. Did you know that the plains used be full of antelope, which are also called pronghorn? But, as more and more people moved and built up the West, there just wasn't as much room for the animals. That's too bad because watching antelope run is something special. They're the fastest mammal in America. They can run up to 50 miles an hour, as fast as a pickup truck. Most of Wyoming's antelopes are now in protected areas. Not much chance of racing trucks there!

Mrs. Rief's Sixth-Grade Class,
Afflerbach Elementary, Cheyenne

State Bird
Meadowlark

State Tree
Cottonwood

State Flower
Indian Paintbrush

The Silly Seasons in Wyoming!

It's windy in Wyoming,
It's snowing in July.
When it's raining in September,
The cows are flying by.

Wintertime is warmer,
Then summertime is bolder.
March is like a lion,
And October is much colder.

WACKY WYOMING!

❋ But it makes life interesting . . . The temperature is totally unreliable. It once snowed in July.

❋ You have to get a permit to plant a cottonwood tree, even though it's our state tree!

❋ Watch those speed traps. People drive 10 miles over the speed limit, and you can still get passed by other cars.

❋ Here's something to moo about. For every one person in Wyoming, there are at least two cows!

A Very Special First

Nellie Tayloe Ross, the first woman governor in the United States, served Wyoming from January 5, 1925 to January 3, 1927. She encouraged people to stand up for women's rights, and they did just that.

Part of His Art

Jackson Pollock liked to feel as if he was part of his huge abstract paintings. Born in Cody in 1912, he was a leading modern painter at his death in 1956. Instead of using a brush, he liked to drip paints onto his canvases with sticks.

A Leading Lady

If you visit the Statuary Hall in the U.S. Capitol in Washington, D.C., you'll see **Esther Hobart Morris**. A statue of her represents Wyoming. Morris got the territory of Wyoming to pass a law, in 1869, that gave women the right to vote. Later, most states based their women's rights laws on Wyoming's. Esther Morris was born in New York but settled in Wyoming in 1868. She died at the age of 88 in 1902.

Blown Through Time

1803
Wyoming is part of the Louisiana Purchase.

1834
Fort William is founded.

1869
Women vote in Wyoming.

1867
Cheyenne is founded.

1843
Fort Bridger is founded.

1872
Yellowstone becomes America's first national park.

Not Just Any Park: Yellowstone National Park

Today, our national parks face a huge problem. Too many people and too many cars are crowding them. In 1872, people at the dedication of the world's first national park, Yellowstone, would have found that hard to believe. The park is in parts of three states: northwestern Wyoming, Montana, and Idaho. It is home to many animals including elk, buffalo, moose, wolves, foxes, coyotes, rabbits, hares, bears, weasels, voles, trumpeter swans, blue herons, bald eagles, white pelicans, and fish. The animals are meant to live undisturbed in the wild.

The animals share the park with about 10,000 geysers (mounds on the earth that blow off hot air and steam) and hot springs, underground heat sources. Even in the park's early days, many settlers traveled through it. But, because of the geysers and springs, they thought that they were in hell.

1892
Wyoming becomes the 44th state.

1896
See the real Wild West as Cheyenne Frontier Days start.

1921
Wyoming gets a new state seal.

1929
Grand Teton National Park opens.

1947
F. E. Warren Air Force Base opens near Cheyenne.

1990
HAPPY 100th birthday, Wyoming!

Splendid Wyoming

F. E. Warren Air Force Base was named after our first state governor. In the 1800s cavalry men lived in its houses.

Grand Teton National Park is one of the greatest national parks of all time. You can climb in the majestic Teton mountains or stop by a stream. It really is spectacular.

The Legend of Devil's Tower

An Indian girl was picking flowers in a field of Indian paintbrushes. A grizzly bear saw her and gave chase. The girl climbed a rock to escape. The Great Spirit saw her and loved her. He raised the rock up to him so that she could be his wife. The bear went away, but he left his claw marks on the side of the rock. This is a legend about Devil's Tower. The real story is that long-ago volcanoes actually created this 865-foot-tall tower. But the legend is more fun!

Yellowstone Park, the first national park in the world. Its beautiful scenery will take your breath away. If you visit you'll think you're in heaven.

Cheyenne Area Convention and Visitor Bureau
309 W. Lincolnway
(307) 778-313
http://www.cheyenne.org

Mrs. Rief's sixth-grade class, 1997, says "hi!"

Notes